Old Testament Studies

BOOK TWO

JOEL THROUGH MALACHI

by

Frank M. Boyd

© Copyright 1967 by
GOSPEL PUBLISHING HOUSE
Springfield, Mo. 65802
Revised 1988

PRINTED
IN U.S.A.

Contents

UNIT ELEVEN Page

UNIT TWELVE

Lesson 23

Introduction to the Prophetic Scriptures

Before we begin the study of the prophetic Scriptures, a principle should be stated without which this portion of the Word is not clearly understandable, namely, that the historical events of the prophet's time have a direct bearing upon his messages. One must know the historical background, including political, economic, and religious conditions, as well as foreign relations, before he can get the full import of the prophet's message.

We shall treat the prophecies not in the order they follow in our English Bible, but in their chronological order as best determined by Biblical scholarship.

The prophets of Old Testament times were men whom God chose and anointed with His Spirit to be the channel through which His Word, His message, His revelation came to His people Israel. We must not lose sight of the fact that God called Abraham, and from him and his seed constituted a nation which we know as Israel. He separated them from the other nations (Gentiles): (1) to be His witness; (2) to be the medium through which His Word (the Scriptures) should come; (3) to be the channel through which the promised Messiah should come and His redemptive purpose for man be wrought out.

The presence of God among them as their theocratic king assured them of the communication of His will (Exodus 25:22), and one way by which His will was revealed was by the prophets.

The ministry of the prophets was twofold. (1) They brought to light and then proclaimed God's message for their own day and time, a message frequently of rebuke of sin, with a declaration of impending judgment and a call to repentance. (2) They foretold future events, which, when they were fulfilled, would prove that "a prophet had been among them," who had declared God's unfailing word. The prophets also foretold of rich future blessings for the encouragement of the faithful in the nation.

7

Up until the time when prophecy came to be recorded for future generations, none of the prophets in the 12-tribal kingdom or in its divisions into Judah and Israel made any reference to Messiah or His kingdom. This can be accounted for by the fact that moral and spiritual conditions after the division were such that there could be no real apprehension in faith of such a national hope.

"The prophets could not speak of future spiritual blessings to those who had no ear to hear. It was their immediate duty, therefore, to convince the people of their sins and to seek to bring them to repentance; see for example the character of the utterances of Elijah and Elisha in the northern kingdom. As the sin had been national, so the repentance must be national, which was never the case."— Gray.

THE PROPHETS' MESSAGES CONCERNING THE GENTILES

Frequently the prophets had a "burden" (cf. Isaiah 13:1; 15:1; 17:1; etc.) or oracle concerning nations other than Israel. These nations bordered upon Israel and came into contact with them in commercial relations (Tyre, for example), and frequently in war, for with Edom, Moab, the Philistines, and Syria the kingdoms of Judah and Israel had frequent conflicts.

Assyria became a great world power, invaded land after land, and finally attacked, overthrew, and took Israel into captivity. This same power almost overran Judah, the southern kingdom, also, but was hurled back by supernatural intervention.

Babylon overthrew Assyria and rose to dominion over most of the known world. It was this power that finally overthrew Judah and took her into captivity.

Furthermore, the messages to and concerning these Gentile nations are to be explained on the basic principle that God deals with them according to their treatment of His chosen people—"I will bless them that bless thee, and curse him that curseth thee" (Genesis 12:1-3). National prosperity or chastisement for Gentile nations has been, is now, and will be given on this basic principle, until the very time the messianic kingdom is set up.

WHY WRITTEN PROPHECY?

The utterances of the prophets for their own time did not need to be written down, but there came the time when their utterances did come to be written and "the transient word took on a permanent form." It was necessary that future generations should have the Word of God for their warning and encouragement.

This recorded Word anticipated a day of "future withdrawal of God's presence, a consequent cessation of prophetic utterances, and hence a delay or postponement respecting the setting up of the messianic kingdom." (Cf. Amos 8:11,12; Lamentations 2:9.)

As far as we can determine, the earliest of all the prophets whose writings have come to us is *Joel*.

Joel

Little is known of the personal history of Joel beyond the bare statement of 1:1. His ministry was presumably in Judah, the southern kingdom, rather than Israel, probably during the time of Joash (2 Kings 12). The allusions in 1:9,13,14; 2:15 to Jerusalem as the center of worship evidence this. The references in 2:27 and 3:16 are evidently to the whole nation of the 12 tribes, which God always has in mind.

Amos is known to have prophesied somewhere about the close of the eighth century B.C. Joel seems to be quoted by Amos. (Cf. Amos 1:2 with Joel 3:16; Amos 5:16-18 with Joel 1:11,12.) Therefore, Joel must have preceded Amos.

The Occasion

The people were faced with the most devastating plague of locusts the land had known. Wave after wave of these destroying pests had destroyed the harvests and had brought on general famine conditions. Drought had come to complete the picture of devastation and ruin. It was a tragic hour.

The Message

The main theme is "the day of the Lord" (1:14,15; 2:1,2,11-14; 2:28-32; 3:14). This expression refers to a day, or period, when God directly and definitely intervenes in the affairs of men on earth, either in judgment or blessing. In this calamity of the locust invasion Joel sees a visitation from God, calls it "the day of the Lord," and views it as a type of later judgment, in fact, the time of final world judgment. Like many of the other prophets, Joel predicts the future in the light of the present, regarding a present and imminent event as a type of a future event.

Threefold Outlook of the Day of the Lord

1. The prophetic vision and message pertained to things present or near, circumstances in which the people to whom he spoke were then living. There was an actual plague of locusts and the resultant desolations were tragically evident (1:1-20). It was a "day of the Lord."

2. The prophet sees in the invasion of the locusts a foreshadowing of an impending invasion of the Assyrian army (2:1-11), which he describes, using the figure of the locust plague for the purpose of explanation and illustration (cf. Isaiah 36 and 37).

3. Looking still further into the future he sees the invasion of the locusts and of the Assyrian armies as typical of a final invasion of Palestine by the confederated armies of Antichrist (3:1-21), leading to the complete establishment of divine authority and sovereignty.

Outline of the Book

Now, keeping this central thought of the day of the Lord in mind, we sum up this threefold outlook as follows: (1) the day of the Lord, as *immediate* in the invasion of the locusts; (2) as *imminent* in the coming Assyrian invasion; (3) as *future* in the final age-end onslaught against the land of Israel.

THE IMMEDIATE DAY OF THE LORD (CHAPTER 1)

1. *An unparalleled calamity* (1:1-3)
2. *A frightful desolation* (1:4-12)
3. *A call to national fast and repentance* (1:13,14)
4. *A mourning prophet* (1:15-20)

Chapter 1 describes what to the Eastern lands is a terror, an invasion of locusts. This is the scourge which Joel describes with an accuracy that astonishes all that have ever experienced its ravages. The following description will make vivid to us the nature of something with which we are not very familiar in the West:

"A traveler in Syria has described his sensations as he approached a hillside, the surface of which seemed literally moving down towards him. So violently did his horse tremble that he was forced to dismount, and stood gazing with wonder at what looked like a stream of molten mortar. In reality it was myriads of young locusts on their resistless march. When the very dust of the earth seems to quicken and to move, day after day, voracious and marauding, over cornland and pasture, no device of man can stay the disaster that must inevitably ensue. Fire will not keep them at bay. Walls will not delay their progress.

"When a wall or house lies in their way, they climb straight up, going over the roof to the other side and blindly rush in at open doors and windows. When they come to water, be it a puddle or river, a lake or an open sea, they never attempt to go around it, but unhesitatingly leap in and are drowned; and their dead bodies floating on the surface form a bridge for their companions to pass over. The scourge thus often comes to an end, but it as often happens that the decomposition of millions of insects produces pestilence and death."

THE IMMINENT DAY OF THE LORD (CHAPTER 2:1-27)

1. *The Day of the Lord* (2:1-11) (A greater calamity)

While these verses probably do depict the ruthless advance of the Assyrian armies, noted for their cruelty, like locusts because of their numbers and destructive effects, there is a supernatural element blended into this description, in which some expositors see a fulfillment of Revelation, chapter 9, where demonic spirit locusts swarm out of the pit of the abyss to torment men in the last days.

2. *The call to repentance* (2:12-17)

There are three wrong attitudes men can take toward calamities which visit them and the works of their hands—earthquakes, tornadoes, famine, floods, storms, pestilences, hurricanes—that (1) of self-pity, with no recognition at all of man's moral responsibility toward God; (2) of cynical hardness, a spirit of rebellion against God, charging Him falsely with vindictiveness and injustice; (3) of stony indifference, the attitude of the Greek Stoics, considering these things as mere blind fate, with no recognition of divine activity.

God's judgments are called "His strange act." They are not punitive and penal, in their final analysis, but always remedial, in order that man might repent (change his mind) and be restored to right relations with God.

3. *Promise of great temporal blessings* (2:18-27)

THE FUTURE DAY OF THE LORD (2:28 TO 3:21)

From 2:28 to 3:21 the prophet's vision is clearly projected into the time of the end, the Tribulation, and the millennial kingdom to follow.

1. *The outpouring of the Spirit upon Israel* (2:28,29)

This prophecy was partially fulfilled on the Day of Pentecost (Acts 2:16-21), but not exhaustively so. It is even being fulfilled in our day in the outpouring of the Holy Spirit upon hungry hearts everywhere, but it awaits a final glorious fulfillment upon a cleansed and restored nation of Israel.

2. *The signs, terrestrial and celestial, of the last days* (2:30,31)
3. *The final deliverance for Israel* (2:32)
4. *The assembly of the nations against Israel* (3:1,2)
5. *Their mistreatment of Israel* (3:3-6)
6. *Recompense to Israel's enemies* (3:7,8)
7. *Final onslaught against Palestine* (3:9-16)
8. *Israel's restoration* (3:17-21)

In 3:9-16 we have the Old Testament picture of the judgment of the nations presented to us in miniature, representative, typical form in Matthew 25:31-46. Joel reveals to us the occasion, the time, the place, the actual carrying out of the judgment of the nations at the battle of Armageddon. (Cf. Revelation 14:14-20; 16:12-16; 19:15-21.)

Note that as the result of and following this judgment of the nations Israel is restored to her land and to her God forever.

Lesson 24

Jonah

Jonah is placed next to Joel in our study for the reason that, as far as can be determined, these two men were contemporary, Joel in Judah and Jonah in Israel. The only reference concerning Jonah as having prophesied to his own people is found in 2 Kings 14:25, but this verse establishes the fact that Jonah was a historical person. A prediction Jonah had made concerning the restoration of the coasts of Israel had been fulfilled in the reign of Jeroboam II, somewhere near 800 B.C., showing that Jonah must have lived at an earlier date. Nor can we ignore the direct testimony of our Lord (Matthew 12:39-41) to the historicity of the prophet. Jesus mentioned him as a type of His own death and resurrection.

The Great Fish

The philosophic attitude of the past half century has created a certain skeptical attitude toward Jonah, which makes it almost impossible to open the book for study and exposition without people's thoughts centering upon a fish and wondering whether the so-called whale could or actually did swallow Jonah.

Let us get this question settled before we study the book. In the first place, while objections have been made from a study of the physiology of certain species of whales that a whale could not have swallowed Jonah, the fact remains that there are species of whales that could swallow and have swallowed a man. But this argument is really beside the point, for the Scripture statement is that "God prepared a great fish"—species, special physiological characteristics, etc., unknown, but God prepared it.

However, there are specific and well-authenticated instances of men having been swallowed alive by great fish and actually surviving the ordeal.

"In *Coronet* (December 1938) there was an article on 'He Played Jonah,' by Irving Wallace. James Bartley was lost in 1891 from the

13

ship *Star of the East* when a whale overturned a boat in the waters off Falkland Islands. The whale was killed. A day and a night was consumed in removing the blubber. When the stomach was opened Bartley was found unconscious inside. For about three weeks he raved, calling upon heaven to save him from the 'furnace' in which he imagined he was being consumed. In the fourth week he resumed his duties on the boat. As recorded in one book, we find his answer to the question as to what his reactions were. He said, 'I remember from the moment that I jumped and felt my feet strike some soft substance. I looked up and saw a big canopy of pink and white descending, and the next moment I felt myself drawn downward feet first, and realized that I was being swallowed by a whale. I was drawn lower and lower, a wall of flesh hemmed me in, yet the pressure was not painful, and the flesh gave way before my slightest movement. . . . Suddenly I found myself in a sack much larger than my body, completely dark. I tried to rise, to cry out, but all action was now impossible; yet my brain seemed abnormally clear, and with full comprehension of my fate I lost consciousness."

"Several years ago in the English Channel a man was swallowed by a Rhinodon shark. This shark was killed some 48 hours after the accident and the man found alive. He was exhibited in a London museum as the Jonah of the 20th century. Dr. Harry Rimmer later met this very man. So here we find that a man had lived for two days and nights in a 'great fish.' Why should it be thought impossible that under God's stated care and protection a man could not remain a day and a night longer in a sea monster?"—Condensed from *Twentieth Century Christian.*

If we believe the God of the Bible we will have no difficulty with the historicity of the book. Four times we read of divine activity—"The Lord prepared a great fish," "the Lord God prepared a worm," "God prepared a gourd," "God prepared a sultry east wind." There is no difficulty to the devout mind regarding the "great fish" swallowing Jonah.

The Times of Jonah

Jonah lived in the days of Jeroboam II of Israel. This king, as previously noted, extended his borders from Hamath in the north to the Sea of Galilee and east of Jordan to the Dead Sea. The Syrians were pushed back to their own land. Other neighbors were weakened. Meanwhile in the southern kingdom of Judah, King Uzziah built up a strong kingdom. Side by side these two kingdoms flourished.

But on the horizon there was appearing a menace, which was afterward to swallow up Israel and to threaten Judah with extinction—the rising power of Assyria.

In such a day of unparalleled success, Jonah, the son of Amittai, did his preaching in Israel. The people of Israel were not disposed to speak or think in friendly terms of their neighbors. An ugly, narrow, selfish nationalism had developed in their hearts. Certainly no one in Israel had any love for the people of Nineveh.

But God, who is "merciful and gracious, long-suffering and abundant in goodness and truth, keeping mercy for thousands, forgiving iniquity and transgression and sin," said, "Should I not have pity on Nineveh?"

Literary Value of the Book

It is considered by one great literary authority and author, Charles Read, as "the most beautiful story ever written in so small a compass."

The Jews esteemed it very highly and chose it as the special portion to be read on the sacred Day of Atonement. The great German scholar, C. H. Cornill, says of the book:

"I have read the Book of Jonah at least a hundred times, and I will publicly avow, for I am not ashamed of my weakness, that I cannot even now take up this marvellous book, nay, not even speak of it, without tears rising in my eyes, or my heart beating higher. This apparently trivial book is one of the deepest and grandest that was ever written, and I should like to say to every one who approaches it, 'Take off thy shoes, for the place whereon thou standest is holy ground.' "

The Man Jonah

The book is not a prophetic utterance, but rather a prophetic story. It is the words of God spoken to a man who knew God so well that he sinned against Him.

1. He was of Gath-hepher, near Nazareth, a Galilean town. The Pharisees in Christ's time evidently overlooked this when they asserted that no prophet ever came from Galilee (John 7:52).

2. He began his prophetic career as Elisha closed his.

3. Opinion of some Jewish authorities is that Jonah was the son of the widow of Zarephath, whom Elijah raised from the dead.

4. A prophecy of his is preserved for us (2 Kings 14:25-27); therefore, he was a fully accredited prophet.

Jonah's Commission
Jonah was commissioned by the Lord to go to Nineveh and preach a message of impending judgment. He desired to escape from the responsibility, because he knew that if Nineveh repented, judgment would not fall upon it. And the one thing for which Jonah was most anxious was that it should be destroyed.

Jonah's Disobedience
Why, then, did Jonah disobey God's instructions? Because he was a coward? No, indeed, for did he not deliberately tell the sailors on the ship to throw him overboard, knowing that he would perish? He had fully counted the cost and made the sacrifice.

His motive was a false patriotism. He hated Assyria and sought escape from his instructions by deliberately rebelling against God. He was a willful, strong, impulsive prophet who could not afford to let God make a serious mistake like this of giving Nineveh an opportunity to repent. He had an antisocial, intolerant mind that could not see good come to a hated enemy. He feared God, yet ran away from Him and deliberately refused to be used in God's plan for a great city.

The facts behind Jonah's apparently patriotic actions are ably stated by Dr. John Urquhart in his *New Biblical Guide*:

"Assyria had been laying her hand for some generations upon the nations on the Mediterranean coast, and it was the hand of a fierce and ferocious mastery. No considerations of pity were permitted to stand in the way of Assyrian policy. It could not afford to garrison its conquests, and it practiced a plan which largely dispensed with the necessity for leaving garrisons behind the Assyrian armies. There was unsparing slaughter to begin with. The kings seem to gloat in their inscriptions over the spectacle presented by the field of battle. They describe how it was covered with the corpses of the vanquished. This carnage was followed up by fiendish inflictions upon individual cities. The leading men, as at Lachish when Sennacherib had conquered that city, were led forth, seized by the executioners, and subjected to various punishments, all of them filled to the brim with horror. Some of the victims were held down while one of the torturers, who are portrayed upon the monuments gloating fiendishly over their fearful work, inserts his hand into the victim's mouth, grips his tongue, and wrenches it out by the roots. In another spot pegs are driven into the ground. To these, a victim's wrists are fixed with cords. His ankles are similarly made fast, and the man is stretched out unable to move a muscle. The executioner then applies himself to his task; and, beginning at the accustomed spot, the sharp knife makes its incision, the skin is raised inch by inch till the man is flayed alive. Then these skins are stretched out upon the city walls, or otherwise disposed of, so as to terrify the people and leave behind long-enduring impressions of Assyrian vengeance. For others, long sharp poles are prepared. The sufferer, taken like all the rest from the leading men of the city, is laid down; the sharpened end of the pole is driven in through the lower part of the chest; the pole is then raised, bearing the writhing victim aloft; it is planted in a hole dug for it, and the man is left to die.

"No man in Israel was ignorant of these things. Jonah may have witnessed them. Without doubt, too, Jonah knew that Assyria, this spoiler of the nations, was the appointed executioner of God's vengeance upon the 10 tribes. It was not hid from the prophets of Judah that their people were to fall under the hand of a nation that had not yet risen to supreme power. They knew that Babylon was to pour out upon Judah the fierceness of God's wrath. In like manner did God deal with the prophets of God in Israel who had a harder task than that, heavy though it was, of their Judean fellow laborers. Hosea predicts clearly that Israel shall be rooted up and 'eat unclean things in Assyria.' Now, say that this counsel of Jehovah had been revealed to Jonah, can we not understand his action? The word of the Lord came: 'Arise, go to Nineveh, that great city, and cry against it; for their wickedness is come up before me' (v. 2). Nineveh's cup, then, was full. The Judge had ascended the tribunal. The cause had been placed before Him. Sentence was about to be pronounced. Gladder news than this, Jonah's ears had never heard. If Nineveh perished, Israel was saved! This fearful scourge would be tossed into the fire, before it had time to fall upon poor Israel's already bleeding shoulders. There was only one thing to be feared: God's mercy might arrest the smiting of God's justice. Jonah knew that He was a merciful God, and that, if even Nineveh cried to Him, Assyria might be saved, and then Israel would perish. But what if Nineveh were left without warning? What if she and her princes were now abandoned to reap the reward of their fearful atrocities?

"It was a choice between vengeance on him, a rebellious prophet, and vengeance on his people. He would sacrifice himself, let Nineveh perish, and so save Israel! That seems to have been Jonah's purpose and the reason of his sorrow at Nineveh's escape. Paul said he was willing even to be accursed—cast out from God's presence—if by that means Israel could be saved. It was Christ's resolve when He saved us; for He was made a curse for us. The Lord has told us that Jonah was a type of Himself. The type may have begun there. The expression that Jonah 'fled from the presence of the Lord' is repeated in 1:10. It is this fact which makes the mightiest impression upon his fellow-voyagers. 'Then were the men exceedingly afraid, and said unto him, Why hast thou done this? For the men knew that he fled from the presence of the Lord, because he had told them.' And it will be noticed that Jonah, though he confesses to these men, makes no confession to God. When he is cast overboard, there is no prayer, no cry to the Lord, from the prophet's lips. He has counted the cost. He has put himself outside God's mercy. He has made himself a curse for his people's sake; and, in the calmness of that eternal sacrifice, he resigns himself to his fate. The time has come to pay the price; and he pays it!"

Cities in God's Purpose

Prince Bismarck's statement concerning cities—"Great cities are great sores upon the body politic"—can hardly be challenged. They have been from the beginning and are still sinkholes of iniquity; and where great numbers of people are brought so closely into contact, moral and spiritual corruption, as well as physical disease, spread rapidly.

The first city was built by a murderer, Cain, and the civilization which merited the judgment of the flood was largely Cainite.

Nevertheless, a city is in the ultimate purpose of God—Jerusalem, the city of the Great King; and its heavenly counterpart, the New Jerusalem, the abode of the bride of the King. But righteousness and just rule will dominate these cities.

Nineveh

Nineveh, at this period, was a city of at least 1,000,000 inhabitants, judging from Jonah's mention of 120,000 babes (4:11). It took three days to walk across it. It was a great area, enclosed by walls for protection. Between the houses were open fields where cattle could graze.

God beheld this city, knew its sins, and yet said concerning it, "Should not I have pity on Nineveh?" (4:11). Jonah and the nation of which he was a member had no thought of pity for Nineveh "and in asking the question, God was inquiring whether they were thinking of Him from the same standpoint. God does pity Nineveh." We are told that at this time it was in a greatly weakened condition from calamities which had befallen it, and would probably be more responsive to Jonah's message. God pities other cities and would have mercy upon them if they would repent.

God even recognized the "cattle" in Nineveh, the animal creation, and had pity upon it. "God is merciful and gracious."

The immortal Faber in one of his hymns puts the truth thus:

"There is no place where earth's sorrows

Are more felt than up in heaven.

There is no place where earth's failings

Have such kindly judgment given."

Dr. G. Campbell Morgan in his *Voices of Twelve Hebrew Prophets* comments: "God is not impassive despite the theologian of great ability, who wrote a volume, the title of which was *The Impassive God*. His arguments were all to show that God is not really affected by emotion in any form. When I read it, I said, 'Thank God! That is not my God!'"

Outline of the Book

The Prophet's—

1. Commission (1:1,2)
2. Disobedience (1:3-17)
3. Prayer (ch. 2)
4. Recommission (3:1-3)
5. Success (3:4-10)
6. Reproval (ch. 4)

Let us observe and discuss a few interesting points from the Book of Jonah.

1. From Jonah's account of his experiences in the belly of the great fish and his prayer we read (2:2): "I cried by reason of mine affliction unto the Lord, and he heard me; out of the belly of *hell* [Sheol, Hebrew] cried I, and thou heardest my voice." This language might be considered as figurative, expressing the great depths of the prophet's anguish and temporary separation from God and normal

life in the interior of a great fish that had dived down to the very foundations of the mountains in the depths of the sea.

But there is the strongest evidence that we should take the word *Sheol* in its literal significance. It means "the place of departed spirits," so the deduction is that Jonah died as to his body and his soul is now crying to God from Sheol. If this be so, it lends greater interest and vividness to the words of Jesus, "For as Jonas was three days and three nights in the whale's belly; so shall the Son of man be three days and three nights in the heart of the earth."

In this language Jesus alludes not to His burial in the tomb, but to the experience of death in which His soul went to Sheol or Hades (Greek) [see Ephesians 4:8,9], remained for three days and nights, and then was reunited to His body in resurrection. Jonah's prayer seems clearly to imply physical death and subsequent resurrection.

2. The events of chapter 2 take on added meaning if we view them in the light of the religious life of the Ninevites. Let Dr. James M. Gray comment from his *Christian Workers Commentary:*

"The Ninevites worshiped the fish god, Dagon, part human and part fish. They believed he came up out of the sea and founded their nation, and also that messengers came to them from the sea from time to time. If, therefore, God should send a preacher to them, what more likely than that He should bring His plan down to their level and send a real messenger from the sea? Doubtless great numbers saw Jonah cast up by the fish, and accompanied him to Nineveh as his witnesses and credentials."

There are two side arguments that corroborate the historicity of this event. In the first place, "Oannes" is the name of one of the latest incarnations of Dagon, but this name with "J" before it is the spelling for Jonah in the New Testament. In the second place, there was for centuries an Assyrian mound named "Yunas," a corrupted Assyrian form for Jonas, and it was this mound's name that first gave the suggestion to archaeologists that the ancient city of Nineveh might be buried beneath it. Botta associated "Yunas" with Jonah, and the latter with Nineveh, and so "pushed in his spade, and struck the walls of the city."

3. Modern critics of the Book of Jonah have attacked the authenticity of a city-wide move of repentance initiated and carried through by decree of the Assyrian king. These questions are listed and answered by Dr. John Urquhart in his *New Biblical Guide:*

a. Is it possible that a great heathen city like Nineveh should be so moved by the preaching of an obscure Hebrew preacher? In answer let it be noted that Jonah preached to them at a time when they were experiencing an alarming decline of power. There was possibly an expectation of coming calamity, and the presence of a prophet who had been thrown up by a fish would be sufficient to stir the superstitious people who believed that their god sent messengers from the sea.

b. But was it at all likely that the state would interfere and a royal edict be issued enjoining a prolonged fast? Was action of this kind in accord with Assyrian custom? "It was just such a fast," says Professor Sayce, "as was ordained by Esarhaddon II, when the northern foe was gathering against the Assyrian empire, and prayers were raised to the sun god to 'remove the sin' of the king and people. 'From this day,' runs the inscription, 'from the third day of the month even the month Iyyar, to the fifteenth day of Ab of this year, for these hundred days (and) hundred nights the prophets have proclaimed (a period of supplication).' The prophets of Nineveh had declared that it was necessary to appease the anger of heaven, and the king accordingly issued his proclamation enjoining the solemn service of humiliation for one hundred days."

c. Was it the Assyrian custom to cause even the beasts to share in the humiliation? (Jonah 3:7). "Herodotus has answered that question long ago. He tells us that, when the Persians were in Greece, a battle was fought in which a general, endeared to the whole army, was slain. 'On their arrival at the camp,' says Herodotus, 'the death of Masistius spread a general sorrow through the army, and greatly afflicted Mardonius himself. They cut off the hair from themselves, their horses, and their beasts of burden, and all Boeotia resounded with their cries and lamentations. The man they had lost was, next to Mardonius, most esteemed by the Persians and their king. Thus the barbarians in their manner honored the deceased Masistius.' "

Jonah's Complaint and God's Answer

It would seem from 4:5 that Jonah "still had a lingering hope that the city might be destroyed." "He was still influenced by a misguided patriotism that had blinded him to mercy. God dealt gently with His servant and by an object lesson rebuked the petulant and vindictive spirit of the prophet. Jonah was willing to spare a worthless gourd, yet was angry because God had spared a great city and its teeming population. If Jonah was willing to spare the gourd, should not God spare Nineveh?"

TYPICAL LESSONS

Jonah is typical not only of the Lord Himself (Matthew 12:38-42), but also of Israel. Jonah is God's ambassador sent to preach repentance and right relations with God to the Gentiles. So was Israel commissioned—"Ye are my witnesses." God's redemptive purpose for them was inclusive of "the stranger," the foreigner (see Isaiah 56:3-8), but Israel became bigoted and swept by an exclusive spirit, due to pride and vainglory. Jonah objects to the Gentiles being blessed and flees from the unpleasant task. So Israel, as exemplified by the apostle Peter (Acts 10), in their exclusiveness would withhold the message of salvation from the Gentiles.

Jonah is visited by a divinely sent storm and is thrown into the sea. So Israel is now cast into the sea of the nations; but like Jonah, as a nation, is not lost, for presently Israel will be cast up and take her divinely appointed place on the earth, and will become ambassadors of Jehovah and conveyors of blessing to the Gentiles.

PRACTICAL LESSONS

Dr. Kyle M. Yates, in his book, *Preaching from the Prophets,* outlines some important spiritual lessons from Jonah:

1. The path of self-will is always downward.
2. In the hour of distress one turns to the God he has grieved.
3. How futile it is to resist the will of God.
4. In every heart there is an inherent capacity for God.
5. God knows and loves and seeks the salvation of all people.
6. One usually runs into a storm when he seeks to run away from God.
7. It is tragic to have to meet the storms of life without God's presence.
8. One tends to limit God by disobedience.
9. True repentance may avert the catastrophe that has been threatened.
10. No divinely given task may be lightly disregarded.
11. It is utterly impossible to escape from God.

12. God would have us love all men as He loves them and give ourselves to the task of winning them.

13. God has a purpose dispensationally for the Gentiles (this lesson particularly directed to the Jew).

Lesson 25

Amos

Remembering the principle suggested in introducing the study of the prophetic Scriptures, let us note the background of the Book of Amos as to political, moral, religious, and economic conditions.

Background

There is a certain sameness in the themes of many of the prophets, but this is because the conditions prevailing in their days were similar. The following sequence applies rather generally to the messages of the prophets: SIN, DENUNCIATION, IMPENDING JUDGMENT, CALL TO REPENTANCE, PROMISE OF RESTORATION.

Amos, whose ministry was mainly to the 10 tribes, views their national sins as especially heinous, because they were a nation of privilege, of special covenant relation with God. Their failure to walk in His ways and according to His laws would bring an even heavier punishment upon them than upon the heathen nations, who did not have the same advantages (3:2).

The theme of Amos may be stated as follows: "The setting forth of the sins of a privileged people, whose privileges brought them great responsibility and whose failure under that responsibility brought them a judgment according to the light they had received."

The Man Amos

Amos was a native of Tekoa, about six miles south of Bethlehem in the hilly country of South Palestine. He was not a prophet by training, not trained in the prophet schools. As he records concerning himself (7:14) he was a herdman, a shepherd, and a "dresser" (RV) of sycamore fruit.

The sycamore was a kind of wild fig that did not ripen unless the fruit was pinched or nipped. A humble occupation indeed, but God called him to be His mouthpiece. The rugged life which he lived, out in the open, under the stars, close to nature, gave opportunity

24

for meditation and the development of a God-consciousness not so readily apprehended by the city dweller.

Note his reference to two of the great constellations in the starry heavens—the Pleiades and Orion. In this is a clear indication of his devout appreciation of "God in creation."

His Times

The time in which Amos ministered would be called by men today "The Golden Age" of the kingdoms of Jeroboam II in Israel, and of Uzziah in Judah, who were contemporary. (See 2 Kings 14:23 to 15:7; 2 Chronicles 26.) Their enemies were subdued or quiescent on every side. Prosperity reached a high point, but it was accompanied by moral and spiritual conditions which deserved the severest rebuke and pronouncement of judgment.

You will recall that it was Jeroboam I who was responsible for setting up two golden calves, one at Bethel and one at Dan, with the evident purpose of keeping the seceding 10 tribes from going to Jerusalem to worship and thus bringing about a return to loyalty to David's dynasty.

Amos evidently gave forth his messages of rebuke and of impending judgment in the midst of the thronging worshipers at Bethel. Dr. J. Taylor comments on Amos' ministry there:

"Bethel was the principal scene of his preaching, perhaps the only one. When he had delivered several addresses there Amaziah, the chief priest of the royal sanctuary, sent a message to the king, who seems not to have been present, accusing the preacher of treason, and at the same time ordered the latter to quit the realm. Evidently there was some reason to fear that the oppressed poor might be stirred up to revolt against their lords and masters. The threats of coming judgment would disturb many hearers. The denunciations of cruelty and injustice would awaken many echoes. Yet the priest's language evinces all the contempt which a highly placed official feels towards an interfering nobody, a fellow who (thinks he) gains a precarious livelihood by prophesying (7:10-17). On reaching home Amos doubtless put into writing the substance of his speeches."

Recall what was said in "The Prophet's Messages Concerning the Gentiles," Lesson 23, about the surrounding nations.

While the Old Testament is mainly concerned with God's covenant people, Israel, He was not without witness in other nations. Cf. Acts 10:34,35. Sometimes God used these nations as scourges or instruments of chastisement upon His own people, but they themselves came under His severe judgments when they exceeded their commission and, in pride and self-glory, avarice and vindictiveness, oppressed His people. (Cf. Isaiah 10:5-19; Zechariah 1:14,15.)

PROPHETIC DISCOURSES (CHAPTERS 1 TO 6)

DISCOURSES AT BETHEL ON NATIONS (1:3 TO 2:3)

How many such nations are addressed in this passage?
Of what nation was Damascus the capital? Gaza? (See map.)
What unusual phrase introduces each discourse? (1:3,6,9,11)

"This does not mean that the given nation had sinned only three or four times, but is a Hebraism indicating that the transgression had been innumerably often."—Gray.

"This is [also] a figurative way of declaring that God does not act immediately in judgment; but that He waits in order to give every nation the chance of repentance."

Dr. Kyle Yates sums up briefly the sin of each nation as follows:

a. *Syria:* merciless cruelty in war (1:3-5).

b. *Philistia:* enslaving captives (1:6-8).

c. *Tyre:* dealing in slave traffic (1:9,10).

d. *Edom:* heartless, unbrotherly conduct, and unforgiving spirit. [Remember the Edomites were descended from Esau, Jacob's twin brother, and thus were a brother nation.]

e. *Ammon:* fiendish cruelty based on cupidity (1:13-15).

f. *Moab:* cruelty, hatred, inhuman treatment of other peoples (2:1-3).

DISCOURSE CONCERNING JUDAH (2:4,5)

How can Judah's sin be summarized? (2:4) [Disloyalty to Jehovah and despising His law.]

DISCOURSE CONCERNING ISRAEL (2:6-16)

From verse 6 of chapter 2, nearly to the end of the book, the prophet is dealing mainly with Israel, the northern kingdom, but in several places his indictment is of the whole nation (cf. 3:1,2), and his promise of a glorious future involves the 12 tribes (cf. 9:7-15). What Amos proclaimed of indictment against Israel might just as fittingly have been said against Judah, except that King Uzziah was godly and the temple in Jerusalem provided for the worship of Jehovah at least outwardly. Conditions politically, socially, and religiously were quite identical. (See Isaiah 1:1-24.)

1. *Israel's sins are charged against them* (2:6-8).

Israel is indicted for her sins against Jehovah, in plain violation of the Mosaic law.

Name four of those sins from 2:6-8.

2. *The prophet recalls their mercies and blessings* (2:9-12).

Jehovah had driven out the Amorites from before them (2:9—cf. Numbers 21:21-30); brought them out of Egyptian bondage; cared for them in the wilderness; separated unto Himself those who would be His messengers and examples; but—

3. *Their punishment is proclaimed* (2:13-16).

Verse 13 is better understood in the RV—*"I will press you in your place as a cart presseth that is full of sheaves."* Their punishment is doubtless to be the heavy calamities that will come upon them by the Assyrian invaders and their final captivity. (Note again 2 Kings, chs. 15 to 17.)

THREE DISCOURSES AGAINST ISRAEL (CHAPTERS 3 TO 6)

These three discourses can be clearly identified by their introductory words—"Hear this word."

1. *The necessity of judgment upon Israel* (ch. 3).

Israel's ingratitude for God's divine favor and their lack of appreciation and recognition of their peculiar covenant relation to Him above all people is set forth. Their greater privilege brought greater responsibility; therefore their punishment must be severe (3:1-3). Then, guilt is intensified because God spoke to them deliberately by His prophets, who could not but fulfill their commission as any effect follows its cause (3:4-8).

Judgment through "an adversary" (3:11), undoubtedly Assyria, is about to strike and only a remnant will escape (v. 12); and Bethel with its idol altars will be wiped out, and their luxurious "summer" and "winter" homes will be destroyed (vv. 14,15).

2. *Denunciation of oppression, idolatry, and impenitence* (ch. 4).

Amos does not hesitate to administer a stinging rebuke to the women of the land, whom he calls "kine (cows) of Bashan." They were as heartless as their husbands, and made such demands upon their men that they in turn heaped great burdens upon the peasants (4:1).

This oppression of the common people by the rich (vv.1-3) and the flagrant idolatry of the nation (vv. 4,5) had ripened them for judgment, particularly because God's chastisements (vv. 6-11) had been unheeded. They are now to come, as it were, face to face with God in the final and worst judgment of all (vv. 12,13).

3. *Oppression, formal worship, and vicious living spell the doom of Israel* (chs. 5 and 6).

Chapter 5 is a remarkable discourse on *seeking the Lord.* If they will do this, impending judgment may be averted (5:1-15); but if they will persist in scornful desire to see the day of the Lord (v. 18) they *will* see it in its awfulness and terror (vv. 16-20). God hates their hypocritical worship. Like their fathers at Sinai (Exodus 32) they have deserted God's true service and set up their calves; they are honoring the vile god Moloch of the Ammonites, worshiped by human sacrifice. They will be led into captivity (vv. 21-27).

Chapter 6 is a vivid picture of a people living in carnal security, as though calamity were far off.

What is the picture in 6:4-6?

These revelers will be the first to go into captivity (v. 7). The instrument of God's judgment will be another "nation," a reference again to Assyria (v. 14).

PROPHETIC VISIONS (CHAPTERS 7 TO 9)

These chapters record a series of five visions indicating God's determination to bring punishment upon Israel:

THE LOCUSTS (7:1-3)

In vision, first, the prophet sees a plague of locusts, or grasshoppers, about to devastate the land. In compassion for his people, the prophet intercedes and his intercession is successful.

THE FIRE (7:4-6)

This probably refers to the intense heat of a protracted drought which would dry up even the underground water supply of springs and wells. Again the prophet's intercession averts the calamity.

THE PLUMB LINE (7:7-9)

The downfall of Israel is announced in the symbolism of the plumb line, not now used to build up, but to mark the defects in the wall,

Israel. "In the midst" (v. 8) is emphatic, for the judgment of God will strike the very heart of the nation. He will smite the idolatrous sanctuaries of the people (v. 9) and obliterate the dynasty of Jeroboam II, for with the fall of his house Israel would soon cease to exist as a kingdom.

A Parenthetical Historical Narrative (7:10-17)

In reading the prophecy it is noticeable that as long as Amos is talking in Israel and denouncing surrounding nations (1:3 to 2:5), there is no evidence of unpopularity or opposition. When his message has to do with the home nation, he is challenged.

Who was his official opponent? (7:10)

What was the object of worship at Bethel? (Cf. 1 Kings 12:25-33)

What false charge does Amaziah bring against Amos and to whom? (7:10)

What language indicates the effect of his utterances?

How positive and direct were his messages? (v. 11) (7:10)

Amaziah's report to the king was to justify what he undoubtedly proposed doing—banishing Amos. "But he represents it to the prophet in such a way as to effect a courteous removal." Hence the advice, "Go to Judah and there you may earn your bread by your preaching, but stop this presumptuous inveighing against this place of worship at Bethel. Don't you know that it is the king's royal house? Nothing should be said against the king."

What showed Amos' personal courage?

What details of his life does this incident bring to light? (vv. 14,15)

What special punishment does Amos foretell upon this wicked priest? (vv. 16,17)

The Basket of Summer Fruit (8:1-3)

The words translated "summer fruit" in the original indicate "gathered fruit," that is, fruit fully ripe (cf. 2 Samuel 16:1). Just as gathered fruit soon decays, the symbolism is of Israel "ripe" for judgment—complete national decay and disintegration is about to take place. Devastation and death will mar their "sacred" sanctuary at Bethel.

The remainder of the chapter catalogs some of the social and national sins for which judgment now impends. List what these sins were, from 8:4-6.

Israel has despised the Word of God; now God will bring on a famine of that same Word. The prophetic voice will be silenced,

and the people will go deeper and deeper into the spiritual darkness
brought upon themselves by rejection of the light of God's truth
(8:11-14).

THE SMITTEN SANCTUARY AND ITS WORSHIPERS (9:1-10)

In vision Amos sees Jehovah "standing upon the altar," that is,
observing, right in the very midst of Bethel, the false worship and
perverted worshipers. He gives the order for a crash that brings
that whole temple to the ground and, like Dagon's temple in Philistia
(Judges 16:21-30), involves the worshipers in its fall (v. 1).

There will be no escape, for is He not the omnipresent God of
all creation, whose "eyes behold, whose eyelids try the children of
men"? (vv. 2-6). God's hand is over the nations to establish them
and set their bounds (v. 7), as well as to visit judgment upon them
for national sin (v. 8).

The prophet's vision (vv. 9,10) reaches the wider scattering of
"the house of Israel" (including Judah, as indicated by v. 8) among
"all nations." The mention of this scattering affords a clear approach
to the message which follows.

THE RESTORATION OF ISRAEL (9:11-15)

All the prophets, no matter how much reproof and threatened
judgment they speak of, see a better day ahead, when through bitter
experience Israel will have learned her lesson, will repent, and be
restored again to divine favor and blessing.

*He will sift His people among the nations, but will there be
nothing left in His sieve?*

How does this compare with 3:12?

The last five verses of chapter nine divide themselves into four
themes:

1. *Restoration* (v. 11)

After the sifting and purification is accomplished, the Davidic
kingdom will be reestablished.

2. *Possession* (v. 12)

The whole nation (12 tribes) will be the head of the Gentile
nations. This is fully in accord with the messages of all the prophets.

3. *Prosperity and fruitfulness* (vv. 13,14)

Bumper crops, rapidly rotating, fully enjoyed by the people, will
be the order of that *really* Golden Age.

4. *Perpetuity* (v. 15)
Israel will inherit their land forever. Note the significance of finality in the words "no more."

Lesson 26

Hosea

Hosea is the first in the order in our Old Testament of what we sometimes call Minor Prophets. They are not minor because of any inferiority of personality or message. They differ from the Major Prophets only in the extent or length of subject matter embraced.

Hosea was a contemporary of Amos, Isaiah, and Micah. The contents of the book indicate that his ministry was to the northern kingdom of Israel, covering a period of 60 to 70 years, ending with the captivity of Israel.

It would be well to review "Background" of Amos in Lesson 25 for the prevailing conditions of the times referred to in 1:1. Also review again the scriptural record of these times found in 2 Kings 15-17.

Let us sum up again in catchword outline the social, economic, religious, and moral conditions of the times of these contemporaneous prophets:

Social and Economic Background

Unprecedented prosperity, wealth, luxury, self-indulgence.

Summer and winter homes for the rich, with plenty of hewn stone and ivory panelling.

Business good, wine plentiful, feasts, banquets. Ivory couches, rich furnishings. Ease and extravagance in contrast with the misery of the slave population.

Cities growing. Merchant class making money. Land concentrated in the hands of a few.

Judges dishonest. Government corrupt.

Usury, extortion, riots, class hatred.

Shallow optimism.

Injustice and oppression by rich. Poor workers in the fields suffering at hands of cruel landowners and heartless creditors.

Religious and Moral Background

Shrines at Bethel and Gilgal. Pilgrimages. Elaborate ceremonies. Regular religious observances.

Moral laxity. Righteous hated and opposed. Much insincerity and cant—all this abetted by religious leaders.

Rich nobles selfishly indifferent to cries and groans of suffering multitudes.

Idling away of precious time in drunken carousals while swift retribution approached.

Hosea's Unique and Distressing Experience

We hear a great deal these days of visual education, pictorial object lessons, appeal to the eye, symbolic actions. But this, after all, is not so new as we might think. God used such methods long ago. Much of Ezekiel's ministry was in the form of pantomimic actions, dramatizing truth in the presence of his hearers.

Hosea's ministry was unique in that he himself was the object lesson. His personal experience of marriage to an unchaste woman was peculiarly ordered.

1. Hosea, like other contemporary prophets, was a conspicuous figure in the land, so his personal experiences would excite curiosity, interest, and inquiry, and would provide a medium through which to give to the people the peculiar instruction which his own life symbolized.

2. As far as the prophet's own spiritual relationship to God was concerned, his family life made him an intimate partaker of the emotion of the divine heart over a favored people to whom He was wedded, yet so utterly unfaithful to Him. God is a God of infinite emotions, of which we can be only the shadow. We must forever dismiss from our minds that God is impassive or unfeeling in any holy direction in which we ourselves are sensible. Hosea has been called "the weeping prophet" of Israel, as Jeremiah was of Judah.

We will discuss Hosea's personal experience in connection with the outline of the book.

Outline

The book falls quite naturally, if we will ignore chapter divisions in our English Bible, into three main themes, keyed by the words *Separation, Condemnation, Reconciliation.*

SEPARATION: ISRAEL'S UNFAITHFULNESS (CHAPTERS 1 TO 3)

Gomer, the Prophet's Unfaithful Wife

"Hosea is commanded to marry an unchaste woman as a sign to the people that they, as the wife of Jehovah, have been unfaithful to their vows of fidelity. This union must have shocked the people; and this it was intended to do, in order that, on their inquiring concerning this union, they might discover that they themselves were represented by Hosea's unfaithful wife. . . . Moreover, the prophet's motive in marrying the woman was a pure and lofty one. He was to give her his name and his protection, and lift her out of her former life of moral degradation to the same high plane on which he lived. But why does he do this? Is it not clear that Hosea's marriage with this unchaste woman illustrates Jehovah's marriage with an unchaste people? Did Israel have anything more to commend her to God's love and care when He took her to Himself, than this woman when Hosea married her (Deuteronomy 9:4-6; Isaiah 51:1,2)?"—Dr. Gray.

Other expositors hold that when Hosea married Gomer she was a clean woman, but that she later fell into sin. Dr. Kyle M. Yates advocates this view as follows:

"The idea that Hosea is illustrating is that Israel was pure and innocent and faithful when Yahweh [Jehovah] chose her as His bride. Hosea had such high ideals of marriage and preached such strong messages against infidelity that we cannot imagine his going out to a woman of impure life and taking her into his own home. Surely he married a woman who was pure and worthy. She became entangled in the web of sin and immoral life about her and became an adulteress after the birth of the first child. The intense pain that came to the pure heart of the husband cannot be weighed. The struggle of his grief and shame when he found that she was unfaithful to him reveals something of the inexhaustible love of the true lover. After several years of the agony she went out from the home to sell herself into slavery to the paramours who promised her more."

The Children's Names

By divine direction the children born of this union were given names which carried significance as messages to Israel. This was true also of the prophet Isaiah and his two sons, Shear-jashub and Maher-shalal-hash-baz—"Behold, I and the children whom the Lord hath given me are for signs and wonders in Israel from the Lord of hosts, which dwelleth in mount Zion" (Isaiah 8:18). Shear-jashub meant, "A remnant shall return," indicating that God would preserve a remnant of His people for their perpetuation in the fulfillment of His covenant. Maher-shalal-hash-baz meant, "In making speed to the spoil, he hasteneth the prey," indicating that the Assyrians in attacking Jerusalem were only hastening their own doom. Isaiah meant, "Jehovah hath saved" or "salvation is of Jehovah."

So the prophet Hosea and his toddling sons, every time they appeared in public, conveyed by their names a message to the people. Notice the names of Hosea's children:

Jezreel (vv. 4,5)—"God will disperse"; a sign of the doom of the dynasty of Jehu, whom God raised up to accomplish His judgments upon the wicked house of Ahab. Jehu had, by one fearful massacre, exterminated the whole house of Ahab in Ahab's royal city of Jezreel (2 Kings 9:30 to 10:17). Though he did this by divine command through Elisha, the bloody deed of Jehu was shorn of all real value by the fact that while destroying Baal worship he retained worship of Jeroboam's calves. Zechariah, the son of Jeroboam II, was murdered and was the fourth and last king of Jehu's dynasty (2 Kings 15:8; 10:30).

Jezreel was also a sign of the doom of the whole nation of Israel— "scattered, dispersed," because of their wickedness (Hosea 1:4).

Lo-ruhamah (vv. 6,7)—"unpitied," "not favored": a sign of the exhaustion of the divine compassion for Israel. "The kingdom owed its preservation in the midst of the prevailing idolatry only to the undeserved compassion of God."

On the contrary, the promise to Judah (1:7) was a keen reproach for the house of Israel. They were not like Judah. In what respect? Judah owed its deliverance to the fact that it acknowledged Jehovah to be its God, and not (as v. 7 implies) to its military force; "while Israel on the contrary, trusting in its military strength instead of Jehovah who is its God no longer, shall for that very reason, and in spite of its warlike resources, utterly perish."—Schmoller.

Lo-ammi (vv. 8,9)—"not my people": a sign that God disclaims any relationship to Israel.

The separation is complete! Nevertheless, however true this present separation is, the prophet looks forward to the restoration of Israel, to their great increase, to their reconciliation to God, in union with Judah in the last days, under one sovereign. This will happen because of God's covenants with Abraham, Isaac, Jacob, and David.

Israel, the Unfaithful Wife

We are now brought to a second experience in the domestic life of the prophet. It seems that Gomer, Hosea's wife, notwithstanding his love for her as the mother of his children, and his abundant provision for her needs, turns back from husband and family to her former lovers and sinful companions and becomes an adulterous wife.

Chapter 2 is difficult to expound in detail, for as Dr. James M. Gray says: "This story is like a dissolving picture, making it difficult to determine where the record ceases to speak of Hosea's wife and begins to speak of Israel's unfaithfulness to God." He suggests that the first idea be dismissed, and the second held in mind, where the intention is plain, and proceeds:

"The teaching clearly is, that notwithstanding God's goodness to Israel, calling them to be His people, providing for and protecting them when they had no more claim on His bounty than that unchaste woman had on Hosea's love, yet they had abused His kindness and committed spiritual adultery with idols, especially in Baalim worship."

What is the prophet instructed to do? (2:1) The terms *Ammi* ("my people") and *Ruhamah* ("finding mercy") voice a pleading, plaintive cry on Hosea's part for the return of his wife, and symbolize the yearning heart of God over the unfaithful people Israel.

What is the indictment of Israel? (2:5)

What punishment will she receive? (2:6,7)

What use did Israel make of God's prosperity? (2:8)

To what historical period do verses 11-13 refer? Cf. 1 Kings 18.

With what verse does the transition from judgment to forgiveness take place?

List the blessings Israel will receive as found in 2:14-23.

Jehovah, the Faithful Husband

Hosea is now commanded to take back his unfaithful wife who had deserted him. Here lies a progression, not only in Hosea's relation with Gomer, but also in God's relation with Israel, depicting the truth that while God must consistently chasten His unfaithful people, He loves them still and will restore them to himself.

It appears from 3:2 that Gomer had been sold into slavery from whence Hosea redeems her. What a picture of Israel's bondage through the centuries, yet the Lord has paid the price for her redemption on Calvary! However, before full conjugal rights are restored to Gomer there was to intervene a probationary period of special provision for her necessities, during which she was to live free from adultery (v. 3). He, too, will keep himself from becoming husband to another woman.

The application is made in 3:4,5. Israel is to remain for a long period free from idolatry.

To what period in her history does this apply?

What is the conclusion drawn from verse 5?

This last prophecy has been remarkably fulfilled in that the Jewish people have for centuries ("many days") had no king or prince, have been without a priest or sacrifice, and since the Babylonian captivity an idolatrous Jew has been as rare as snow in summer. The transition days between Israel's long "wilderness" (2:14) experience—her "Lo-ammi" and "Lo-ruhamah" period, the period of her scattering—and her regathering are upon us, and we see the nation now established in Israel. True, there is still before her the "time of Jacob's trouble" (Jeremiah 30:4-7), but this will be followed immediately by a glorious salvation (Jeremiah 30:8,9).

CONDEMNATION: ISRAEL'S SIN CATALOGED (CHAPTERS 4 TO 13)

Dr. James M. Gray observes that the first three chapters of Hosea are "historico-prophetic"; "historic, as alluding to the personal life of the prophet, but prophetic, as prefiguring God's relations to and dealing with Israel."

The second division of the book encompasses a series of general discourses making up a continuous prophecy, plainly cataloging in detail the sins of Israel. A few of these might be noted: falsehood and faithlessness (4:1), licentious idolatry (4:11-14), murder (5:2), pride (5:5), adultery and drunkenness (7:4,5), backsliding (11:7), self-sufficiency (12:8), etc.

Note the use of the tribal name *Ephraim* for the whole northern kingdom, just as *Judah* is used for the southern kingdom, composed of Judah and Benjamin.

Israel had destroyed herself through willfulness and sin, as exemplified in their demand for a king to be like the other nations

(13:9-11, RV). These leaders had largely led her astray, bringing the judgment of God upon them.

RECONCILIATION: ISRAEL RESTORED (CHAPTER 14)

This section begins with a strong plea from the heart of God for Israel's return to Him. As one teaching a child to pray, Jehovah through the prophet gives her the very words of a prayer for restoration, accompanied by acknowledgment of the futility of leaning upon Asshur, "the arm of flesh" (14:1-3).

Israel's heart preparation and words of repentance will find Jehovah ready to fulfill words of blessing and restoration (14:4-9).

Lesson 27

Isaiah 1-35

Before beginning the study of Isaiah, review the historical records contained in 2 Kings 15-20 and 2 Chronicles 26:32. It is utterly impossible to understand the message of any of the prophets apart from the political, economic, and religious conditions present at the time of writing, and the national and international relations of the kingdoms of Israel and Judah when the prophets ministered. The historical background or setting is made the occasion of further prophetic messages which concern the future, of which the immediate events of the prophet's time are often a foreshadowing.

Political Background

Isaiah's ministry covered a period of more than 60 years during the reigns of four kings of Judah—Uzziah, Jotham, Ahaz, and Hezekiah. Uzziah in Judah and his contemporary, Jeroboam II in Israel, were great and powerful kings, whose reigns were long and prosperous. The prophet Amos was God's mouthpiece in Israel, while Isaiah was filling a vitally important role as prophet and statesman in Judah.

Isaiah began his ministry in the tragic close of the reign of Uzziah (Isaiah 6) whose stubborn sacrilege brought upon him the judgment of leprosy. Jotham his son became regent during Uzziah's last days, and was God-fearing and faithful to the end. Jotham was succeeded by the wicked and idolatrous Ahaz. Hezekiah, his son, was pious and God-fearing, but in the latter part of his reign became lifted up in pride and self-glory, after the miracle of his healing.

Before Isaiah's ministry was half over, the northern kingdom of Israel was overthrown and taken captive, during Hoshea's reign, by Sargon II, king of Assyria, 721 B.C. The contemporaneous history of Israel during Isaiah's life reveals a succession of wicked and idolatrous kings. Intrigue, conspiracy, and assassination removed one king after another. During the reign of Menahem, the Assyrian encroachments began, and Israel was put under tribute. These invasions increased in frequency and power until the tribe of Naphtali was taken captive by Tiglath-pileser III during Pekah's reign. Hoshea assassinated Pekah and succeeded him: Shalmaneser IV invaded Israel and put Hoshea to tribute. His rebellion and alliance with So, king of Egypt, enraged Shalmaneser, and he continued the siege of Samaria, which fell in 721 B.C., and Israel was removed to Assyrian bondage by Sargon, the successor of Shalmaneser.

The Man Isaiah

Isaiah, the son of Amoz, was born in Jerusalem about 760 B.C. He preached for about 60 years in his native city. His messages were directly to kings, princes, and people. His name means "Jehovah has saved," quite appropriate to the man and his message, both for his own times and for later (looking forward to the consummation of redemption). Isaiah was also a statesman of no mean ability, entering freely into the national councils during the stormy times in which he lived.

He was married and had two sons, Shear-jashub and Maher-shalal-hash-baz, whose names, with his, carried a message to the people of Jerusalem. (See 8:18. We shall discuss this point of interest later.)

"His equipment and training were the best that his age afforded. In body, in mind, in temperament, in personality, he was superbly endowed with the qualities that fitted him for highest usefulness. His intimate knowledge of the city, the kingdom, the surrounding nations, and the history of the world fitted him to interpret the meaning of all the movements of peoples in the light of God's will. It is highly probable that he was influenced by contact with Amos, Hosea, and Micah. The greatest influence in his life was the compelling grip of God's hand upon him that kept him constantly at the task of preaching."—Yates.

Theme of the Book

The warnings of the first 35 chapters were made necessary by current political, moral, and religious conditions, and in dealing with this situation the prophet was a preacher of righteousness. At the same time Isaiah's vision swept the far reaches of the centuries, and some of his wonderful prophecies still await fulfillment in the glorious reign of Messiah in the millennial age. The consolations of the latter part of the book find no permanent resting place short of the millennial kingdom.

"The reason for his dispensational outlook is not hard to find. In the first place, the words of Hosea are true of the inveterate disposition of Israel: 'My people are bent to backsliding from me' (11:7). God's entreaties, warnings, and chastisements availed but little and only temporarily. 'They mocked the messengers of God, despised His words, and misused His prophets, until the wrath of the Lord arose against His people, and there was no remedy' (2 Chronicles 36:16).

"Yet, in the second place, God had unconditionally promised to bless Abraham's seed and make them an everlasting blessing to all nations. He had with equal positiveness promised David an everlasting throne for his house. The problem before God was, then, how to fulfill for a people so persistently rebellious His irrevocable covenants to give them glory and dominion, and yet to do so on the necessary conditions of their fulfilling righteousness. Isaiah unfolds the solution of this problem. Christ is the key . . . and hence He is the focus of Isaiah. In brief, the plot is this: while the tribulations of the generations and the centuries passing by do humble the Jews in part and temporarily, yet their true and final repentance awaits the purifying fires of the great tribulation of the last days under Antichrist, from whose devouring jaws their Messiah, crucified by them in His first advent, will at His second coming snatch the little penitent and trusting remnant, and make them the nucleus of the fully restored and exalted Israel of the millennial age. The prophetic focus is very often indicated in Isaiah by the phrase 'that day,' the key, we may say, to Isaiah, meaning the day of Christ's advent in glory to be Israel's king and to rule the world as King of kings and Lord of lords."—Stevens.

Form of the Book

The Book of Isaiah is a miniature of the whole Bible. First, in form: having a chapter for each book of the Bible and having two clearly defined divisions, chapters 1-39 and 40-66, corresponding chapter for book to both Old and New Testaments. Second, in message: the first 39 chapters are condemnatory and correspond to the Old Testament message of law and judgment; while the last 27 chapters are consolatory, corresponding to the message of grace and restoration to God's favor. Third, in doctrines: presenting clearly somewhere almost every phase of evangelical truth.

Possibly Isaiah, like Jeremiah, had a secretary who recorded his messages so that we have them today.

It will be helpful to dismiss from your mind the chapter divisions found in our English Bible, which are man-made after all. Often they divide a message or theme in the wrong place and make clear understanding of the book more difficult. On the other hand, there should be divisions right in the midst of some chapters, where they do not occur in our English Bible.

Further, let your imagination picture the prophet, not seated at a desk or table writing down his message, but standing before the people, priest, or king, as the occasion may be, mightily under the anointing of the Holy Spirit, either giving forth a denunciatory message against the sins of the people, or looking with prophetic, telescopic foresight into the future and revealing the calamities or blessings to befall them.

Sometimes the prophet speaks in the third person and refers to what the Lord has revealed to him to say to the people; again he speaks in the first person as the direct mouthpiece of God; again he takes into his mouth the cry of his own people (cf. 2:1-4; 1:15,16; ch. 64).

PART I (CHAPTERS 1 TO 35)

Judah, far from heeding the warnings, followed Israel's evil example and even exceeded her in abominations. Jehovah repeatedly entreated the nation through the prophet Isaiah and endeavored to lead her to repentance by using the goad of foreign foes—Syria and Israel, Edom and Philistia, and then the repeated incursions from Assyria. But Judah stubbornly persisted in her sins.

THREE DISCOURSES (CHAPTERS 1 TO 5)

Isaiah begins Part I with vigorous denunciation of the sins of Judah and Jerusalem. Expositors differ as to whether these messages precede or succeed chapter 6, which records Isaiah's call, but this point is not too important.

First Discourse (ch. 1)

This discourse opens with a scathing denunciation of the people for their sins, their callousness and ingratitude (vv. 2-4). Then comes a vivid picture of the consequences of their national sins (vv. 5-9).

They are likened to a desperately sick man (vv. 5,6); and to an abandoned, disintegrating temporary booth, once used to shelter a watchman in a vineyard or garden; and to a besieged city (vv. 7,8). Their apostasy was so great that only the presence of a remnant, preserved by Jehovah, kept them from the fate of Sodom and Gomorrah (v. 9).

Rulers and people are addressed metaphorically as the vile cities of Sodom and Gomorrah (v. 10) and their hypocritical worship is exposed (vv. 11-15). Then follows a call to repentance, followed with assurance of forgiveness and cleansing even from the deepest-dyed sin, with warning against incorrigibility (vv. 16-20).

The fruitlessness of the appeal is recognized, so judgment is inevitable (vv. 21-24), but with the result that in the end God will purify a faithful remnant in the last days through whom He can fulfill His covenants (vv. 25-27). Warning follows (vv. 28-31). Reference is made in verses 29 and 30 to their idolatrous worship on high places.

Second Discourse (chs. 2-4)

The second discourse begins where the previous one ended—with the "last days." The millennial days of Israel's restoration, universal unity of worship, universal sovereignty, and worldwide peace are pictured (2:2-4).

The prophet, probably in a message given later, returns to the indictment of Israel in her present condition of ungodliness, soothsaying, and idolatry (2:5-9). The day of the Lord, both immediate and in the remote Tribulation, will humble all classes, deal with misrule and oppression, and judge the haughty spirit and vainglorious gaudy fashions of the Jewish women (2:10 to 4:1). Dr. James M. Gray comments: "Seventeen of the 21 ornaments mentioned in 3:16-26 were of the kind worn by the heathen goddess Ishtar. The Babylonian women copied the dress of their favorite goddess and the Israelite women were copying their fashions."

The passage clearly indicates that there will be a reverting in "the day of the Lord"—the last days of the present order of things—to the same gaudy display, the foreshadowings of which we see now in the bold modern fashions and display everywhere of the female physical form.

The state of war prevailing in the last days shall so reduce the male population (3:25) that seven Jewish women, to whom childlessness was a reproach, will seek after one man, who will be "more precious than fine gold" (Isaiah 13:12).

As the prophet sees the dark shadows of the tribulation days fleeing away, he beholds (4:2-6) the glorious day of the kingdom of Messiah ("the Branch of the Lord" cf. Jeremiah 23:5) breaking upon the remnant of Israel bringing material prosperity (v. 2), spiritual transformation (vv. 3,4), and the return of the glorious manifest presence of Jehovah as in the days of the pillar of cloud and of fire (vv. 5,6).

Third Discourse (ch. 5)

In the third discourse Judah is likened to a vineyard which Jehovah had carefully planted and tended, but which rewarded Him with wild grapes (vv. 1-7). This symbolism pictures the sins of the nation, which failed to live up to its privileges and responsibilities, a catalog of which, with the inevitable judgments to follow, is given in verses 8-30. The spirit of greed and grasp (compare with modern monopolies) and its resultant judgment (vv. 8-10); drunkenness and its consequences (vv. 11-17); moral perversion, defiance of God, haughtiness, and revelry and its fruitage (vv. 18-25); and the summoning of foreign nations as executioners of judgment upon His own people (vv. 26-30) are all set forth.

CHAPTER 6

Whether this account of Isaiah's call antedates the visions of the first five chapters is open to differences of opinion, but its chronological position at the close of Uzziah's life is clear. The book indicates that Isaiah could well have been of aristocratic lineage, a man who had access to the court, the king, and the princes. He had intimate knowledge of the city, the kingdom, the surrounding nations, "and the history of the world fitted him to interpret the movements of peoples in the light of God's will."—Yates.

No doubt the Lord granted to Isaiah the majestic vision of Himself, both to reveal the prophet's helplessness and dependence and to encourage him by showing the might of Him who had commissioned the prophet. Isaiah's ministry was a most difficult one, for it was to a people utterly unresponsive, hardhearted, and callous (vv. 9,10).

Note: (1) the vision—the glory of Christ (vv. 1-4; cf. John 12:41); (2) the effect of the vision—Isaiah's consciousness of his sinfulness and unfitness (v. 5); (3) his cleansing and call (vv. 6-8); (4) the judicial hardening and blinding of Israel for their willful rejection of the light (vv. 9,10; cf. Matthew 13:14,15; John 12:39,40; Acts 28:25-28).

"God's purpose was not to harden the nation further in its sin, but rather to bring it to repentance in order to save it from destruction. Isaiah's whole ministry, with its marvelous visions, climaxed with one of the most stupendous miracles of the ages [the supernatural destruction of the Assyrians], was, if we may so speak, as if God were frantically waving a red flag to halt the nation in its mad sweep toward the whirlpool. But when a nation sets itself against God, even His wondrous mercies result only in further hardening."—Halley.

(5) Isaiah's cry—"How long?" (v. 11); that is, how long would Israel's blindness last? Answer: till the land be desolate, the people gone far away into captivity and exile, and a return of a faithful remnant—"tenth." (Cf. Matthew 23:39; Luke 21:24; Romans 11:25.)

CHAPTERS 7 TO 10

A Warning and a Promise to the House of David (7:1 to 9:7)

The occasion of this prophecy was the invasion of Judah by the confederate kings of Syria and Israel. They attacked Judah separately (2 Chronicles 28:5,6), then jointly (2 Kings 16:5). Their object was to displace Ahaz and begin a new dynasty (7:6). Ahaz appealed to Tiglath-pileser of Assyria for help (2 Kings 16:7). He responded with an invasion of Syria and North Israel and carried their peoples away into captivity (2 Kings 15:29; 16:9). This was the Galilee captivity in 734 B.C.

Isaiah's message to Ahaz was in the early part of this joint attack on Jerusalem, and it carried assurance that the invasion would fail. The 65 years of 7:8 is thought to cover the period from the first deportation of Israel, 734 B.C. to the settlement of foreigners in the land by Esar-haddon about 670 B.C. (2 Kings 17:24).

The Virgin Son

The perpetuation of the "house of David" meant more to God than it did to Ahaz. It is in line with the fulfillment of the Davidic covenant (2 Samuel 7:12-16) that the "sign" of the "virgin son, Immanuel" is given, not so much to the ungodly Ahaz, but to the godly in the nation of Israel to assure them that God's covenant could never fail, enemies or no enemies.

Some scholars believe that Isaiah 8:1-4 should follow immediately after 7:16. Note that 8:1-4 divides a context referring definitely to the Assyrians and to confederacies against Immanuel's land—7:17-25 and 8:5-22—into two parts, which actually belong together.

If we place 8:1-4 after 7:16 we can more clearly see the relationship between the son of Isaiah and the "virgin son." The birth of Isaiah's son, Maher-shalal-hash-baz, was unusual in that it was strikingly witnessed to. He was a "sign" in his name—"In making speed to the spoil he hasteneth the prey"—that these enemies in hurrying to the conquest of Judah were only hastening their own doom. Furthermore, a prophecy accompanied his birth that before he was able to articulate the words *father* and *mother* the enemies of Judah, Syria, and Israel would be overthrown. In this he was a "sign" (8:4).

It is true also, in the prophecy of 7:16, that before the "virgin son" would come to years of accountability the same enemies would be overthrown, but He would be no "sign" to that generation, for His birth came so many centuries later. So, putting the various elements of this seeming enigma together, we come to the conclusion that the events and prophecy of 8:1-4 are a partial fulfillment of 7:14-16. In other words, Maher-shalal-hash-baz was a *type* of the "virgin son," a sign to that day of deliverance from foreign foes, completely fulfilled by Messiah who would bring final deliverance from foreign foes and from every confederacy against Israel (cf. 8:9,10) and would sit "upon the throne of David" (9:6,7).

Immanuel is prophesied to be a light, when He comes, to the people in the region of Galilee, where the darkness of spiritual death and national calamity has been deepest—in the very northernmost tribes (9:1,2). Here in the very region which was first overrun and the people taken captive by the Assyrians, Christ ministered "light" in His gracious ministry of teaching and healing (cf. Matthew 4:15,16; 2 Kings 15:29).

The Assyrians (7:17-25; 8:5-22; 10:1-4)

We must not lose sight of the fact that in Isaiah's day the Assyrian Empire had reached the zenith of its power, was threatening the whole West, and almost (as we shall see later) swallowed up these nations.

Now Isaiah prophesies to Ahaz, as the representative of the "house of David," that the very Assyrians to which he was turning for aid against Syria and Israel (Kings Rezin and Pekah) would themselves overrun Judah, bringing desolation and famine conditions (7:17-25). Furthermore, as an overflowing river they would engulf Immanuel's land making it like a man up to his neck in water (8:5-8).

Isaiah makes this impending Assyrian invasion the occasion for a prophecy that any confederacy or association of nations against Palestine—Immanuel's land—would be broken and fail (8:9,10). It is *His* land, though in those days He was not yet manifest in the flesh; and He is watching jealously over it. Thus will it be in the last days when the nations of the earth attempt to swallow up the land of Israel and the Jews. (Cf. Zechariah 14:1-4.)

In chapter 8:11-18 Isaiah reveals the divine instructions to him personally that in these stormy times of national crisis he was to remain aloof from all proposals of alliance with other powers for help, and to look only to the Lord. He and his children by their very names—Isaiah, "Jehovah is salvation"; Shear-jashub, "a remnant shall return"; and Maher-shalal-hash-baz, "in making speed to the spoil he hasteneth the prey"—were a constant testimony, wherever they went, to God's faithfulness to deliver the nation, preserve it in perpetuity, and overthrow Israel's enemies.

Verses 19-22 warn of the dire consequences of looking to the various dark arts—spiritualistic mediums, astrologers, soothsayers, etc.—in times of national crisis. "To the law and to the testimony," the divine revelation, they should resort. The region of Galilee, the tribes of Zebulon and Naphtali, had gone into spiritual and tribal eclipse because they had fallen into these very idolatrous practices. But even here, as we have already noted, the glorious presence of the "virgin son," Immanuel, the manifest God, would diffuse His light (9:1-7).

"Following his habit of frequent and sudden shiftings back and forth between his own times and the future, Isaiah abruptly turns his eyes toward Samaria."—Halley. So we have here in 9:8 to 10:4 a sort of parenthesis, containing an account of the calamities which Jehovah had sent upon the 10 tribes (Israel), but which had gone unheeded. The most of Israel was carried away in 734 B.C., but Samaria held out until 721 B.C. These calamities were: foreign invasion (9:8-17); anarchy (9:18-21); and impending captivity (10:1-4).

The Assyrians—a Divine Instrument (10:5-34)

Isaiah has not yet left the theme of the Assyrians in the early chapters and sets forth this nation as God's instrument of judgment upon Judah. Their ally at Ahaz's plea has now become a scourge against them because of their "hypocrisy" (vv. 5,6). Because of the Assyrians' pride and arrogance, and because they cruelly exceeded their commission, God will turn and judge them (10:7-19). Israel will then learn not to put their trust in idolatrous nations (v. 20). However severe Israel's chastisements may be in any age, God in His mercy will always leave a remnant who will form the nucleus of a new nation (vv. 21-23).

Judah is not to fear the Assyrians, for even though they relentlessly swallow up town after town in their advance (vv. 28-31), they will only *threaten* Zion. God will cut them down like the felling of trees (vv. 32-34; cf. chs. 36,37) for the fulfillment of this prophecy.

CHAPTERS 11 AND 12

The Assyrian invasion of Palestine in those centuries long ago is a type, a foreshadowing of a final invasion of Israel. Consequently the prophetic perspective in chapter 10, continuing into chapters 11 and 12, focuses on this greater invasion of the land in the latter days by the final Assyrian. Note the mention of Assyria in 11:11,16 in connection with the last days, and Israel's restoration.

Note also that in the prophecy of Micah, a contemporary of Isaiah, mention is made of the deliverance which the Messiah, to be born in Bethlehem, will bring to Israel from the *Assyrian* (Micah 5:5).

Chapter 11 is specifically messianic, because it sets forth the anointing (Messiah means "the anointed One") of one from David's stock (vv. 1-3); His beneficent reign (vv. 4,5); the wonderful transformation of the animal kingdom (vv. 6-8); and the era of righteousness and peace (v. 9).

The prophet sees the resultant blessings to the Gentile nations (v. 10) when Israel is again (for the second time) restored from her worldwide dispersion (vv. 11-16). Verses 15 and 16 seem to hint of a miraculous working of God in preparing a highway for His people then, such as was wrought in the passage of the Red Sea when they came out of Egypt.

Chapter 12 records a joyous millennial song of the forgiven and restored nation, back in the land, exalting Jehovah for His fame. What a day it will be when Jerusalem is again a praise in the earth!

Note: The law of prophetic perspective is the method of describing future events as if they were continuous and in immediate sequence. (Cf. Isaiah 61:3 and Luke 4:17-20.) In reading the Book of Isaiah, the Lord Jesus leaves off after the words "the acceptable year of the Lord," closes the book, and tells the people, "This day is this Scripture fulfilled in your ears." Had He continued to read and then given such an explanation of the passage, His word would have been untrue, for the "day of vengeance of our God" has not yet come, and already a gap of almost 2,000 years has elapsed. In other words, the prophet sees both advents as one would look at distant ranges of mountains, the intervening valleys not being visible until one climbed to the top of the nearest range. This is called "prophetic perspective."

CHAPTERS 13 TO 23

This section records special "burdens" or oracles which the prophet spoke concerning some of the nations bordering on Israel. Assyria invaded land after land, finally attacking Israel and Judah, and became a world power. Then Babylon overthrew Assyria and rose to dominion over most of the known world. She was afterwards conquered by Medo-Persia, which became the greatest of all the oriental monarchies. These chapters foretell God's judgment upon these powers, covering a period of two centuries, for their attitude toward His chosen people.

"The relation of Judah to neighboring nations is important to remember. With Moab, Edom, and the Philistines, Judah had continued conflicts. Though within the boundaries of Judah, and subdued by David, they were constantly endeavoring to maintain an independent position; and during the reign of godless, feeble kings their efforts were generally successful. Assyria had increased in strength and was increasing her conquests on every side. Egypt had been subdued by Ethiopia, and both countries were united under one dynasty. Assyria and Egypt were both preparing for the coming struggle, and each in succession sought the alliance of both Israel and Judah as a bulwark against the other. The right policy, in regard to the temporal interests or to the religious character of the Jewish kingdoms, was clearly to stand aloof from both."—*Angus-Green Cyclopedic Handbook.*

(Refer again to "Introduction to the Prophetic Scriptures," Lesson 23.)

"Consequently, prophecy throws all these movements of God's hand over the nations in the perspective of the coming of His Son as King of Israel and the Judge of all nations. In connection with His return, Israel's tribulations will reach their climax and successful termination, and vengeance upon Gentile nations, for their mistreatment of Israel, will be exhaustively visited; whereupon Israel, i.e., the remnant left, will be glorified in the earth, and all nations that are permitted to remain as such will be reconstructed with reference to God's workings through Israel for the world."—Stevens.

Babylon (chs. 13:1 to 14:23)

Babylon was at this time an ancient kingdom struggling against Assyria for independence and rising slowly into importance. Hence the necessity of the divine revelation concerning the future power of Babylon and Judah's overthrow by her a century and a half later (39:6). Hence also the policy of Merodachbaladan in sending an embassy to Hezekiah (39:1-3).

These two chapters are continuous in theme and should not be separated in consideration. Babylon and the house of Israel are seen in the nearer "day of the Lord," one the instrument of chastening upon the other: the overthrow of Babylon for her haughtiness and pride by the Medes (vv. 17,18), the restoration of Jacob to God's favor (14:1-3), and the humbling of the proud and arrogant king of Babylon down to the pit of the underworld (14:4-23). However, this section comprehends a relationship between Babylon and Israel yet to be fulfilled, and final in the destruction of the one and the establishment of the other, with resultant blessing to the whole earth (14:7,8).

The question then arises—"Will Babylon be rebuilt as a literal city?" We believe so. This statement may contradict the views of some of our eminent Bible teachers, notably Scofield (see Scofield Reference Bible, footnote on Revelation 18). A careful examination of the details of this prophecy will reveal the fact that Babylon has never been destroyed after the manner there described. First, it states that the city should be destroyed as were Sodom and Gomorrah. When these cities were visited by Jehovah not a trace of them was left, and the Dead Sea now covers the site. Secondly, "it shall never be inhabited." A city called Hillah occupies the site of Babylon, and it was built of the very stones of the ruins, although Jeremiah prophesies (51:24-26) that a stone should not be taken for a foundation from the city. At present it is not a "possession for the bittern and pools of water," but heaps of ruins.

The first organized opposition against the Almighty arose from the valley of the Euphrates. Babylon was founded by Nimrod; and from the city and community which he founded arose the first blasphemous attempt to dethrone the Almighty—the building of the tower of Babel (Genesis 10:8-12; 11:1-9). Babylon was the seat of the first world empire which was allowed to have supremacy over Israel in the beginning of the "times of the Gentiles." Why might not Satan's last efforts at the close of this period arise from the same quarter? This is only conjecture, but let us look at the scriptural reasons for believing in the rebuilding of the city:

1. Isaiah locates the destruction of Babylon (and we have no doubt that the literal city, as well as the false system of worship and all her commercial activities, is meant) in "the day of the Lord." That day in literal fullness has not yet arrived, for that day comes when Christ appears (13:6).

2. Babylon has never been destroyed as were Sodom and Gomorrah—neither as completely nor as suddenly. (Cf. Jeremiah 51:8; Isaiah 13:19; Revelation 18:10.) The nearest it came to this was when Sennacherib leveled the city to the ground in 689 B.C. and turned the Euphrates River over it, making the city "pools of water" for a time. It was rebuilt by Sennacherib's son, Essarhaddon. At the time of the apostles it was a populous place. Peter and Bartholomew preached the gospel there. Five hundred years after Christ there were Jewish academies there which produced the Babylonian Talmud.

3. It is still inhabited (Isaiah 13:20). A town named Hilla, of some 10,000 inhabitants, occupies the site of the old city. It was built of stones taken from the ruins of the old city (Jeremiah 51:24-26).

4. The physical phenomena spoken of in Isaiah 13:10 were not seen at the time of its overthrow by Cyrus, nor since, as far as we know.

5. The Lord did not then visit Israel with rest nor has He yet done so (Isaiah 14:1-3; cf. v. 4).

6. The king of Babylon described in Isaiah 14:4-20 fits Tiglath-pileser who took that title two years before he died. He seems to be a type of an august and powerful being yet to appear.

7. The 18th chapter of Revelation seems to require the rebuilding of the city. The language used here is so literal and local that one

can hardly avoid the conclusion that a city, a great commercial center, is meant. Note especially verses 10-12,16,21-23. The kings of the earth who destroy mystical Babylon, the false religion of the 17th chapter, in order to give their worship to "the beast," lament the overthrow of the literal city.

8. World government is being proposed in our day by eminent statesmen and intellectuals as the only solution for the problems of nationalism, international disagreement, world economic instability, etc. Elaborate plans have been drawn for a world center of exchange, a great clearing house of ideas and ideals with carefully planned buildings and means of communication which would reach every corner of the world.

Furthermore, the site of Babylon has been proposed repeatedly as the best one for such a center, because of its position at the juxtaposition of land areas of three continents and the natural agricultural resources of this region.

From the groundwork which has been laid, a new prosperity is beginning to flourish in the regions of old Babylon and Nineveh. According to the 1969 edition of *Encyclopedia Americana,* "Iraq's economy, primitive and stagnant until 1914, has been remarkably transformed since then in the scale of its agriculture, its immense oil development, its industry and trade, and its means of transportation. Every potential of the economy has been studied by experts of many nationalities and science, engineering, and technology in many forms have been pressed into service."

Arnold Toynbee in his book, *Civilization on Trial,* published by Oxford University Press, after giving scientific reasons for a new locus of the center of gravity of human affairs, makes the following amazing statement:

"The center point of human affairs . . . is now toward some locus approximately equidistant from the western pole of the world's population in Europe and North America, and its eastern pole in China and India, and it would indicate a site *in the neighborhood of Old Babylon,* on the ancient portage across the isthmus between the Continent and its peninsulas of Arabia and Africa."

Philistia (ch. 14:28-32)

Philistia, originally called Palestine, from which the whole land afterward took its name, was Judah's inveterate enemy on the southwest. A double calamity was to befall her, one probably from Sennacherib and the other later from Nebuchadnezzar (v. 29). The last verse of the chapter seems to require its final fulfillment in an inquiry of the people of this region as to the meaning of events in the latter days.

Moab (chs. 15,16)

Moab was another relentless enemy of Judah, even though the Moabites were of kindred blood. Moab was a constant menace and became lifted up in arrogance and pride. She was always tributary, as long as God's people and the kings walked in the way of the Lord; but at times of Judah's backsliding Moab threw off the yoke of Judah. Isaiah 11:14 points to the national resuscitation of this people in the latter days, and Jeremiah 48:47 implies that they will exist during the Millennium along with restored Israel.

The cities named were pillaged by Tiglath-pileser, 734 B.C.; by Sargon, 713 B.C.; and by Sennacherib, 701 B.C. Isaiah may refer to one or all of these invasions. However, he advises them that it would be to their advantage to renew their allegiance to the house of David (16:1-5).

The picture of these two chapters seems to be: (1) the desolations to come upon Moab at the hands of the Assyrians in one or all of the invasions aforementioned in chapter 15; (2) the counsel from the prophet to seek help and protection from Judah and to give allegiance to the house of David, which they had a hand in founding in the person of Ruth the Moabitess, David's great-grandmother. They were to send the tribute of lambs (cf. 2 Kings 3:4) to Jerusalem from Sela (called Petra by the Romans), capital city of Edom, just across their southern border (16:1).

Note that Edom and Moab are mentioned together so much in Scripture that they might almost be considered one country. They were neighbors in the area east and south of the Dead Sea.

According to 15:7 it would seem that the Moabites had arrived in Sela as fugitives. But the fugitives are not in Edom only. According to 15:8,9, they are dispersed on every side. Therefore fleeing crowds are seen at the brook Arnon on Moab's northern border (16:2).

Verses 3,4 are a petition of the prophet to the Moabites in the name of his people. They are exhorted not only to put themselves in subjection to Judah, but they are also to afford protection to Judah, for the prophet assumes that there will come upon Judah a visitation of judgment such as he pictures for Moab in chapters 15 and 16. This was fulfilled by Nebuchadnezzar, for in Jeremiah 40:11 Moab is expressly included among the lands into which scattered Judah had fled.

Moab is exhorted in vivid figures of speech to grant protecting shelter and asylum to those whom Isaiah designates as "mine [God's] outcasts."

The prophet now gives the reason why Moab should seek shelter from Judah and afford shelter to the fugitives of Judah. It is a prophetic word in which Isaiah sees the end of despotic world power as represented in his day by Assyria and Babylon. He sees also the setting up of the kingdom of God under a great personage in the line of David (16:4,5). If Moab would participate in this glory of Israel, God's people, then they should prove worthy by doing what is asked of them in 16:1-4.

Here is unquestionably an allusion to the messianic kingdom and, by the law of double reference, a foreshadowing of the escape of the faithful remnant of the Jews in the last days from Antichrist to find shelter in the "wilderness" of Edom and Moab. (Cf. Matthew 24:15-21; Isaiah 63:1-6; Revelation 12.)

Damascus (ch. 17)

While the greater part of the section under consideration (chs. 10:5 to 35:10) belongs to the first part of Hezekiah's reign, evidently this chapter is a somewhat earlier utterance of Isaiah concerning the coming overthrow of Syria and Israel at the hands of Shalmaneser. On account of the confederacy between Syria and Israel, the prophecy seems to concern Israel more prominently. The overthrow of both kingdoms is revealed (vv. 1-3), the escape of a remnant of Israel is described (vv. 4-6), the vanity of idols realized (vv. 7,8), the result of forsaking God seen to be "desperate sorrow" (vv. 9-11), demonstrating the utter vanity of the nations and the futility of confederacy against His chosen people, even though for a time the nations are allowed to have ascendency over them (vv. 12-14).

Concerning an Apparently Undesignated Land
Beyond the River of Ethiopia (ch. 18)

Cush, or Ethiopia, was a land south of Egypt occupying the Nile valley above the First Cataract, including what is now known as Nubia and the Sudan. The prophet speaks of a land "beyond the rivers of Ethiopia." A better rendering of verses 1,2, and 7 may help somewhat in the interpretation, although various ideas have been propounded. The United States, England, and other countries have been mentioned as possibilities. The writer does not see the appropriateness of designating either of these countries by a reference to "beyond the rivers of Ethiopia." Beyond the Great Sea would be more fitting.

"Ho [same word here as in Isaiah 55:1] to the land of buzzing wings, which is beyond the rivers of Ethiopia; that sendeth ambassadors by the sea, even in vessels of papyrus upon the waters! Go, ye swift messengers, to a nation tall and of glossy skin, to a people terrible from their beginning hitherto; a nation sturdy and that treadeth down, whose land the rivers divide" (Rotherham and Jewish Version).

In verse 7 read "tall and of a glossy skin," instead of "scattered and peeled"; and "land the rivers divide," instead of "have spoiled."

The possible reference is to some African tribes near Ethiopia who sent an embassage to Palestine (cf. Isaiah 37:9 and Acts 8:27) for contact of African people with Judea. In the end time when the Kingdom is set up, they will send an embassage to Jerusalem, possibly at the Feast of Tabernacles (cf. Zechariah 14:16-19). They will come to acknowledge the King and to bring congratulations to Jehovah and His people. (Cf. Psalm 68:29-31.)

Egypt (ch. 19)

The Lord's people, in time of apostasy, were ever prone to "go down to Egypt" (the great type of the world, the "arm of flesh") "for help." The contempt with which Egypt is regarded by the Lord is apparent, also the ease with which He can humble her pride and vainglory. "He doeth according to His will . . ." (Daniel 4:35). The idols of Egypt shall be abolished, the spirit of the people fail, civil war shall follow, and in their consternation and fear of the impending scourge from the north (Assyria) they shall seek to the powers of darkness instead of to the Lord (vv. 1-3). The bondage of Egypt to Esar-haddon, the most warlike of the Assyrian kings, is shown (v. 4). The agriculture and industries of Egypt shall be paralyzed (vv. 5-10); the counsel of their wise men shall fail and seem utterly foolish, because God will pervert their wisdom (vv. 11-15); the courage of their mighty men shall languish (v. 16); and Judah, hitherto regarded with contempt, will be a source of terror (v. 17). Verses

18-25 clearly belong to "the day of the Lord," when Egypt, by reason of her calamities in the Tribulation, shall cry to Him for deliverance. Their cry will be regarded, the nation restored, and Egypt, Israel, and Assyria will be a threefold blessing to the world in the millennial age.

The Humiliation of Ethiopia (ch. 20)

Philistia was depending upon help from Egypt and Ethiopia to successfully resist the invasion of the Assyrians. A historical statement is given here concerning her overthrow by Tartan, an Assyrian general. (For a long time Isaiah was thought by critics to have "slipped a cog" when he named Sargon as an Assyrian king; but from excavated tables the history of Sargon was discovered after 25 centuries.) The prophet uses this victory over Philistia, and the object lesson of his walking naked and barefoot, to bring to Judah a striking admonition not to put their trust in Egypt or Ethiopia, for both of these are to be completely overthrown by the Assyrian hosts. The lament of the Philistines for the failure to receive help from the south is given in the sixth verse.

Babylon (ch. 21:1-10)

A minor vision concerning Babylon is given in these verses under the name of "the desert of the sea," referring to the time when Sennacherib dug trenches from the Euphrates in 689 B.C. and made a swamp out of the city. Nothing like this happened when the city was captured in 539 B.C. by Cyrus. The prophetic watchman then describes how he received the news of the destruction of Babylon and its images by Sennacherib. Instead of, "and he cried, A lion," the Dead Sea Scrolls read, "and the seer cried" (v. 8). The threshing refers to the fact that Isaiah sees this as a harvest or fulfillment of his prophecies concerning the destruction of Babylon (v. 10). The importance of this vision is emphasized by Isaiah, for it was from this nation that great calamity was yet to come.

Dumah (Edom) (ch. 21:11,12)

The messengers of Seir are pictured as coming to the Lord (or the prophet) with an inquiry as to the meaning of impending events (possibly the invasion of the Assyrians). The reply of the watchman is that the morning (prosperity, deliverance) cometh, followed by the night (trouble). If they desire further information they are to return.

Arabia (ch. 21:13,14)

The inhabitants of Arabia are seen in the vision of the prophet, hard-pressed by the invader, fleeing before the incoming, well-armed hosts (v. 15). This calamity was to fall within a year. The land would be brought low and the remnant of the fighting men of Arabia would be small after the conflict (v. 17).

Jerusalem (ch. 22)

"The valley of vision" here referred to is possibly the valley of Jehoshaphat, where the prophet may have received his revelations. The reference is clearly to Jerusalem and its environs. Isaiah predicts the tumultuous gathering of the people because of the impending incursion (vv. 1-4), the multitude of the invading host (vv. 5-7), the weakness of the city's defenses, and the hasty diversion of the water supply in another direction to keep the city supplied (vv. 8-11). While the Lord's call was to repentance and humbling, the people are seen indifferently and brazenly feasting and carousing right in the face of imminent death (vv. 12-14). The proud and vainglorious Shebna is rebuked by the prophet for exalting himself and preparing a grand mausoleum to his memory; his removal from office, his humbling, and ignominious death are foretold (vv. 15-19). Eliakim, the son of Hilkiah, a trusted servant of the Lord, is given authority and responsibility (vv. 20-25). The stability of God's promise to the house of David is pictured here in the Lord's confidence in Eliakim and his firm establishment as a statesman.

Tyre (ch. 23)

Tyre was a very important, prosperous, commercial city in Phoenicia on the Mediterranean Sea. It was "the mart of the nations," its trade reaching as far as Spain in those days. The relations between Israel and Judah and Tyre were for the most part friendly and peaceful. However, Tyre and her sister city, Zidon, were wicked, proud, idolatrous centers and justly deserved the judgment of God. Zidon is not especially dealt with here. We read the lament of regions which traded with her, over her destruction (vv. 1-12), and the quarter from which her judgment was to come, Babylon (v. 13). Tyre was besieged 13 years by Nebuchadnezzar and finally taken by assault. The desolation of Tyre was to last 70 years (vv. 15-17). Tyre was rebuilt and 240 years later was besieged by Alexander and destroyed. "The last verse, after the law of prophetic perspective, sights the far-distant future, when Tyre would entertain Christ Himself and bring Him an offering of unparalleled faith, and when, in the earlier centuries of the Christian era, she would make lavish offerings for Christian worship."—Stevens.

CHAPTERS 24 TO 35

This section views Judah and Jerusalem in a wider scope of judgment and restoration preparatory to the establishment of the millennial kingdom. "We have already seen that the kingdom of Jerusalem was to be greatly depleted and humbled by Assyria, although in the end gloriously delivered and even enriched through the spoil of her enemy. We have also had some inklings of the Babylonian captivity and the restoration from that captivity as a later stage of history. These judgments, in order to put restoration on a better basis, carry the prophetic vision on down the ages to final judgment and restoration, the overthrow of the inferior prior to the establishing of the superior and lasting kingdom."—Stevens.

The Great Tribulation (ch. 24)

The terms *earth, land,* and *world,* in verses 1-12, while applying to the whole globe, specifically allude to the land of Palestine, and the language used in this section pictures the desolation which would accompany God's judgments upon the land and people because of transgression. The believing Jewish remnant of the latter days is seen repentant, rejoicing, and glorifying God among the Gentiles (vv. 13-15). The Great Tribulation occupies the prophet's vision, worldwide in extent (v. 16), impossible of escape (vv. 17,18), terrible in its visitations (vv. 19,20). The ejection of Satan with his principalities and powers from the heavenly places (Revelation 12), along with the judgment of the kings of the earth confederated under Antichrist, is shown in verse 21; their confinement in the underworld awaiting later judgment (v. 22). The glory of the Lord at His appearing to reign in Mount Zion transcends the glory of the sun and moon (v. 23).

Triumphs of the Millennial Age Through the
Reign of Messiah (ch. 25)

The prophet ascribes praise to Jehovah for His faithfulness to His people (v. 1); He foretells the destruction of Israel's enemies (v. 2); and their acknowledgment of Jehovah as God (v. 3); His protection of His waiting people from their enemies (vv. 4,5); and their vindication in the sight of all peoples, to whom the Lord will make a feast of fat things (v. 6); the removal of the influence of the powers of darkness—by the binding of Satan (Revelation 20:1-3)—from all peoples (v. 7); the mighty triumph over death and sorrow (v. 8); the removal of the reproach which had attached itself to Israel (v. 8); the reception of Messiah by the waiting, believing remnant (v. 9); rest from all their enemies, of which Moab is a type (vv. 10-12).

Another Wondrous Millennial Song of Israel
(chs. 26:1 to 27:1)

A mighty paean of praise will ascend from Jerusalem to Jehovah in the day of their final deliverance from all oppression and especially their release from "the covenant of death" with Antichrist. The strength of Jerusalem in the coming age is not to be walls of masonry but the "salvation," the presence, of the Lord himself (vv. 1-4). Peace will reign outside the city because Jehovah has brought down the pride of all Israel's oppressors (vv. 5-11). Peace will reign within the city because of the presence of the Lord Himself and hearty submission to His rule (vv. 12-15). The prophetic lament, yet to be in the mouth of Israel, is their failure to fulfill their mission as His witnesses among the nations (vv. 16-18). A glorious promise of the resurrection of the faithful fathers is given (v. 19), while the prophet again returns to the theme of the Great Tribulation and exhorts the believing ones to flee to the Lord, their secret chamber for refuge (vv. 20,21).

Verse 1 of chapter 27 belongs in sequence with the latter part of chapter 26. It foretells the destruction of the dragon Satan, the archenemy of God and His people, as well as "leviathan" (doubtless the Antichrist), Satan's final instrument designed for their overthrow.

The Lord's Tender Care of His Vineyard
(ch. 27:2-13)

Again "that day," the day of the Lord, is before our vision. In contrast to the picture of Israel as the rejected vineyard of chapter 5, we see her as one tenderly cared for (vv. 2,3), carefully protected (vv. 4,5), and fruitful (vv. 6-8). Through just chastisement the rebels are purged from the nation and the way is prepared for the penitent to return to Mount Zion (vv. 9-13).

Denunciation of the Egyptian Party in Jerusalem
(chs. 28 to 31)

These chapters constitute a series of rebukes against the party in the city, chiefly the rulers and influential, who, instead of heeding the prophet's call to national repentance and obedience to Jehovah, persisted in leading the people to alliance with Egypt against Assyria.

Warning to scoffers in Jerusalem (ch. 28)

The fate of Ephraim (this tribal name was given to designate the whole of the northern kingdom), already gone into captivity, is used by the prophet as a warning to similar scorners in Jerusalem. Notice the self-sufficient and unteachable spirit of these men (vv. 9-13). Paul cites verses 11 and 12 in 1 Corinthians 14:21,22 as one of God's ways of communicating His message, a sign (the speaking in tongues) to the unbeliever. The proposed agreement of the rulers with Egypt is called "a covenant with death," which shall be disannulled and come to nought, for God Himself will overthrow it (vv. 14-23). Verse 16 is quoted by Paul in Romans 9:33 and 10:11 as referring to Christ, a stumbling block to Israel, who would be found in the same spiritual condition as these rulers in Isaiah's days. The example of the farmer plowing, harrowing, sowing, and reaping, then threshing his different kinds of grain in the appointed way, is used to show that God will have everything done orderly and according to His counsel (vv. 23-29).

Denunciation of Jerusalem for lack of spiritual apprehension (ch. 29)

Jerusalem is addressed here as Ariel, the lion of God. The visitation of God's wrath is sure to come if rebellion is persisted in, but even then judgment is tempered with mercy (vv. 1-8). Refusal to heed God's message leads to judicial blindness (vv. 9-14). Judgment upon the rebellious serves to bring conviction and repentance, with spiritual illumination, to the lowly (vv. 15-24).

Denunciation of turning to Egypt for help (ch. 30)

The only result of turning away from the shelter of God's protection to Egypt would be shame and confusion, for even the Egyptians when they saw the ambassadors of Judah would despise them, and insolently make no move to help Judah (vv. 1-7). See Rotherham for verse 7. "Insolent they sit still." Isaiah is told to make special note of the rebelliousness of the people in refusing the warning of God and deliberately perverting His truth and despising His messengers (vv. 8-11). How true of conditions today! (2 Timothy 4:3,4). This attitude would provoke the Lord to bring sudden ruin (vv. 12-14). Again His call to repentance and faith in Him meets with no response (vv. 15-17). Their stiff-neckedness postpones but does not frustrate Jehovah's promises of grace to Israel, for "He is faithful that promised, who also will do it" (v. 18). A glorious promise of restoration, change of heart, and rich blessing from the Lord, is given (vv. 18-26); and the extinction of their enemies is assured (vv. 27-33).

Tophet (the same as the Valley of Hinnom, the place of idol worship and sacrifice), after the reformation, became the place for the burning of refuse, dead bodies, etc., and became, consequently, the type of hellfire, the place of perpetual burning. Christ uses this expression in Matthew frequently, where "hellfire" is literally "gehenna of fire," referring to this valley of burning. See 2 Chronicles 33:6.

Further denunciation of turning to the "arm of flesh" (ch. 31)

Dependence upon Egypt will prove futile, for she will fail Judah, but the Lord will not fail her (vv. 1-5). He calls to turn from idols to the Lord, who will defend Jerusalem against the Assyrian (vv. 6-9).

A Rapturous Vision of Victory for Israel
Against All Her Foes (chs. 32 to 35)

"The stupendous miracle of Jerusalem's deliverance from the Assyrian, just depicted prophetically, opens up the prophetic perspective upon the advent of the Deliverer in human form and manifestation, and upon the blessings, temporal and spiritual, of His reign, when He shall have put down all enemies. Quite likely Hezekiah is in view immediately, and Josiah more remotely, but only as types of the real Deliverer, the Son of God, upon whose advent and reign in Jerusalem this passage is focused. God gave Isaiah to see Jerusalem, then imperiled by the Assyrians, carried through by unseen hands until the ever-present unseen One comes in the flesh in all heavenly glory and power to make Jerusalem the joy and admiration of all the earth."—Stevens.

The blessings of Messiah's reign (ch. 32)

The Messiah is to come in righteousness, jointly reigning with His princes (v. 1; Matthew 19:28) in the form and nature of a man for a shelter (v. 2) to enlighten and teach (vv. 3,4), to displace the vile with the largehearted (vv.5-8), and through the effusion of His Spirit to transform desolation into fruitfulness (vv. 9-16). Righteousness shall bring peace and quiet, with freedom to carry on agricultural pursuits (vv. 17-20).

The spoiler spoiled and the Lord exalted in Jerusalem (ch. 33)

Of course, the Assyrian is immediately in view, but again the vision reaches down to the spoiling of Israel's final enemy and the enriching of Jerusalem by the spoil (v. 4), the exaltation of the Lord (v. 5), and the discomfiture of the sinners (v. 14). A place of dwelling in the fiery and glorious presence of the divine holiness is only for the righteous; but, robed in the righteousness of Christ, we are safe in the very bosom of God (vv. 14-17). After the removal of Israel's foes, Jerusalem shall be a quiet, holy, glorious city because of the presence of the Messiah, as Judge, Law-giver, and King. The righteous shall be delivered from the curse and scourge of sickness (vv. 18-24).

The judgment of Edom, a type of all Israel's enemies (ch. 34)

This chapter predicts a general judgment of all nations, and a heavy calamity to fall upon Edom in particular. Edom was an inveterate enemy of Judah and type of the world, the enemy of the Church. The judgment of Edom was necessary to the establishment of Israel; so will the judgment of the whole world system be necessary to the establishment of God's people, earthly and heavenly, in the place of the Lord's appointment. This chapter also views the "day of the Lord," when Edom, probably reestablished as a people, shall be visited with vengeance (cf. Isaiah 63).

Millennial blessings upon land and people (ch. 35)

A repetition of the happy story of the final issue for Israel in glorious restoration. Fruitfulness of now arid regions—a literal physical transformation (vv. 1,2), "salvation of the long intimidated Jews" (vv. 3,4), healing for the needy through the abundant outflow of the divine life (vv. 5-7), a highway built for the speedy return of the nation, "the way of holiness"—probably a literal one up to the city, over which the people and nations will travel to the Feast of Tabernacles (v. 8), the safety of their passage (v. 9), and the abounding joy of the returning, regathered Israel (v. 10).

Lesson 28

Isaiah 36-66

HISTORICAL CONNECTING LINK

(CHAPTERS 36 TO 39)

This is a most helpful appendix. It reveals historically what was foretold prophetically in the previous part. It is a fitting introduction to chapters 40-66.

SENNACHERIB'S INVASION AND OVERTHROW (CHAPTERS 36,37)

In 701 B.C. Sennacherib overran all the defensed cities of Judah and surrounded Jerusalem (vv. 1,2). We find Eliakim next in authority, according to Isaiah's word in chapter 22:20,21 (v. 3). The policy of leaning on Egypt is disclosed by the ambassador of Sennacherib, Rab-shakeh. The believing party in Jerusalem is despised by the Assyrians (vv. 7-22) who were aware of Jehovah's commission to come against Jerusalem (v. 10). This was in fulfillment of Isaiah 10:5,6.

The next chapter relates the supernatural deliverance of the city in answer to prayer. Isaiah proves to be not only God's mouthpiece, but a real counselor and statesman in this crisis hour: Hezekiah's distress (v. 1); the visit to the prophet (vv. 2-5); message of assurance of victory (vv. 6,7). The Assyrians insolently sent a message to Hezekiah, before leaving Jerusalem temporarily, saying that they would return and finish the siege and would be victorious as they had been against other nations (vv. 10-13). Hezekiah resorts to the Lord in this crisis. He acknowledges His almightiness (v. 16), also his own helplessness against the Assyrians (v. 18) despite the vanity of their gods (v. 19), and calls upon the Lord to vindicate His own name among the nations by not allowing the people of His choice to be overthrown, and for His own glory to save the kingdom (v. 20). God answers the king through the prophet, takes up the haughty challenge of the Assyrians in His own name, and gives the king assurance of glorious deliverance. He reminds the Assyrians that it is only by His own sovereign permission that they had been victorious against other kingdoms (v. 26) and says that He will turn them back (vv. 28,29). He tells of the escape of the remnant of the people and the complete defense of the city against the shooting even of an arrow (vv. 31-34). God's mercy upon Jerusalem is pure grace, for His own name's sake, and on the ground of His covenant promise to David (v. 35). Then follows the record of the supernatural overthrow of the Assyrian hosts, and of the assassination of Sennacherib (vv. 36-38).

"The literalness of the fulfillment of the foregoing prophecies in this judgment upon Assyria is proof to us that we are to expect all other prophecies of this book to be as literally fulfilled. We also have in this judgment and deliverance a type of the drama of the last days. Sennacherib typifies Antichrist in power and self-assertion, and in the marvelous success of his worldwide ambitions and operations up to the point of threatening helpless Israel with utter annihilation. The supernatural blow and timely rescue of the remnant of God's people typify the stupendous tragedy of Antichrist's overthrow and the rescue of the final remnant of Israel at Christ's appearing. And it is equally true that Israel's rescue will be without their merit, but for God's own Son's sake."—Stevens.

HEZEKIAH'S HEALING AND SIN OF PRIDE (CHAPTERS 38,39)

Hezekiah's Healing (ch. 38)

This experience of the king is a beautiful example of grace in lengthening the span of a life in answer to a heart-cry and for the glory of God. In every sense it was miraculous. It was contrary to the sentence of death upon him (v. 1). It was a direct answer to prayer (vv. 2-5). It antedated the deliverance to the king of God's further faithfulness (v. 6). It was accompanied with a supernatural sign (vv. 7,8). "It was by prophecy that the lump of figs was used, not as a remedy, even as the anointing oil now" (v. 21).

Hezekiah's song of thanksgiving is given (vv. 9-20). Hezekiah was aware that he was departing at the command of the Lord. He was prepared spiritually to go, but unwilling to die prematurely. His plaint was a bitter one; and the Lord heard his cry and saw his tears. He magnifies the grace of Jehovah for deliverance. Even if his sins

might prove a barrier to his healing, the mercy of God had cast
them all behind His back. God is glorified in the supernatural manifestation of His power in healing by the testimony of the healed
one to His name.

Hezekiah's Sin of Pride (ch. 39)
Cf. 2 Chronicles 32:25,26,31

Hezekiah evidently failed to glorify God for his healing and miraculous deliverance from Assyria, in the eyes of the Babylonian
ambassadors, but magnified himself. The ambassadors went away
coveting the material treasures of his kingdom, rather than receiving
the spiritual benefit a faithful testimony to Jehovah would have
conveyed. Babylon was a small kingdom at this time, but came into
great power about a century later. Hezekiah repented and humbled
himself, but the Lord had settled it that Judah and Jerusalem should
be taken captive to Babylon.

PART II (CHAPTERS 40 TO 66)

This part is consolatory, being in direct contrast with Part I. The
word *comfort* occurred only once in the first part (12:1), but frequently we find it throughout Part II (40:1,2; 49:13; 52:12; 61:2;
66:13). This part is not addressed to the impenitent, but to the
remnant in the nation who were "sighing and crying for the abominations" of the nations and needed the encouragement of these
messages. The last part closed with a distinct prophecy concerning
Babylonian captivity; and while this word was not fulfilled for more
than a century later, "still we have not to read far in this part to
find that prophetically we are seated alongside the weeping remnant
in their captivity."

There is a formal division of this part into three sections of nine
chapters each, noted by the repetition of the words, "There is no
peace, saith my God, to the wicked" (48:22; 57:21).

"As has been said, the exiles in Babylon are especially addressed
in their earlier chapters, with strong and comforting assurances of
a happy release and return to Jerusalem. But as the event proved,
this was such an imperfect restoration that it could not fill the cup
of consolation permanently, but could only serve as a token of something better. This higher comfort is especially emphasized in the
second section in the coming of the Redeemer in the form of God's

true servant and the Minister of the gospel. But even this comfort is seriously shadowed by His predicted rejection by His own, so that consolation passes on, in the third section (v. 3), for its final resting place to the coming of the King in glory and in perfect restoration of Israel. These three objective points form the climax respectively of these three sections."—Stevens.

CONSOLATION IN VIEW OF THE RETURN FROM BABYLONIAN CAPTIVITY (CHAPTERS 40 TO 48)

God's Ability to Bring Israel Back from Exile (ch. 40)

Consolation in view of the fact that the full measure of chastisement had been meted out, iniquity pardoned (vv. 1,2). The prophetic call to prepare the way of the Lord, a providential opening for their return as well as a spiritual preparation in the hearts of Israel (vv. 3-8). Verse 3 really requires a three-fold fulfillment to exhaust it: (1) the decree of Cyrus (2 Chronicles 36:22,23) with the consequent leadership of Ezra and Nehemiah in bringing the exiles back from Babylonian captivity; (2) the ministry of John the Baptist (Matthew 3:3) as the forerunner of Christ in His first advent; (3) the ministry of Elijah, as witness and forerunner of the second advent to Israel (Malachi 3:1; 4:5; Matthew 17:11,12; Luke 1:17). The ministry of Messiah as the strong and yet tender Shepherd of His flock is seen (vv. 9-11). A sublime picture of Jehovah in His glorious majesty (cf. Job 38-41) and infinite ability to accomplish His purposes for His people, and the vanity of the boasted idols of the nations (vv. 12-26). The confession of weakness on the part of His people brings the comforting assurance of the full supply of His strength, unwavering, unfainting (vv. 27-31).

The Inability of the Nations to Frustrate God's Purposes to Restore His People (ch. 41)

The fulfillment of His promises to bring back Israel involved complete political changes and the overthrow of the mighty Babylonian Empire. God raised up Cyrus as the agent to fulfill His purposes to deliver the exiles. Cyrus is called "the righteous man from the east," into whose hands the Lord puts the scepter of power (v. 2). The consternation of the idol people and the vanity of their resistance is pictured (vv. 1-7). The Lord through the prophet reassures Israel of His abiding covenant with Abraham (vv. 8,9), of His presence in time of need, and even though Jacob be a "worm," in alliance with God's strength every enemy shall be subdued (vv. 10-16). Even Jehovah's power over nature will be manifest, if need be, in behalf of His people (vv. 17-20).

The prophet mentions the use of prophecy as evidence that the Lord, knowing and declaring the end from the beginning, has ample power to bring His purposes to fulfillment. The vanity of idols is again revealed (vv. 21-29).

The Faithful Servant, Christ, to Whom Redemption Is Entrusted (ch. 42)

At the time of the prophecy, working unseen was the Holy One of Israel, Messiah; but now it is revealed that He shall be manifested as the "Servant of the Lord" to accomplish His will. He is pictured in His ministry of grace and healing, His mission to Gentiles, etc., in His first advent (vv. 1-7) and in His mighty power as Judge, Deliverer, and Establisher of righteousness. The joy of the inhabitants of the world, when His rule is established, is foretold (vv. 8-17). Israel, the faithless servant, is seen (vv. 18-25).

Assurance of Return from Babylonian Captivity (ch. 43)

Here is assurance of God's faithful interest in Israel, even though they are unworthy (vv. 1-7). The fuller restoration of the latter times is again seen in the earlier fulfillment of return from Babylon. God calls Israel to reflect on His faithfulness to them in the past and reminds them of His call to them to be His witnesses. He alone is the Saviour (vv. 8-13). Babylon is shown to be the object of His wrath for Israel's sake (vv. 14,15). He calls upon Israel, after remembering His faithfulness in the past, to look from that to better and more glorious things, which in His grace He has prepared for them (vv. 16-21). He reminds them of their rejection of His covenant and neglect of His worship; yet in grace He is the One who can and will blot out all their sins, when true repentance is seen (vv. 22-28).

Assurance of the Spiritual Transformation Necessary to Bring About the Return from Babylon (ch. 44)

The reason for the Babylonian captivity was Israel's idolatrous imitation of the nations about them. The chastisement of the exile was efficacious in completely transforming their bent on this line. Today there is not a nation on earth that hates idolatry more than the Jew. As Jehovah had chosen Jacob for His special servant, He promises to pour out His Spirit upon him, causing spiritual fruitfulness and a full change of heart toward Him (vv. 1-5). The Lord points out His claim to preeminence and calls Israel again to witness to His care of them (vv. 6-8). Then follows a most clear and graphic description of the utter folly and vanity of idol worship (vv. 9-20). Further assurance is given of His unchanging love, mercy, and purpose to yet glorify Himself through them and to bring to nought the rebellious (vv. 21-26).

The chapter closes with a definite revelation by name of the deliverer Cyrus, the Shepherd, who will perform God's pleasure (vv. 27,28). Nearly two centuries later Cyrus was to issue the decree for the laying of the foundation of the temple and the rebuilding of Jerusalem. "Notice how minutely accurate prophecy is here as elsewhere, in that only the foundation of the temple was laid under Cyrus, the rearing and completion of the structure waiting for the decree under Darius" (Ezra 1:4; 3:11; 4:4; 5:16; 6:7,15).—Stevens.

Appointment of Cyrus as the Agent of the Regathering from Babylon (ch. 45)

"This is a most wonderful portion of prophecy, committing God to the execution of Israel's restoration from Babylon by a king whose very name is given a century and a half before his birth, and nearly two centuries before the empire arose, of which he in his work was to be the head. No wonder the present chapter exults in the name of wonders of such a God!"

Cyrus receives his prophetic appointment as the special instrument in the hands of the Lord to bring about for the sake of Israel, His elect, their deliverance from Babylon. Cyrus himself understood that his commission had come from the Lord, and that his ascendency over the nations (Ezra 1:2) was ordained of God (vv. 1-5).

The relationship between the heavenlies and the earth is seen (vv. 6-8), "the former the reservoir of righteousness, the other as a vessel for its reception" (see Scofield's note on verse 7).

In view of this, submission to the will of God is the only attitude of rulers and peoples, and it is as futile to resist His will as to imagine clay rising up in resistance to the potter's hands (vv. 9-12).

Cyrus' commission is repeated (v. 13), to be executed fully for the glory of God and not for any lesser motive. The mightiest nations of those days shall acknowledge God in this restoration, and lose confidence in their idols, humbly acknowledging Israel as His covenant people (vv. 14-17).

"This crowning destiny of Israel is shown to be essential to God's original and unchangeable purpose for the earth (vv. 18,19); 'He created it not in vain, He formed it to be inhabited.' God neither created the earth a chaos, nor will He let it end in chaos. He created it for habitation; somebody (Satan) brought it to ruin; God renewed it for man, as an everlasting habitation for endless generations. Again Satan stepped in and wrought man's downfall. God gave a Redeemer through the seed of the woman, more specifically the seed of Abraham. Through Him the earth is to be recovered for its original purpose. But this is impossible without the restoration of the full salvation. This great plan has been directly revealed by God, to whom its accomplishment belongs. He has not said to Jacob, 'Seek ye me' in vain. He will bring Israel back to Himself and perfect that which He has designed" (vv. 20-25; compare Acts 15:16,17)—Stevens.

The Mighty Idol Divinities of Babylon
Proven Utterly in Vain (ch. 46)

"Bel and Nebo, together with Merodach (Jeremiah 50:2), constituted Babylon's trinity of divinities, corresponding to the Trinity of the true God. Bel, or Baal, meaning Lord, headed the list. Merodach, the Jupiter of the Romans, was called king of heaven and earth, over against God's King. Nebo was the god of wisdom, 'Scribe of the universe,' over against the inspiring Spirit. The name Nebo is found in such proper names as Nebuchadnezzar, Nabopolassar, Nabonidus."

A striking contrast between the idol gods of Babylon and the true living God is given (vv. 1-4). The heathen gods are burdens to be borne by the beasts, while the living God carries His people from the womb to old age. The infinite distance between Jehovah and the idols is pictured (vv. 5-7), and this is given as the reason for trusting Him (vv. 8-13). Cyrus is again mentioned in verse 11.

Complete Abasement of the Proud City of Babylon (ch. 47)

Almost two centuries before the queen of ancient cities rose to glory among the nations, she is prophetically viewed as debased (vv. 1-5). The reasons for this were her exceeding God's prescribed limit for the chastening of His people (v. 6), refusal to heed God's judgment upon Israel, and haughtily boasting herself against him (vv. 7-9). She even trusted in her own wickedness, foolishly forgetting His omniscience (v. 10). Evil would surely come upon her, and no seeking to divination and the dark arts, or the counsel of her wise men, could avert the calamity (vv. 11-15).

Summary of God's Dealings with Judah, Culminating in the Return from Captivity (ch. 48)

The captives are reminded that the Lord had foretold the situation in which we see them prophetically (v. 3), and the reason for it was their obstinate apostasy (vv. 1-6). The purpose of the exile is revealed as a refining process, the result of which would be to make them a praise to His name and a glory among the nations (vv. 6-11). Through His chosen instrument, the Almighty (vv. 12,13) will visit judgment upon Babylon, Israel's "furnace of affliction" (vv. 14-16). The design of Jehovah in this chastening, as with all His dealings with those He loves, is to teach them "to profit." The Lord regrets that this chastening was necessary, but assures of a glorious and happy issue out of it all in release (vv. 17-21). The wicked have no part in these blessings (v. 22).

CONSOLATION IN VIEW OF MESSIAH'S FIRST ADVENT (CHAPTERS 49 TO 57)

The restoration from Babylon, while a signal event in the history of Israel, was only preliminary to a more glorious dealing of God, a "new thing," which He had in reserve. Only a remnant returned from Chaldea under Ezra and Nehemiah, and while the purifying fires of the exile were powerful in burning out the idolatrous spirit, yet the result fell far short of fulfilling the promise of their ultimate blessing to the whole earth. Hence this section points to the advent of their Messiah. "The evangelist Matthew, sketching in chapter 1 the chronology of Israel from Abraham to Christ through the genealogy of Christ, puts three events into a series like mountaintops, with 14 generations between successive peaks, namely, Abraham to David, David to Babylon, Babylon to Christ."—Stevens. Babylon is now viewed as prophetically past, and the view is forward to the coming of the personal Deliverer, the true "consolation of Israel" (Luke 2:25-32).

The rejection of Messiah, vividly portrayed in this section, and its most prominent theme, suspends the final rest of the nation until the glorious second advent of Christ, pictured in the last section of the book.

Messiah, the Servant of God, the Preserver of Israel, and the Light to the Gentiles (ch. 49)

The Servant of Jehovah here is very evidently the Christ, "the Anointed One," foreordained to this calling. The failure of His ministry for a time is suggested in verses four and seven (vv. 1-7). The second advent, by contrast is seen in full success in fulfillment of the covenant promises, the setting up of the Kingdom, deliverance from the curse (8-10), the gathering of the nations unto Israel—even China (v. 12)—in joyful acknowledgment of the Lord's love to them (vv. 11-16). The fulfillment of the promise to Abraham, that his seed should be as the dust of the earth, is seen (vv. 17-21), with the ready response of the nations in that day of marvels in worship and humble acknowledgment of the Lord (vv. 22-26).

Messiah Under the Humiliation of His First Advent (ch. 50)

This chapter clearly pictures the rejection of the Messiah at the time of His first advent. In the words of the prophet He remonstrates with them for their rejection of Him, as if the nation had been divorced from Jehovah, or as if He had no power to save (vv. 1-3). We see the dependence of Christ daily upon the Father for wisdom and words to speak, as He aims to do His will (vv. 4,5)—"I can of my own self do nothing." His obedience even unto submission to shame and contempt (v. 6). His complete confidence in the Lord to vindicate His claims and put His enemies to shame; consequently His purpose to endure unto the end (vv. 7-9). The prophetic exhortation of Messiah to the believer to trust the Lord in unwavering faith even in the midst of darkness and perplexity, with a warning to the unbeliever that his false faith, in any other than Himself, shall result in sorrow and destruction (v. 11).

Millennial Restoration to Full Favor with the Lord and Redemption from All Affliction (chs. 51:1 to 52:12)

Assurance is given to the believing remnant that He has not forgotten His covenant promise to Abraham, that joy and comfort shall surely come, justice be done, and that even though the heavens and earth vanish, He will surely vindicate His Word (vv. 1-6). Assurance to the "righteous" that He will vindicate not only His Word but them also and that every adversary shall disappear (vv. 7,8). He reminds them that just as He made a way for them through the sea, He will exert His mighty power in their behalf, bringing them, joyful, back to Zion (vv. 9-16). The cup of sorrow and judgment that Jehovah has caused them to drink, because of their sin, will be given to them who have afflicted His people (vv. 17-23). The prophetic call is given in this Gospel Age. As we, with "feet shod with the preparation [firm footing] of the gospel of peace," tread the mountains of sin, so will Israel, God's witnesses, publish the "gospel of the kingdom," announcing the advent of the King to all nations (52:7-10). Just as the remnant under the leadership of Ezra and Nehemiah were called to go forth from Babylon, so will the remnant of the latter days be called to separation from the corruptions of Antichrist, with the assurance that the Lord himself will both lead and guard them fore and aft (vv. 11,12).

The Vicarious Suffering of Messiah (chs. 52:13 to 53:12)

It is indeed worthy of note that this marvelous portion depicting Messiah's sufferings occupies the central place in the middle section of this message of consolation of Part II.

The first advent of Christ was specifically for the purpose of putting "away sin by the sacrifice of himself" (Hebrews 9:26). This passage graphically portrays the sufferings of Christ and the reason for them—His redemptive work for Israel and "the nations." The first and second advent are brought into contrast here, the first appearing more clearly against the background of the second in glory.

The first and second advents contrasted (ch. 52:13-15)

Nations and kings are astonished at the "Servant," first, in the marred aspect of His countenance in the first advent and then in the majesty of His glorious second advent. "The literal rendering is terrible: 'So marred from the form of man was His aspect that His appearance was not that of a son of man'—i.e., not human— the effect of the brutalities described in Matthew 26:67,68; 27:27-30."—Scofield.

The unbelief of Israel (53:1-3)

The prophet describes the lowly character of the Messiah and the utter abhorrence and rejection with which He was met by the blinded nation.

His vicarious atonement (vv. 4-6)

"The hardest part of His trial was that He appeared to be cursed of God on His own account, while in reality it was all on account of His people and for all men. Every line of these verses emphasizes the substitutionary character of His sufferings. All other explanation of the atonement than as vicarious, i.e., taking our place penally and sacrificially, is precluded."—Stevens.

1. *Atonement for bodily healing* (v. 4). The rendering from the Septuagint Version in Matthew 8:17 clearly reveals the fact that the work and atonement of Christ has freed us from the curse upon our bodies, making it possible to have divine deliverance from sickness, and finally from mortality, which shall be swallowed up of life. The Jewish Version renders verse four, "Surely our diseases He did bear, and our pains He carried."

2. *Pardon for our sins as individual transgressors* (v. 5). Provision is made for the immediate cleansing, upon apprehension by faith of the sinner, of all the black record of the past. "I will blot out as a thick cloud thy transgressions." The blessed truth of provision for healing is again seen in the last clause, rendered by Leeser as follows: "Through His bruises was healing granted unto us."

3. *Purification from the evil principle within* (v. 6). Not only must the specific transgressions be forgiven, but provision must be made for the evil nature from which the sins spring. "Here is something common to all men, born in sin and not pardoned and healed out of us. Our common, inherited sin, as well as our sins and sicknesses, has been imputed to the Crucified. Our deliverance is, therefore, an act of God's grace through faith in Jesus for this very thing. The cleansing rectifies our wayward, self-assertive will, and brings us into perfect love according to the fundamental law of God."—Stevens.

The lamblike submission of Messiah (vv. 7-9)

The amazing self-submission of the Lord to the ignominy and shame of an unjust trial in the judgment hall, to the cruel death of the Cross, and to death and the grave in the company of malefactors, is vividly portrayed by the prophet here. Who but the Spirit of God could have written beforehand such an accurate account of the events recorded in the Gospels.

The reward to Messiah for His faithfulness (vv. 10-12)

The suffering of Christ is seen to be the result of the displeasure of God because of the sins of the world imputed unto Him. "He was made sin for us, who knew no sin. . . ." The result of this vicarious sin offering would be the salvation of many. This is the prominent note in the last two verses.

Israel's Rich Blessing After Being Received Back into Jehovah's Favor (ch. 54)

This chapter pictures the resultant blessing to Israel through the sacrifice of Messiah as a sin offering. Israel is here viewed as the wife of Jehovah once put away for unfaithfulness, but now received back into full favor. Barrenness now gives place to fruitfulness (vv. 1-3). The shame, sorrow, and desolation caused by her unfaithfulness now gives place to the fulfillment of the covenant of everlasting preservation and peace (vv. 4-10). The affliction and unrest passes away and glorious restoration in peace and righteousness is seen (vv. 11-14). No enemy shall ever disturb, nor slander arise from any quarter, because He has established them in His righteousness (vv. 15-17).

Spiritual Conditions of the Restoration (ch. 55)

Real spiritual longing on the part of the nation will meet with a full supply of the richest provisions of grace, causing real "fatness." Their reception of the Messiah, the Son of David, will not only mean rich blessing to Israel, but will cause other nations to desire the Holy One of Israel, as they see "the glory of Israel" (vv. 1-5). Genuine repentance will bring abundant pardon and blessing beyond their highest thought (vv. 6-9). Trusting in God's Word will be to realize abundant joy and peace amid the glad chorus of praise even from renewed and transformed nature (vv. 10-13).

Practical Righteousness (ch. 56:1,2)

"While salvation is not by works, yet it brings forth works of righteousness; it changes practices, as well as hearts. Sabbath observance is everywhere in the Old Testament made a test of real heart religion. The reason is because the Sabbath, the same as the rite of circumcision, was the peculiar sign of God's everlasting covenant with Israel (Exodus 31:12-17). Kept merely as a work of merit, the Sabbath was an offense to God and a stumbling block to Israel, even as to us. But kept as a mark of faith in God's fidelity to His covenant with Israel, it is well-pleasing to Him. This old Sabbath, the sign of God's covenant with Israel, is not transferred to Sunday, or the Lord's Day, which rests upon another foundation than that of the fourth commandment or God's relation to Israel. And, just as no one can call Jesus Lord but by the Holy Ghost, so no one can truly keep the Lord's Day under mere conscience or legal requirement, but only as a new creature and by the Holy Ghost."—Stevens.

The Open Door (ch. 56:3-8)

"Exclusiveness is absolutely foreign to grace. God's regulations for the seclusions of Israel of old from corrupting relations with Gentiles were never intended to cultivate 'bigoted exclusiveness. This long-standing characteristic of self-righteous Israel shall be utterly wanting in her millennial transformation. Consequently the blessings of consecration to God, so richly promised to the godly remnant of Israel, as we have seen, will be open to all classes of people. The church may obtain a better name than of sons and daughters; strangers, of spiritual character, will be equally accepted with Israelites; God's temple shall be indeed 'a house of prayer for all nations,' and God will gather many Gentiles to His 'regathered Israel.' "—Stevens.

Warning to the Wicked of Exclusion from the Blessings of the Restoration (chs. 56:9 to 57:21)

In strong contrast to the foregoing is this section which pictures the unbelieving and rebellious among Israel as lazy, gluttonous dogs, selfish shepherds, and blind revelers (56:9-12). These are blind to the virtues of the righteous and ignorant of their blessed and peaceful end (57:1,2). "They are accused of spiritual adultery, because of idolatry and worldly alliance, so hateful to God!" (vv. 3-12). The end of the wicked is seen (v. 13), but also the gracious response of the Almighty to the humble penitent, even though his sins had before separated him from the Lord (vv. 14-19). The section closes with a repetition of the warning of unrest and lack of peace to the wicked (vv. 20,21).

CONSOLATION IN VIEW OF MESSIAH'S SECOND ADVENT (CHAPTERS 58 TO 66)

The coming of the Messiah in humiliation and rejection now passes from view, and the focus of the last section of the book is the second advent when Christ comes in glorious manifestation and power as Avenger, Judge, and Destroyer, setting up His reign in majesty upon the throne of David and perfecting Israel's restoration in the millennial dispensation.

Warning Against Hypocritical Religion and Its Consequences;
the Consequences and Reward of Real Piety (ch. 58)

Israel is rebuked for her hypocrisy (vv. 1,2), and her complaint at not being rewarded for her fasting (v. 3) is met with the charge that her fasting has made no change in her heart nor brought about practical righteousness (vv. 4,7). Real repentance and practical righteousness would soon bring, in answer to prayer, the manifestation of the Lord's presence in rich blessing (vv. 8-10). He would guide, rebuild, and refresh (vv. 11,12), and, if His Sabbaths were again regarded, their delight would surely be in Him, as they realized His goodness and faithfulness in supplying their need fully (vv. 13,14).

The Consummation of Sin (ch. 59)

Israel in the "latter days" will fill up her cup of iniquity with the same sins which caused the judgment of the captivity, probably becoming intoxicated with her own new effort, now expressed in the modern state of Israel.

Murder, lying, perverseness, injustice, malice, and violence will characterize Israel, as well as the Gentile nations in the latter days of this dispensation (vv. 1-8). Spiritual blindness will follow and they will be left to reap the crop of their own planting, in injustice and violence done to them (vv. 9-15). Salvation for the ones who depart from evil, and therefore are accounted mad (v. 15), will be wrought by the Lord himself in delivering them from their oppressors (vv. 16-18), and, in their hour of deepest need, when almost swallowed up by their enemies, He, the Redeemer, will come to fill them with His Spirit and fulfill His covenant to give abiding peace and rest forever (vv. 19-21).

The Exaltation of Millennial Israel (ch. 60)

This chapter closely follows the latter verses of the preceding and pictures the exaltation of Israel among the nations of the earth during the Millennium. In the midst of the darkest hours of the Great Tribulation, at its close, Israel is bidden to arise and fulfill her commission when the "sign of the Son of man" shall be seen (vv. 1-3). She is bidden to look at the stream of sons and daughters coming Zionward from all directions in the time of her real restoration, also the wealth of the nations as a mighty river flowing unto

her, an acceptable offering, with which the Lord will glorify His
people with Him (vv. 4-9).

Does not verse 8 suggest swift-flying aircraft in clouds bringing
Israel back laden with the wealth of the nations? Or does it represent, as in verse 9, vessels in fleets, like white clouds or flocks of
doves on the wing? The Gentile nations shall contribute labor and
wealth to rebuild her walls, their kings recognizing the good hand
of the Lord upon them. Such nations as do not respond in those
wonderful days shall perish. Her gates shall be open continually
because of the multitude of people passing in and out in steady
streams bringing their gifts with them (vv. 10-12).

The resources of the beautiful Lebanon shall be used to beautify
Jerusalem; the nations shall vie with each other in offering obeisance
and bringing goodly presents (vv. 13-16). The baser metals shall be
replaced in her ornamentation by the more valuable; policemen and
tax collectors shall be part of the past, their activities directed into
other channels of constructive character. Violence and robbery,
plague and pestilence shall be no more; the glory of Messiah's presence shall be their light, and a transformed, righteous, and obedient
people shall dwell safely in the land. In a short time a small clan
shall become a mighty nation. Marvelously will this all be wrought
in a short time, when the silence of Jehovah toward His people shall
be broken. Glory to God! (vv. 17-22).

The Anointed One Who Will Bring Israel
To Millennial Blessings (ch. 61)

Messiah himself speaks of the Spirit's anointing upon Him for the
ministry of the gospel, and for His glorious millennial work (vv. 1-
3). His gospel work is described down to verse 2, first clause (cf.
Luke 4:17-21). Thereafter His millennial work is described. Then
follows a condensed repetition of what has been already revealed
in the previous chapters (vv. 4-9). After this comes a song of rejoicing, put into Israel's mouth prophetically, over her restoration
to Jehovah's favor.

Hastening the Millennial Day (ch. 62)
The intercession of Messiah himself (vv. 1-5)

While these verses may be considered as the words of the prophet,
it would seem more appropriate to consider them as the yearning
of the Lord Jesus Christ himself, the heavenly Intercessor, that His

people Israel might realize her salvation and become "a crown of glory in the hand of the Lord, and a royal diadem in the hand" of their God (cf. Matthew 23:37-39). He surely is awaiting the day when her sun shall rise upon the nations, her desolation give place to fruitfulness, and she become the delight of His heart.

The intercession of God's watchmen for the coming of the Lord (vv. 6-9)

Like Daniel of old, who saw by the books that the time of restoration from Babylonian captivity was at hand and immediately began to intercede for the fulfillment of the promise as a priest before the Lord, so should we, as we see the day approaching, give ourselves to this priestly ministry in Israel's behalf. Our destiny is inseparably linked with the destiny of the earthly people, we as the heavenly Bride and Israel as His earthly bride. The redemption of the earth from the curse, the end of war, the only solution of the multiplied problems of the present day among the nations, all await Israel's restoration. See Psalm 122.

Jewish evangelism (vv. 10-12)

The ministry of John the Baptist was one of evangelism in preparing the way for the advent of the Messiah. The ministry of the Early Church and down to the present day has been to prepare the way of the Lord; for salvation is "to the Jew first," and we can help to gather out the "remnant according to the election of grace" now. These verses doubtless will find their exact fulfillment in the ministry of the "144,000" during the Tribulation days, and then in the opening days of the millennial dispensation, when Jewish evangels shall proclaim the advent of the King throughout the wide world, and a nation shall be born in a day. Lord, hasten the day!

Christ the Avenger of Israel (ch. 63:1-6)

These verses have been interpreted by commentators in the past as referring to Calvary and the shedding of the blood of the Savior there; but the context clearly shows that the reference to Him is not as the sacrificial Lamb, but as the Avenger, whose garments are stained with the blood of His enemies. The figure here is of the Treader of Grapes, trampling out with His feet the red juice of the grapes in the winepress, as was done in Oriental countries, the juice of the grapes bespattering the garments of the treader. The reference to Bozrah, the ancient capital of Edom, as the point from which the great Judge appears, may signify that from the direction of ancient Edom the glorious sign of the Son of Man will appear in the time of Israel's direst need. Then again, Edom may be mentioned as a type of the enemies of Israel in the "latter days." Edom was always an implacable foe of the Jewish nation. Much life blood will be shed in the awful closing days of this dispensation. There is a possible reference to this scene in Revelation 14:16-20; 19:11-21.

The Prayer of the Godly Remnant (chs. 63:7 to 64:12)

Isaiah voices the pleadings and the heart cry of the remnant of the latter time as, in their time of extreme need and pressure from Antichrist, they remind the Lord of His lovingkindness and faithfulness to the nation of old, confess the reason for His averted face, and call upon Him again to manifest himself in their behalf (vv. 7-14). Prayer for Him to again turn toward them follows as they remind the Lord of His former yearnings over them and of the fact that even though Abraham and Jacob, their ancestors, should fail to acknowledge them, He is their Father. They remind Him that their adversaries have possessed the land for a long time and they, to whom it rightfully belongs, have been tenants only a short time, as if He never bore rule over them.

Then follows an urgent and insistent cry for immediate help, doubtless in the time when Antichrist would swallow them up. They urge the necessity of the manifestation of His power to the ungodly nations (vv. 1-3), and the fulfillment of the things inconceivable to the natural man, which He had promised to the righteous waiting ones (vv. 4,5). Real repentance and acknowledgment of their unworthiness follows (vv. 6,7). This very condition calls for His divine interposition as their Father, His forgiveness, and the restoration of the desolate land and city (vv. 8-12).

Jehovah's Reply to the Prayer (ch. 65)
The church (vv. 1-7)

Romans 10:20 sheds light upon this portion, where Isaiah reveals the calling out from the Gentiles of a "people for his name" (Acts 15:14). The time of Israel's rebellion, self-righteousness, and apostasy is the time when the Lord gathers from the Gentile nations a bride for himself. Israel, meanwhile, pouts in rebellion and self-righteousness over this "calling of the Gentiles" until God fully and finally measures "their former work into their bosom" by the closing Tribulation (vv. 6,7).

The godly remnant in the midst of the unbelieving masses (vv. 8-16)

While the Lord is visiting the masses of Israel with judgment, He has His eye upon the faithful "little flock" in the midst of them—the living seed, the godly remnant. These He separates (cf. Ezekiel 9) from the ungodly, who are reserved for the sword (vv. 11,12). His "servants" shall sing for joy, take upon themselves the name of the Lord, and forget all their tribulations in the great joy of their restoration (vv. 15,16).

The millennial city, people, and land (vv. 17-25)

The thought of God for the final "new heavens and new earth" is to be preceded by the creation of a New Jerusalem, to be a joy and a rejoicing in the earth. There will be no more sorrow, no more untimely and premature death, no more enduring of sinners in the midst, no more fruitless labor, no more violence, no more unanswered prayer; and all ferocity and bloodthirstiness will be gone from the animal creation. This is the glowing picture of the renewed land and nation.

Summary of Millennial Consummations (ch. 66)

The old nation (vv. 1-4)

"God, whose throne is in heaven and whose footstool is the earth, can take no rest in temple or offerings of a hypocritical people, such as Israel ever proved to be. He prefers the temple of a humble and obedient heart. Hence, He does away with the old nation of Israel, as a nation of false, self-willed worshipers."—Stevens.

The new nation (vv. 5-9)

"Jerusalem is to be the scene of a nation's birth in a day. A persecuted remnant, who fear the word of the Lord, shall suddenly emerge from the midst of national catastrophe and destruction, and be constituted by their Messiah into the new nation of millennial glory and worldwide honor."—Stevens.

The other nations (vv. 10-21)

"The new nation, unlike the old, so far from despising and excluding the Gentiles, and so far from making itself an object of hatred and prejudice to them, shall share its joys and blessings freely with them, on the one hand; and they, the Gentiles, on the other hand, 'shall be delighted with the abundance of her glory,' i.e., Jerusalem's

glory (vv. 10-14). For God not only will destroy the incorrigible
Israelites but also the incorrigible Gentiles; those who gather for
Israel's destruction will be gathered likewise for their own destruction (vv. 15-18). After this double judgment, the remnants of the
nations that escape from the general catastrophe shall return from
Jerusalem to their own lands to tell the tale of Messiah's arrival and
glory (v. 19), and to stir up the Gentile nations to bring back the
scattered members of Israel (v. 20). God will even take of godly
Gentiles that emigrate to the Holy Land, for priests and Levites,
i.e., for the sacred offices of priests and Levites" (v. 21)—Stevens.

The everlasting nation (vv. 22-24)

"The things seen are now temporal, but are not always to be so.
New heavens and a new earth are to be constituted that shall remain
before God forever. Even so, this new Israel and its seed are to
remain before God forever (v. 23). They shall be the rallying point
of worship for the whole world perpetually (v. 23). And the perpetual
signs of the destruction of transgressors, Israelites and Gentiles
alike, shall be among the objects of instructive interest and awful
warning to all who visit Jerusalem" (v. 24)—Stevens.

Lesson 29

Micah

Historical Background

While Amos and Hosea prophesied in the north, Isaiah and Micah were contemporary in the south and ministered directly in Judah, although Micah's vision also takes in Samaria, the northern kingdom of Israel (1:1). "It was a period of turmoil, strife, change, and growth. Assyria, coming rapidly to front rank as a world power, invaded and destroyed both Syria and Israel. The shadow of Assyria's armies was cast over Judah and the lowlands of Philistia."—Yates.

We have discussed some facts concerning the times of these early prophets in the study of Amos and Hosea, but the ministries of Micah and those of Isaiah, his fellow-prophet in Judah, occur a few years later in the stormy period following the Golden Age of Jeroboam II and Uzziah.

To serve as background for the study of both Micah and Isaiah we cover the reigns of these four kings in Judah—Uzziah, Jotham, Ahaz, and Hezekiah—during which the northern kingdom of Israel disintegrated rapidly and finally reached its tragic end.

About 745 B.C. the Assyrian king, Tiglath-pileser III, began his conquest of the West. He was the Pul or Pulu of 2 Kings 15:19, having changed his name for that of the illustrious Tiglath-pileser I, a great Assyrian conqueror *(Encyclopedia Britannica)*. He first broke the power of the Arameans (northeast of Palestine near the river Euphrates) and their allies in northern Syria. The year 738 B.C. found the Assyrians conquerors of Syria, Israel's northern neighbor, and Rezin of Syria (Isaiah 7:1) and Menahem of Israel paying tribute (2 Kings 15:19). This invasion marked the beginning of the end for both of these kingdoms.

Just a few years later, depending upon Egypt for help, Rezin of

Syria and Pekah of Israel determined to unite the people of the West against Assyria. They had grown tired of paying tribute to the Assyrians. Jotham, king of Judah, a godly son of Uzziah, refused to be drawn into this plan and later his son Ahaz was attacked by Rezin and Pekah. (See Isaiah 7:1-9.) Ahaz invited Tiglath-pileser to come to his aid, which he was only too quick to do. He immediately struck at Syria, captured Damascus, slew Rezin, and in 732 B.C. practically overran Israel. Samaria was left as a small city with a vassal king, Hoshea (2 Kings 17:1) as its ruler.

Hoshea was content to pay tribute for a short time only. He revolted and Shalmaneser, Tiglath-pileser's successor, besieged Samaria. After 3 years it fell (722 B.C.) and was destroyed by Sargon II, who had come to the throne during the siege. Captivity then came for the kingdom, founded 209 years earlier by Jeroboam I.

The land of Israel was practically depopulated, and colonists, brought from various lands by the Assyrians, occupied it under Assyrian governors. (See 2 Kings 17:24.)

Hezekiah, a godly king, son of the wicked Ahaz, came to the throne in Judah about 728 B.C. and gradually turned away from Assyria. The official policy of the court at this time was to lean upon Egypt for help against the increasing Assyrian encroachments upon the south. Apparently Hezekiah personally was not too much in sympathy with this policy. This reformer king threw out the Assyrian altar which Ahaz had brought from Damascus in 732 B.C. (See 2 Kings 16:10-16.)

About 715 B.C. the Philistine city of Ashdod led a general revolt against the Assyrians. Judah, Edom, and Moab, relying upon Egypt, refused to pay tribute to Sargon II. In 711 he attacked the West with a powerful army and inflicted heavy punishment upon the rebels. But the people of Jerusalem itself escaped and the city was spared.

Upon Sargon's death, 705 B.C., the powerful young Sennacherib came to the Assyrian throne. In 701 B.C. he overran all the defensed cities of Judah (see Isaiah 36) and his armies under the leadership of his general Rabshakeh arrived before the very gates of Jerusalem. Hezekiah's faith in Jehovah and Isaiah's statesmanlike counsel and confidence in the divine word, kept the inhabitants of Jerusalem from surrender; the Assyrian armies were supernaturally destroyed;

and Sennacherib fled to Assyria, soon to be assassinated by his sons (Isaiah 37:36-38).

During these stormy times Isaiah and Micah preached and counseled in Judah.

The Man Micah

Very little is known of the prophet other than the statement of 1:1, except what we may gather from the tone of his message. His name is a shortened form of Micaiah, meaning, "Who is like Jehovah?" He was a native of the town of Moresheth in the western part of Judah. "It was formerly a dependency of Gath, one of the cities of the Philistines, but by the conquests of Uzziah this whole territory came into the possession of Judah. Unlike Isaiah and Jeremiah, this prophet did not belong to the capital, but lived in the country. He lived by the great international highway [from Assyria to Egypt] and was in a position to observe the political movements in Western Asia."—Kaye.

"Through this quiet village passed the messengers and diplomats from the court of Jerusalem en route to Egypt. It was an ideal place for a young prophet to live and learn and preach. Micah was a country man who looked with distrust upon the residents of the cities, and yet he must have learned to love his capital city with a sincere devotion. He was keenly aware of world events and their significance. His lowly origin made him capable of seeing things in a light that might well be coveted by statesmen the world over."—Yates.

He was probably the writer of his own messages, we judge from the personal references in 3:1,8. The testimony to his ministry by the elders in the reign of Jehoiakim (time of Jeremiah the prophet) indicates that he died in peace. He is frequently described as a prophet. His utterances are quoted in Isaiah 41:15 (cf. Micah 4:13); Ezekiel 22:27 (cf. Micah 3:2); Zephaniah 3:19 (cf. Micah 4:6,7); Matthew 2:5 and John 7:42 (cf. Micah 5:2). Jesus quotes him in Matthew 10:35,36. His prophecy of the destruction of Jerusalem was an indirect means of saving the life of Jeremiah when the latter was about to be put to death for making a similar prediction (Jeremiah 26:10-19).

His Personality

We must not disassociate the prophets from their times, as though they were emotionally impassive toward prevailing conditions in their nation. Even though anointed of God as His messengers, they were men very much alive to the social, political, and economic conditions and keenly sensitive to the wrongs and injustices of their day. Undoubtedly Jehovah clothed, as He always does, the personality of these prophets with himself and gave them much freedom to express, in line with His ultimate purpose, their own feelings.

"It belongs to the theanthropic [God and man combined] element in the nature of prophecy, that the prophets, on the one hand, standing above the people, utter with seeming mercilessness the decrees of God's justice; while on the other, as members of the people, they enter sympathizingly into the deepest popular suffering."—Kleinert.

In his likes, his dislikes, his convictions, and his emphasis on social righteousness, Micah was definitely akin to Amos and Elijah. "He was a true patriot who loved his land, his capital city, but most of all his own poor, downtrodden people. His convictions were rooted and grounded so deeply that he was able to maintain a stern, powerful, fearless front in denouncing the evils of his day. His unfeigned sincerity carried weight wherever he went. His passion for righteousness drove him forth with a flaming word for those who lacked ethical standards. The 'unsophisticated rustic' was always seeking justice and mercy for his peasant friends who suffered so bitterly. He was an artist in using figures, similes, descriptions, and words that carried peculiar weight."—Yates.

The personality of this man Micah is clearly reflected in the language he uses in denunciation of prevailing conditions.

Social Conditions

Dr. Kyle M. Yates in his excellent book, *Preaching from the Prophets,* sums up the social conditions and Micah's reactions toward them.

"The country preacher knew the tragic situation in Judah and Israel. Out where social wrongs are more keenly felt than anywhere else, he was able to sense the suffering of the peasants under the cruel pressure of men who had power. The judges were venal, the priests were immoral and corrupt, the prophets were hirelings, the nobles took peculiar delight in fleecing the poor, and the entire group had built up a wall of enmity, fear and hatred that made life miserable for all classes.

"*They covet fields, and seize them and houses, and take them away: and they oppress a man and his house* (2:2).

"*Haters of good and lovers of evil, tearing their skin from upon them and their flesh from their bones* (3:2).

"The nation was ready for a collapse. The princes, the priests, the prophets, and the people were responsible for its downfall.

"*Ye abhor justice, and twist all that is straight, building Zion with blood, and Jerusalem with iniquity. Her chiefs judge for a bribe, her priests teach for hire, her prophets divine for money; and yet they lean on the Lord, saying, Is not Yahweh in the midst of us? Evil cannot come on us* (3:9-11).

"Callous greed and cruelty mark the ungodly conduct of men who should behave humanely.

"*Ye strip the robe from off the garment from these who pass by unsuspectingly, averse to war. The women of my people ye tear from their pleasant homes; from their children ye take away my glory forever* (2:8,9).

"The people were so greedy for wealth that no step was too low for them if a bit of money was involved. The Naboth vineyard experience was reenacted on all sides. Certainly a prophet was sorely needed."

Religious Conditions

Dr. Yates' comments on these also are so clear and pertinent that we quote again:

"On every hand there was a spirit utterly foreign to the sort of religious fervor that the prophet desired. A scornful, reckless type of irreligion was prevalent. The people did not want any preaching done except the weak, insipid variety that would allow them to go on in their way without embarrassment. It is a tragic hour when people will hear only the man who panders to their selfish, immoral nature.

"*If a man who walks in wind and falsehood should deceive thee, saying, I will preach to thee of wine and strong drink; he would be the preacher of this people* (2:11).

"Soothsaying, witchcraft, superstition and idolatry were prevalent in the land. The Assyrian practices and cults were still influencing religious behavior. The people were lacking in integrity to such an extent that no one could be trusted.

"*The good man has perished from the land, and of the upright among men there is none; they all are lurking for blood; every man hunts his brother with a net. The best of them is like a thornbush, the most honest is like a thorn hedge. Trust not a friend, put not confidence in a familiar friend: a man's enemies are the men of his own house* (7:2,4,5,6).

"The prophets and priests were corrupt, selfish, immoral, and greedy. What good could come from such leadership? These men were guilty of the sort of behavior that kills spiritual glow. They merely wanted money, ease, cheap popularity, and some assurance that they could continue to live in luxury. They were willing to make war on all those who opposed them.

"*Who lead my people astray; biting with their teeth they preach peace; and against him who gives them nothing for their mouth they consecrate war* (3:5)."

The Message of the Book

Both the nothern kingdom of Israel, represented by its capital city, Samaria, and the southern kingdom of Judah, represented by Jerusalem, are condemned as guilty in the eyes of the great Judge of the universe (1:2). Destruction, captivity, and exile, the prophet says, are inevitable for both. Micah rebukes the social injustices; denounces general unfaithful-ness and dishonesty; inveighs in vivid figure of speech againstpriestly corruption and heathenish abuses; announces judgment upon Samaria and upon Jerusalem and its temple; promises return from exile and the reconstitution of city and nation.

One has said that the prophecy of Isaiah is an enlargement of that of Micah. Isaiah clearly falls into two main divisions: Condemnatory or Denunciatory (chs. 1-39) and Consolatory (chs. 40-66). Micah's prophecy falls quite easily into the same categories: Denunciation (chs. 1-3) and Consolation (ch. 4-6).

Some expositors make a threefold division: Impending Judgment (chs. 1-3); A Vision of Hope (chs. 4,5); A Vivid Contrast (chs. 6,7). We shall follow the latter outline.

IMPENDING JUDGMENT (CHAPTERS 1-3)

These chapters contain a description of the approaching judgment of Israel and Judah.

Chapter 1

What indications are there here that both kingdoms are involved?
Which is mentioned first and how severe is to be her judgment?
(vv. 6-9)

How is the transition of the prophet's message from Samaria to Jerusalem made? (v. 9)

What towns of Judah are particularly mentioned in verses 10-15?
Note from a map of "Palestine—southern division" that they are all in the vicinity of Moresheth or Mareshah, the prophet's hometown. This specialization seems to indicate the prophet's concern with conditions prevailing in his own part of the country which reflected the general national condition.

Chapter 2

Chapter 2 unfolds the causes of the impending judgment. First, the conduct of the nobility or higher ranks is under indictment. "Wickedness is more criminal in proportion as it is more deliberate." Here this social class is seen on their couches at night deliberately planning how they can rob others of their possessions. The next day they execute those vile plans (vv. 1,2). God beholds this iniquity and will judge it (vv. 3,5), for He hears the lament of the oppressed (v. 4).

The people will not listen to genuine prophecy (v. 6). They are ready to accept any kind of drivel such as verse 11 depicts—a prophecy of abundance of wine and strong drink.

The promise of restoration (vv. 12,13) was probably given on another occasion than the foregoing to a minority group who, as Ezekiel describes them, "sigh and cry for all the abomination that be done in the midst." It is the promise of a restored "remnant." This word is frequently used by Micah's contemporary, Isaiah.

Chapter 3

The princes or rulers of the people came under indictment for their complete moral perversion and their oppression of the people. At the time of the revelation of the wrath of God their cry for mercy will be unheeded (3:1-4).

The false prophets, who prophesied for gain and who were leading God's people—"My people"—astray, are judged (3:5-8). In verses 9-11 Micah recapitulates his charges against these two classes, rulers and priests, and follows it with a terrific prophecy that Zion, the temple area, and the whole city of Jerusalem would be leveled to the ground (v. 12). This prediction was most literally fulfilled.

So both "bloody" (3:10) capitals, Samaria and Jerusalem, will be desolated (1:6 and 3:12).

A VISION OF HOPE (CHAPTERS 4 AND 5)

Chapter 4

A complete change of vision characterizes these chapters. Though Zion is to be destroyed (3:12), it will be restored, gloriously rebuilt, and will become the center of the world kingdom of God (4:1-8).

As you study, notice verses 1-4 are in language almost identical to that of Isaiah 2:2-4. Remember that these men were contemporaries, but which one quotes the other? We do not know. Maybe God gave both the same revelation in the same terms.

At what time will these kingdom glories be fulfilled? (4:1). We shall discover from prophecy that this expression—"last days"—points to the end of the times in which we now live, the Christian dispensation. After God has called out a people for His name, He will "return, and will build again the tabernacle of David, which is fallen down" (Acts 15:16). The "age to come," following this Christian dispensation, is the Kingdom Age or the Millennium.

Under what figure is the exaltation of Zion depicted? (4:1)

Who is to participate in these glories and under what conditions? (4:2)

What language clearly shows that these conditions have never yet prevailed and that the fulfillment belongs to the Millennium? (4:2)

How do verses 3,4,7, further prove this point?

The scope of future blessing revealed in 4:1-8 is worldwide. Let us sum up these thrilling blessings:

1. Worldwide government (v. 1). (The word *people* is "peoples" in the original.)

2. A worldwide capital (v. 2)

3. Worldwide participation (v. 2)

4. Worldwide justice (v. 3)

5. Worldwide peace (v. 3)
6. Worldwide prosperity (v. 4)
7. Worldwide sovereignty (v. 7)

But this glorious vision is for the future. Before its realization Israel is in dismay and turmoil; she is under the chastisements of God; she will be in bondage to foreign powers (Assyria, Babylon), who vindictively seek her destruction (vv. 9-11).

These nations do not know God or His purposes. They do not recognize that Israel, despite her sins, is a nation covenantly related to Him. Israel's ascendency and the punishment of these nations is certain (vv. 12,13).

Chapter 5

The common teaching of all the prophets is that Israel's deliverance and blessing are related to the advent of their Messiah, the Son of David. His coming is treated in this chapter as one advent. True, verse 2 is quoted in Matthew (2:6) in reference to the first coming of Christ, as we now designate it, but the perspective of all the prophets views the first and second advents as one, and does not see or recognize the time gap between them, which we now know as the Christian church dispensation.

Consequently in this chapter there are elements which were not fulfilled in the first advent of our Lord and clearly await His return from heaven. Note that the emphasis in verse 2 is not upon the lowliness of the birth in Bethlehem. In fact, the language is not necessarily that of a birth at all, but the place from which the Messiah will arise. Note further that the element of *rulership* is the prominent factor.

Let us notice some of the events listed which did not occur at His first coming, but which are clearly related to His second advent.

Verse 3 indicates a time when "she which travaileth hath brought forth," that is, the final phase of Israel's national birth pains, the time of the tribulation (Jeremiah 30:4-9), as the result of which she shall realize her national fruitfulness, her national destiny.

In verse 4 the reference is to Christ's establishment as the shepherd or sustainer of His people in regal majesty and His being "great unto the ends of the earth," certainly not yet fulfilled.

In verse 5 "this man" (again, Messiah) is spoken of as "the peace" of Israel "when the Assyrian shall come into our land," a clear

allusion not to the invasions of the prophet's own time, but to the
latter days. Comparison with verse 6 proves this.

It is true, as Isaiah reveals, that since Palestine is Immanuel's
land (cf. Isaiah 7:14; 8:8-10), it was His invisible protection that
brought deliverance from the Assyrian hordes in history now past
to us (Isaiah 37:36), but the reference in Micah 5:5 is to a future
"Assyrian," likely the Antichrist. Either the land of Assyria (now
Iraq, which is experiencing great reviving) will have a signal re-
surgence in the last days (cf. Isaiah 19:23-25 for the final outcome)
or else it stands as a type of the Gentile power which shall rise up
as the last enemy of Israel before her final restoration. We prefer
the literal interpretation.

Verses 7-15 reveal Israel's ascendency, her freedom from dependence upon military might, her deliverance from occult practices, her cleansing from idolatry, and her complete victory over all
her foes.

A Vivid Contrast (Chapters 6 and 7)

These chapters have been described as presenting a "contrast
between the reasonableness, purity, and justice of the divine requirements and the ingratitude, injustice, and superstition of the
people which caused their ruin."—*Synthetic Bible Studies.*

Chapter 6

In chapter 6 the prophet voices the "controversy" which God has
with His people. His constant faithfulness and Israel's faithlessness
are in striking contrast. So poignant are Jehovah's feelings in the
matter that He would have even the mountains reverberate with
His voice as He calls His people, if they have a charge, to witness
against Him.

He challenges His people to testify if He, their true God, ever
did seek other than their welfare from their beginning as a nation.
In other words God says, "Can you produce any excuse for forsaking
me?" (6:1-5).

Their religion is mere formality, pure hypocrisy (6:6,7), that does
not produce that practical righteousness which Jehovah requires.
Micah's accurate acquaintance with the Law, which appears
throughout his messages, stands forth again (v. 8; cf. Deuteronomy
10:12).

In this "controversy" Jehovah's judgment follows and proves His indictment of Israel. They have continued in the Baalism of Omri and Ahab (v. 16); consequently His rod (v. 9) must descend in penalty upon them (vv. 9-16).

Chapter 7

The prophet voices, as the representative of his people, the prayer of a faithful remnant (no doubt present even in his day) who will be sincerely repentant in the last days. They lament in sincere confession their sinful condition (7:1-6); voice their intercession for their nation; and express their full confidence in God's returning favor and in victory over their "enemy" (vv. 7,8).

Verses 9 and 10 express their humble submission to God's chastening, and their expectation of ultimate justice and victory and the turning of the enemy's reproach back upon himself.

Note how the prophet voices God's promise of restoration and how he refers to the land covenant of God with Abraham (vv. 11,12, ASV; cf. Genesis 15:18) which will be fulfilled; nevertheless, chastening must precede their restoration (v. 13).

Micah prays for divine provision and protection as of a shepherd. God had prospered His "flock" of old, like sheep grazing in abundance on the rich pasture lands of Bashan and Gilead (East Jordan). The divine response is voiced and God assures Israel of His divine intervention on their behalf as directly and positively as when He brought them out of Egyptian bondage (vv. 14,15).

Gentile nations will be in confusion at Israel's triumph and at their own discomfiture. The terror of the Lord shall seize upon them, because of their oppression of His people (vv. 16,17).

In the closing verses (18-20) the prophet praises the faithful Jehovah who will in mercy bring about the restoration of His people on the ground of their return to the Lord and His forgiveness of their sins.

Thus will He fulfill His unconditional covenant made with their fathers (Genesis 12:1-3; Deuteronomy 7:8,12; Psalm 105:9,10; Luke 1:72,73).

PREDICTIONS

Note the definite predictions of future events in the Book of Micah:

1. Samaria, capital of Israel, to fall (1:6,7)
2. Jerusalem and its temple to be destroyed (3:12; 7:13)
3. The people of Judah to be taken captive to Babylon (4:10)
4. Israel and Judah to return from captivity (4:1-8; 7:11,14-17)
5. Messiah to be born in Bethlehem (5:2-4)
6. Universal peace and prosperity when men of all nations look to Zion (4:1-4)

Lesson 30

Nahum

Expositors are agreed the Book of Nahum is peculiarly the prophecy of divine vengeance. In modern history we have seen the ruthless cruelty of dictators who seek to overrun the earth. For a time they seem to "flourish like a green bay tree," but the turn of events comes and, like a Mussolini or a Hitler, they perish in ignominy and shame. "Vengeance still belongs to God. Such monstrous disregard of God and His righteous standards will bring swift and certain judgment. Any nation that deliberately sets itself to defy God and trample upon innocent peoples must feel the terrible touch of the divine hand."—Yates.

Nahum's book is a terrible arraignment and pronouncement of judgment upon a nation (or any nation) that seeks glory by war and oppression. "God still hates brutality, violence, and wrong." See Lesson 24 on Jonah for data on Assyrian cruelty.

The Book of Nahum complements the Book of Jonah. About one hundred years separate them. It is a prediction of the utter destruction of the great city of Nineveh, capital of the Assyrian Empire. As we read it, we find history represents a complete fulfillment of the prophecy.

It still stands (as Professor Kennedy in Hastings' *Bible Dictionary* states it) as "an object lesson to the empires of the modern world, teaching as an eternal principle of the divine government of the world, the absolute necessity, for a nation's continued vitality, of that righteousness—personal, civic, and national—which alone exalteth a nation."

The Times

Nahum lived and preached sometime between the fall of Thebes (called No in 3:8), the great capital of Upper Egypt, in 663 B.C., and the fall of Nineveh in 612 B.C. Most recent scholars place the date *near* the time of Nineveh's collapse.

Esarhaddon of Assyria, 681-669 B.C., built a great kingdom. He conquered Egypt and made it a part of his empire. (See Isaiah 19:4 for a prophecy concerning this.) "Assurbanipal, 669-626 B.C., continued the work of his illustrious father throughout a long and stormy reign." To him is credited the building of beautiful palaces and the establishment of great libraries. He is remembered "as the greatest known patron of literature in the pre-Christian centuries."

Upon the death of Assurbanipal in 626 B.C. an enemy of Assyria, Nabopolassar, became king of the Babylonians. A confederacy of the Medes and Scythians joined forces with the Babylonians to bring about the ruin of Nineveh.

You will be interested, no doubt, to note some of the facts concerning this great city. The completeness of its overthrow becomes all the more impossible from the human standpoint, and all the more dramatic from the divine standpoint, when we know the actual greatness of the city in Nahum's day.

Nineveh was founded by Nimrod (Genesis 10:8-11) and had been famous for centuries. Any invader was confronted with the walls as Diodorus Siculus, Greek historian, says, 100 feet high, nine miles in circumference, and wide enough for three chariots to drive abreast. It had 1,200 defense towers and a moat outside the walls 140 feet wide and 60 feet deep.

The city fell in 612 B.C. never to rise again. Its destruction was so complete that the armies of Alexander the Great, in 331 B.C., marched right over the site and did not notice it. It was not until 1842 that it was discovered by the archaeologists Layard and Botta.

The Man Nahum

The name Nahum means "consolation" or "compassion." We do not know exactly where he lived. Some expositors have contended that his home was at Elkosh on the banks of the Tigris River, but this is hardly tenable. Jerome claimed he was a native of Galilee, living near Capernaum ("city of Nahum"). Still another would make him a resident of a small village near Micah's home in southwest Judah.

He prophesied, as far as we know, in the reign of Josiah, possibly after an unsuccessful attack on Nineveh by Cyaxares in 623 B.C.

The book itself reveals to us in its very language the character of the man.

Remember again that God never obliterated the personality of His prophets; He never made them mere automatons, or mechanical voices; but He used the prophet's distinctive personality to lend a naturalness, as well as supernaturalness, to his message.

Dr. Kyle M. Yates in *Preaching from the Prophets* characterizes Nahum thus:

"Nahum was a patriotic saint, who had a deep hatred for the Assyrians. His sensitive nature, strained almost to the breaking point by the godless cruelty of the inhuman warriors, was almost fanatical in his exultation over the horrible suffering of the enemy. He was keenly observant. To him the seas, the hills, the storms, the clouds, and the river were symbols of God's wrath and fury. His quick imagination, coupled with his keen intuition, made him a vivid painter with words. His sense of a holy God so tragically outraged by unscrupulous men drove him to lengths unreached by others. As a poet he has few equals. His soul, on fire with righteous indignation, flashed and blazed in dramatic poetry."

The Theme

The impending doom of Nineveh flashes from every page of the book. The people of Nineveh had repented at the message of Jonah, but as one has put it: "It is evident that they repented of their former repentance, and so gave themselves to idolatry, cruelty, and oppression that 160 years later Nahum pronounced against them the judgment of God in the form of utter destruction."

If we are correct in placing Nahum chronologically in the time of Josiah, when Israel had already fallen, along with other northern nations and their cities, under the iron heel of the cruel oppressor, and when Judah had already been overrun and Jerusalem itself threatened, we can better understand the purpose of the book. It was undoubtedly to inspire his countrymen with the assurance that this threatening giant that God had kept from capturing Jerusalem was about to come to an end. Nineveh, his own capital, would be destroyed and the Assyrian Empire overthrown, as the result of their own iniquities.

The Style

"For sheer beauty, poetic imagery, dramatic description and vivid imagination Nahum is unsurpassed among the prophets. He describes the swift, relentless sweep of the enemy with all the vividness and color of an eyewitness. He was charged with emotion. His whole being was under the spell of a mighty torrent of feeling."—Yates.

Brice calls it "the most vivid and passionate fragment of declamation in all literature." It consists of a single poem, but its content may be clearly outlined.

Outline

Various expositors outline these three chapters in different forms, but all most appropriately:

A Sublime Picture of God. Chapter 1
A Graphic Picture of the Fall of Nineveh. Chapter 2
A Statement of the Reasons for the Utter Ruin of the Wicked City. Chapter 3

—Yates

Judgment on Nineveh *Declared.* Chapter 1
Judgment on Nineveh *Described.* Chapter 2
Judgment on Nineveh *Defended.* Chapter 3

—Scroggie

The Verdict of Vengeance. Chapter 1
The Vision of Vengeance. Chapter 2
The Vindication of Vengeance. Chapter 3

—Morgan

THE VERDICT OF VENGEANCE (CHAPTER 1)

The eternal God, despite appearances sometimes to the contrary, is in active control of the affairs of this world. The nations are as *"a drop of a bucket, and are counted as the small dust of the balance"* (Isaiah 40:15). *"All the inhabitants of the earth are reputed as nothing: and he doeth according to his will in the army of heaven, and among the inhabitants of the earth: and none can stay his hand, or say unto him, What doest thou?"* (Daniel 4:35).

God is fully aware of the world's injustices and oppressions, and it would seem is slow to act against them, but this is to give men an opportunity to correctly estimate their conduct and to repent. He is long-suffering and full of tender mercy.

Nineveh, the great city of Assyria, was doomed at an earlier date when Jonah was sent to preach to her, but repented temporarily. But Assyria became more and more powerful and arrogant, cruel and oppressive, consequently God's patience was exhausted. "When

He lifts His finger in judgment the mightiest nation with the most elaborate equipment is doomed to fall."

Nahum describes Jehovah, the Judge, in chapter 1, not as an "unjust, capricious executioner, but one who is slow to anger, who waits patiently for the fruits of repentance before punishing."

"Do not let us imagine, when we think of the anger of God, that it is anything like the hot, passionate, blind, foolish, blundering of a man in a temper. He is slow to anger; yet once having crossed over in the presence of things which demand a new attitude of vengeance, He is as irresistible as a hurricane that beats the sea into fury, or the simoom that sweeps the land with desolation. Note how the words, 'jealous, vengeance, wrath, anger, indignation, fierceness, fury,' describe the overwhelming fact of the anger of God. In man, wrath becomes his master, and drives him; God is always master of His wrath and uses it."

The end of Hezekiah's reign marked the captivity of the ten tribes of Israel to the ruthless Assyrians. Says Dr. Joseph Angus:

"At this period of perplexity, when the overthrow of Samaria must have suggested to Judah many fears for her own safety, when Jerusalem had been drained of its treasure by Hezekiah, in the vain hope of turning away the fury of Sennacherib, and when distant rumors of the conquest of part of Egypt added still more to the general dismay, the prophet is raised up to reveal the power and tenderness of Jehovah, to foretell the subversion of the Assyrian empire, the death of Sennacherib, and the deliverance of Hezekiah."

What is God's character, as revealed in 1:2,3?

What revelation does Nahum give of His power, and to what natural phenomena does he refer? (1:4-6)

To what is Judah exhorted in 1:15, and on what ground?

THE VISION OF VENGEANCE (CHAPTER 2)

This chapter depicts in most vivid language the siege and capture of Nineveh and the consternation of the inhabitants.

Greater Nineveh included the whole triangle between the Tigris and Zab rivers, from their junction northward to Korsabad, all heavily fortified. The inner city (described under "The Times") was considered impregnable.

Nineveh, as Nahum describes it in 2:8—"like a pool of water"— was made so by the great number of protecting canals along the edges of the walls. The prophet foretells a detail of the means of

Nineveh's overthrow in 2:6—the river gates shall be opened. "After two years of siege a sudden rise of the river washed away part of the walls. Through the breach thus made, the attacking [armies] swept in to their work of destruction."

Huzzab, referring to the queen of Assyria, is pictured as going into captivity (2:7), and the spoiling and utter destruction of the city is described (2:9-12).

Note the repetition of the expression, "Behold I am against thee" (2:13; 3:5).

THE VINDICATION OF VENGEANCE (CHAPTER 3)

Nahum continues with a vivid detailed forecast of the siege. He had mentioned the chariots in 2:3,4, and now he pictures the prancing horses, cracking whips, rattling wheels, and the bounding, raging chariots, the flashing swords, and the great heaps of dead bodies (3:1-3).

The prophet states the various causes contributing to this fearful slaughter. The example of No-amon (or Thebes), the great city of Egypt, once populous and powerful, which fell under the judgment of God, is cited to illustrate the similar punishment coming upon the Assyrians (3:8-10).

Note the figurative pictures Nahum presents to describe the weakness and the fall of Assyria (vv. 11-19)—ripe figs, women warriors, devouring fire, destructive cankerworms, locusts, grasshoppers, slumbering nobles, an incurable disease.

So complete was the obliteration of this great city that, as before noted, even Alexander the Great's armies marched over the site without being aware that Nineveh once stood there. The archaeologist Botta began his labors there in 1842, Layard in 1845, Rassam in 1852, and Loftus in 1854. "The results of their researches as to extent, character, and variety of marbles, sculptures, and inscriptions brought to light, have confounded cavilers at the sacred Scriptures, entranced with delight antiquaries and archaeologists, and astonished the whole world."

Nineveh's former greatness and its complete ruin are clearly evidenced by archaeological research.

PRACTICAL LESSONS

Observe a few practical lessons from the Book of Nahum for our present benefit:

1. God's patience is limited.
2. God is in *active* control among nations.
3. God's judgments are remedial, not vindictive.
4. Nations, as well as individuals, reap what they sow.
5. National arrogance that ruthlessly and cruelly oppresses other nations meets with divine wrath.
6. In the light of God's eternal redemptive purpose for the people of the world, the destruction of one wicked city is but a small thing.

Lesson 31

Zephaniah

Period of Zephaniah's Ministry

Between the cessation of the prophecies of Isaiah, Micah, and Nahum, and the days of Zephaniah, Jeremiah, and the later prophets, there was an interval of two generations during which there was no prophet whose message has reached us.

The truly great reformer, King Hezekiah, was succeeded by a son, Manasseh, and a grandson, Amon, whose wickedness was as intense as Hezekiah's righteousness, if not greater in degree. Manasseh had a long reign of 55 years during which all of his father's work was undone. The nation was converted back to heathenism. The worship of Jehovah was banished. Baal and his black-robed priests (Chemarim) returned; and the worship of the vile god Malcham (Molech) was revived.

The princes of Judah had become so corrupt that justice was impossible. Injustice, oppression, and violence flowed out from the court and swallowed up the people like a flood. The true prophetic voice had been stilled for over 50 years. Reformation by prophetic teaching would have been hopeless, for the people were callous to any spiritual stimulus.

"In Zephaniah's indictment of Jerusalem he pictures the people as unteachable, the rulers as predatory, the courts as merciless, the prophets as traitors, and the priests as profane. It was a dark day for God's land."—Yates.

The youthful King Josiah set out to clean up the desecrated temple and to turn the people back to Jehovah. In the course of repairs on the temple a copy of the Pentateuch was found, which made a deep impression on king and people. As a result of the reading of the Law, Josiah undertook a vigorous reform. Idols, groves, images, high places, heathen altars were thrown down. This reform did much for the kingdom, but lacked sufficient depth to change individual hearts and lives. Outwardly it was a great success and the zeal of the young king is to be commended.

Zephaniah and Jeremiah, whose ministry began in the thirteenth year of Josiah's reign, undoubtedly encouraged the king in his efforts. "It is a safe assumption that this prophecy was uttered before the reformation, in which Zephaniah was himself a prime mover, about 25 years before Judah's captivity."—Halley.

The Man Zephaniah

Unlike Micah, the peasant prophet, or Amos, the sheepherder, Zephaniah was an aristocrat. He traces his ancestry back to Hezekiah (cf. "Hizkiah," 1:1). This fact establishes the principle that God has a place for all types of men. His kingly lineage would undoubtedly give him standing with princes and rulers as he stood forth to make his stern denunciations.

He was well acquainted with Jerusalem and the court life of that city, as his book reveals. "His grim, austere, sober nature has gained for him the name of 'puritan' or 'protestant.' He seemed obsessed with a terrible conception of the doom that was coming upon the wicked world about him. No hope was in sight, for the certain doom was richly deserved and must come on friend and foe alike.

"He had a comprehensive view of history. One is tempted to speculate on the type of educational institutions that prepared young men in the way so many of the prophets were educated. Zephaniah reminds us of Isaiah in his broad understanding of the guilt and needs of other nations. He thought of his civilization as incurably corrupt. All the surrounding nations were equally enmeshed in sin and guilt. His own beloved land was involved and must suffer the cruel tortures of a just God who could do no other thing in the light of men's behavior. Yahweh was to sweep away, as with a devastating flood, all the nations; and Judah must suffer the full severity of the onslaught. A new era of peace, plenty and happiness was to follow in the wake of the destruction.

"Zephaniah was not a poet. He was deeply impressed with the fact that God had laid His hand on him and that he must warn his beloved people of the impending calamity. He was sensitive to the faintest whisper of God. Imagination and emotion play a large place in his preaching. He was a flaming evangelist who spoke with fury and effectiveness a burning message of rebuke to a people who were

rapidly losing all power to respond to such serious challenges. Being
violently opposed to world conditions he left the impression that he
was pitiless and harsh and unsympathetic. Some have called him
fanatical. However this may be, he was vitally concerned with the
proclamation of the divine denunciation."—Yates.

The Book

Our English translation would give the impression that the prophet
sat down and wrote this book in three chapters, but the fact is that
it consists of a series of brief oracles, undoubtedly given at different
times in the early days of King Josiah's preparation for the reformation.

The prophet announces in scathing language the nearness of "the
great day of the Lord," "a day of trouble and distress," "a day of
wrath" . . . (1:14,15) for all who have "turned back from the Lord."

It has been divided as follows:

1. An impending Day of Wrath for Judah (1:1 to 2:3)
2. A Day of Wrath for the Nations (2:4-15)
3. A Day of Wrath for Jerusalem (3:1-8)
4. A Day of "A Pure Language" (3:9-20)

Day of Wrath for Judah (Chapter 1:1 to 2:3)

Zephaniah pronounces certain doom on the idol worshipers—the
adherents of Baal, their black-robed priests; the worshipers of the
heavenly bodies; the deluded worshipers of the vile god Malcham
(Molech) and all who have deserted Jehovah (1:1-6). Even King
Manasseh sacrificed children to this image (2 Chronicles 33:6).

The unfaithful rulers are denounced along with every class of
sinner, whom God will search out as with candles (1:7-13).

God's jealous wrath like a blast of fire (1:18) is about to fall upon
the whole earth, but "striking with peculiar fury upon the inhabitants
of Jerusalem." The "Great Day of Jehovah" is to be a terrible day
from which there is no escape.

Chapter 2 opens with an urgent call to repentance that they may
be "hid in the day of the Lord's anger" (2:1-3). Nothing can avert
the nation's doom, but a praying remnant may be saved through
repentance.

Day of Wrath for the Nations (Chapter 2:4-15)

Gaza, Ashkelon, Ashdod, and Ekron, four wicked idolatrous cities
of the Cherethites (Philistines), inveterate enemies of God's people,

are threatened with dire destruction (2:4-7). Moab and Ammon, nations which had their beginning in incest (Genesis 19:30-38), and whose vile idolatrous practices smelled to high heaven, come under the judgment of complete obliteration (2:8-11). These lands are still waste and desolate today and give scarcely any evidence of former occupation by powerful peoples.

Ethiopia, southern Egyptian nation whose rulers at this time controlled all Egypt, and Assyria, with Nineveh its proud capital, within 20 years lay desolate under the power of Babylon (2:12-15).

DAY OF WRATH FOR JERUSALEM (CHAPTER 3:1-8)

Chapter 3 brings a further indictment of Jerusalem, the prophet's native city, for her obstinacy and rebellion. Princes, priests, and prophets are especially singled out for punishment. The universality of this "great day of the Lord" upon all nations of the then known world is seen in 3:8.

DAY OF "A PURE LANGUAGE" (CHAPTER 3:9-20)

In commenting upon chapter 3, especially this latter portion, Dr. G. Campbell Morgan observes: "A modern expositor has said that it is perfectly patent that this was not written by Zephaniah because the contrast is too great between the picture of the awful, sweeping, irrevocable judgment and that of the restoration. No one can imagine, he declares, that the same man wrote them both. All of which is the result of the expositor's blindness. The last picture is that of the enthroned Jehovah, the picture of a new order; songs instead of sorrow, service instead of selfishness, solidarity instead of scattering. That is the intent of judgment. . . . The very contrast demonstrates the unity of the authorship."

This section of the book is like the quiet calm after a tremendous storm. It is a message of assurance of God's protecting care for and preservation of a hidden faithful remnant. Three times Zephaniah speaks of the salvation of a remnant (2:3,7; 3:12,13); and twice of their return from captivity (2:7; 3:20) with the introduction among the peoples (plural) of the earth of a "pure language" (3:9).

This may have reference to the unity of language among the nations as existed before the confusion of tongues at Babel. But it certainly has reference to the unity of worship of the "peoples" as proven by the fact that they "call upon the name of the Lord to serve him with one shoulder" (literal), meaning that they all bear the same yoke of Jehovah (cf. Zephaniah 3:9, ASV).

This will be fulfilled at the end of this age and the ushering in of the Millennium.

"Jehovah will purge from Israel those who reposed in a self-righteous pride of their covenant privileges; and purged from these sinners, Israel will be a humble, trustful and holy nation" (vv. 11-13). Cf. also Ezekiel 20:33-38.

The chastening hand of God will be lifted from Israel; they will be greatly blessed and rejoice in His presence after their enemies are punished; great national and international rejoicing will follow Israel's restoration (vv. 14-20).

Note the sublimity of the language in 3:17. The long-suffering and patience of God with His people, the constancy of His love, and His own overflowing joy in His people are beautifully expressed.

Lesson 32

Jeremiah 1-25

Background

To understand the book we must be informed of the times. Jeremiah ministered from about the thirteenth year of King Josiah to the early part of the Babylonian captivity, a period of about 40 years, 626-586 B.C. You should read 2 Kings 22 to 25 and 2 Chronicles 34:1 to 36:21.

But no estimate of Jeremiah is complete without a brief study of the reign and influence of Manasseh, Josiah's grandfather. He began his long reign of 55 years over Judah in 698 B.C. upon the death of good King Hezekiah. The Assyrian kings, Esar-haddon (681-668 B.C.) and Assurbanipal (668-626 B.C.), wielded powerful influence over him; he was "forced to acknowledge the religion of the empire and to put down any local prophet or teacher who opposed such tendencies."

It is quite probable, and according to Jewish tradition, that Isaiah was put to death by King Manasseh. The vilest idolatrous practices were revived and introduced by Manasseh and continued also through the two years his son Amon reigned. The worship of Jehovah was completely suppressed.

Josiah came to the throne about 641 B.C. during the days the Assyrian Empire was declining under the hammer blows of the Scythians. Nabopolassar of Babylon began to reign in Babylon in 626 B.C., the thirteenth year of Josiah, and in 612 B.C. Nineveh fell under the combined forces of the Medes, the Babylonians, and the Scythians. Babylon rapidly assumed top place as head of the world empire.

Josiah's tragic death at Megiddo ruined all hope for Judah. It continued for about 20 years, but with ungodly leadership. "Judah's sun was gradually sinking. Exile was certain."

In 605 B.C. Nebuchadnezzar (or Nebuchadrezzar) became king of Babylon and Jehoiakim was placed on the throne of Judah by the Egyptians who had slain Josiah. Nebuchadnezzar defeated the Egyptians at Carchemish and Egypt's door was closed as a world power.

Jehoiakim was proud, sinful, idolatrous, a rejector of Jehovah—a constant thorn in Jeremiah's side. In 598 B.C. Nebuchadnezzar was forced to come against Jerusalem because of Jehoiakim's rebellion. His son Jehoiachin succeeded him, but his reign ended in three months, when Jerusalem was captured by the Babylonians. The best of the citizens along with the royal family were taken captive to Babylon with the sacred vessels of the temple.

Mattaniah, Jehoiachin's uncle, was made ruler by the Babylonians. Daniel and Ezekiel were in Babylon. Jeremiah and Habakkuk were prophesying in Jerusalem. Judah's position was like a tottering wall. After 11 years of weak, vacillating rule, the Babylonians in 587 B.C. besieged Jerusalem and took it. The walls were thrown down, the temple was destroyed, Zedekiah's sons were slain, and he was blinded and taken to Babylon. The people were taken into bondage.

Gedaliah was left as the representative of the Babylonian government to govern the people who remained in Judah. "Jeremiah chose to stay with these same people, although he could have gone to Babylon as a guest of the royal house." When Gedaliah was murdered by Ishmael, a Jewish hothead, the fear-stricken Jews fled to Egypt and took Jeremiah forcibly with them. Here he passed his latter days.

Social Conditions

"The social conditions faced by Jeremiah during his long career called for a wise head and courageous action. On every side he saw problems of class and family and foreign cults with their attendant miseries. The rich were powerful, unscrupulous, oblivious to the real needs of the poor, and interested only in that which would bring gain to themselves. The poor were driven to toil as slaves with almost no advantages for improvement of any kind. Discontent, hatred, and envy filled their minds as they endured the misery of the passing days. Family life was deplorable. Slavery was common as early as 600 B.C. Robbery, murder, lying, and emphasis on a selfish hunt for material things, characterized the life of the people."—Yates.

Religious Conditions

"The religious conditions were not more pleasing. Jeremiah found a strange mixture of Canaan's nature religion, Jezebel's Baalism, Babylonian cults, and a natural tendency to an utterly meaningless formalism. Religious syncretism had done its worst and the merger was far from satisfactory. To the sensitive soul of Jeremiah the people were as bad as the heathen inhabitants of Canaan. He indicts them for unreality, sensualism, double-mindedness and outright degeneracy.

"Josiah's reforms in 623-621 B.C. attempted the elimination of the superstitious practices, the suppression of the heathen sanctuaries, and the purification of the Temple and its worship. Much good was accomplished, but the movement failed to bring about the sort of revival of religion that the nation so sorely needed. Jeremiah realized how superficial and weak it was and how incapable the people were of understanding the basis for genuine spiritual religion. It was impossible to lift the people, the priests, and the other prophets into the clear atmosphere of spiritual religion. They could not understand his language."—Yates.

Jeremiah the Man

Jeremiah was the son of Hilkiah, a priest of Anathoth in Benjamin. Abiathar, David's great priest, established the village and his descendants continued to dwell there. The accession of the boy king Josiah to the throne produced radical changes in the nation. Jeremiah must have strongly favored the king's reforms, and it is conceivable that they were personal friends.

It would seem that he remained in his native village for several years. At length, by divine compulsion and in consequence of the persecution of his fellow townsmen, and even of his own family (11:21; 12:6), he moved out into a field of ministry which took him to Jerusalem, even into the king's court, in the gates of the city among the swarming populace, and into other cities of Judah. Cf. 11:16; 19:2; 20:1-3; 22:1; 34:2.

Jeremiah had a distinct call to the prophetic office (ch. 1). He was diffident, shy, and timid, but was prepared to hear God's voice and implicitly obeyed, despite his own feelings of inability. He was overwhelmed with the terrific responsibility that rested upon him, but went forth with the certainty of God's call and of His hand upon him.

Although he is called "the weeping prophet" (cf. Lamentations),
he was no weak sentimentalist. He was a fearless man, yet moved
with deep emotion over the deplorable spiritual condition of his
people and over the impending consequences of their sins. He was
"shocked by the vulgar religion with its hollow mockery, its shallow
stupidity, and its worldly materialism."

"The history of Jeremiah brings before us a man forced, as it were,
in spite of himself, from obscurity and retirement into the publicity
and peril which attended the prophetical office. Naturally mild,
susceptible, and inclined to mourn in secret for the iniquity which
surrounded him rather than to brave and denounce the wrongdoers,
he stood forth at the call of God, and proved himself a faithful,
fearless champion of the truth, amidst reproaches, insults, and threats.
This combination of qualities is so marked, that it has well been
regarded as a proof of the divine origin of his mission."—Dr. Joseph
Angus.

The Book

The book contains a wide variety of material. Baruch (36:4) was
his friend and secretary and was largely responsible for the collection
and preservation of the material. The arrangement of the various
prophecies and memoirs is not too systematic and chronologically
sequential, so it is sometimes difficult to follow for logical study.
The best explanation is that there has been some dislocation of the
order by early copyists of the manuscripts. From the account in
chapter 36 we know that a second edition of the prophetical messages
was produced after Jehoiakim had destroyed the first. "Much of the
biographical narrative was contributed by Baruch who spent his
entire life in the company of the great prophet."

Content of the Prophecy

Due to the lack of chronological order in the prophecies, aforesaid,
it is difficult to make a satisfactory analysis of the chapters in our
English Bible.

As to location of the chapters in the reigns of the kings during
which Jeremiah prophesied, and subsequently, the following will
be helpful, as outlined by Dr. Joseph Angus in his *Cyclopedic Handbook to the Bible:*

1. In the reign of Josiah (chs. 1-12). The beginning of chapter 11
seems to mark the time when the book of the Law was newly
discovered in the temple. Cf. 2 Kings 22:3-13.

2. Under Jehoiakim (chs. 13-20) in connection with which series of discourses is recorded the conspiracy against the prophet, with his deliverance (chs. 25,26). Chapter 22:1-19 denounces the unrighteousness of Jehoiakim and declares his fate and the fate of his brother and predecessor, Jehoahaz (or Shallum). Chapter 35 draws lessons of constancy and obedience from the conduct of the Rechabites. Chapters 45 (to his secretary, Baruch) and 36 refer to the roll of prophecies as read to Jehoiakim in the fourth year of his reign, and by him cut to pieces and burned.

3. Under Jehoiachin (22:20-30). The fate of the king (called Coniah) is pathetically depicted. He is to be a lifelong prisoner in Babylon, and to leave no heir to the throne, which virtually declared he would be childless.

4. Under Zedekiah. The following passages belong to this period. Chapter 21; chapter 27:1-18 (counselling submission to the Babylonian yoke); chapter 28, recording the prediction of the false prophet Hananiah of deliverance within two years; chapter 34, concerning Zedekiah's fate and the punishment of the slave-owner's perfidy; chapters 37 and 38, giving an account of the prophet's arrest and imprisonment; chapter 39 and 52:1-30, the capture of Jerusalem; chapters 30-33, giving the assurance of restoration, and of the New Covenant, with the remarkable episode (ch. 32) of the purchase by the prophet of his ancestral property at Anathoth, in the assurance that the land would be regained.

5. The prophecies concerning the nations (chs. 46-51) were probably uttered at different times and are gathered into these six chapters from their similarity of subject. The brief discourse against Elam (49:34-39) was delivered at the beginning of Zedekiah's reign; the prophecy against Babylon (chs. 50,51) in Zedekiah's fourth year when the king went with the chief officer of his court into Chaldea on some errand unknown to us. This discourse was to be cast into the Euphrates bound to a stone, a symbol of the sinking of the proud city. Cf. Revelation 18:21.

6. After the fall of Jerusalem. One of the most striking parts of the book is in chapter 29, a letter sent by Jeremiah to the exiles in Babylon with Jehoiachin, counseling them as to their conduct in captivity. Instead of rebelling and repining they were to settle down as peaceful and industrious inhabitants of the country, and to re-

pudiate those false prophets who sought to stir up discontent. After 70 years, the prophet declares (29:10), the captivity would cease.

7. To the end of Jeremiah's life (chs. 40-44). This section is mainly historical (see "Background"). The chief prophetic discourse is a protest against the idolatry of the Jews in Egypt (ch. 44).

JEREMIAH'S CALL AND COMMISSION (CHAPTER 1)

We shall have to believe in foreordination and predestination when we read the account of Jeremiah's call (vv. 4,5). But we shall have to note also Jeremiah's recognition of the difficulty and danger of this divine commission and his plea of inability to speak (v. 6), and the fact that his opposition was broken down, and he yielded to God (v. 9).

His commission was to give forth messages of the fall and rising again of nations (v. 10).

VISIONS

In the process of his induction into the prophetic office he is given two visions. One is of a rod of an almond tree (vv. 11,12) which the context reveals an instrument of chastisement is meant, indicating the vigilance of the Lord to "watch over" (ASV) His Word to perform it. (If this were a green shoot of almond it would symbolize the early execution of God's purposes, for the almond is "the wakeful tree." It awakes from the sleep of winter earlier than the other trees, flowering in January and bearing fruit in March.) The second vision is of a seething pot, open toward the north, symbolizing the invasion from the north by the Babylonians (vv. 13-16).

PROTECTION

Jeremiah is assured of divine protection in his most difficult task (vv. 17-19). The evidence of the book completely confirms this. His feet were thrust into the stocks in the gate of Jerusalem, where he was an object of reproach and scorn (ch. 20). He was put into a dungeon, where he would have perished had not Ebedmelech, the Ethiopian, rescued him (38:4-13). He was imprisoned (38:27,28), but God preserved him.

GENERAL MESSAGES OF REBUKE TO JUDAH
(CHAPTERS 2 TO 25)

FIRST MESSAGE TO JUDAH (CHAPTERS 2:1 TO 3:5)

Verses 1-3 form an introduction both to this first discourse and at the same time to the whole of Jeremiah's prophecies. They contain the thought which lies at the heart of all the history of the theocracy, "that notwithstanding the revolts on the one side and the punishments on the other, love is the keynote of the relations between God and Israel."—Naegelsbach.

The Lord challenges the nation to impeach Him as their God; reminds them of His providential care and blessing, and of their backsliding (2:4-9); and compares their unfaithfulness to Him with the fidelity of the surrounding nations to their gods (2:10-13).

The prophet views them in the imagery of slaves, evil-entreated, dragged away by enemies, their land desolated, their cities destroyed. Why? It was in consequence of their backsliding and devotion to their idols (2:14-19). Their propensity to idolatry, like harlotry, was deeply rooted (2:20-22) and expressed most violently (vv. 23-25), but causing deep shame on account of the nothingness of its objects (vv. 26-28).

The Lord challenges them again to bring charges against Him (v. 29); reminds them of His faithfulness (vv. 30-32) and of their backsliding (vv. 33-37); and pleads with them to return to Him (3:1-5).

SECOND DISCOURSE (CHAPTERS 3:6 TO 6:30)

The Lord reminds Judah of the fact that the ten tribes had been put away by Him because of their idolatry, but that they had failed to take warning from Israel's fate. Judah's sin was all the more glaring (3:6-10). Jehovah then directs His appeal through the prophet to Israel (then in captivity) to repent. He reaffirms His unchanging love for them and promises restoration in the last days (3:11 to 4:2).

The call to "return" is unheeded, so Jeremiah proceeds to announce the punishment. First, he announces the approaching calamity (ch. 4:3-31); second, he gives the cause in the moral corruption of the people (ch. 5); third, he further threatens punishment and reveals that it will originate "from the north country," Babylon (ch. 6).

DISCOURSE IN THE TEMPLE GATE (CHAPTERS 7 TO 10)

While Dr. Joseph Angus places this discourse in Josiah's reign there is strong evidence that it belongs to the beginning of the reign of Jehoiakim. Chapter 26 seems to give us information concerning the historical circumstances in which the discourse was delivered. (Read ch. 26.) We learn that Jeremiah was commissioned in the early part of Jehoiakim's reign to place himself at the vantage point of the fore-court of the temple, where the thronging people—princes, priests, prophets—could not fail to hear (cf. 26:2 with 7:2). Jeremiah was an outdoor preacher.

His message was this: if they continued to act in opposition to the repeated admonitions of the true prophets (cf. 26:5 and 7:13,25) the Lord would make the temple like Shiloh (cf. 26:3-13 and 7:3-14).

This total discourse may be divided into three main charges against Judah.

First Charge (7:1 to 8:3)

It begins with a friendly admonition and promise (vv. 1-7). This introduction carries with it the outlines of Jeremiah's whole discourse—false worship of Jehovah, idolatry, impenitence, falsehood, deceit and violence, and finally exile. It is a summons at the very outset to Judah to turn back from what they must know is contrary to the law of God.

Jeremiah first exposes their trust in the outward temple service, but points out their absolute lack of righteousness. He makes an admonitory reference to what God had done to Shiloh (7:8-15). Cf. Joshua 18:1,10; Judges 18:31; 1 Samuel 4:10,11.

The utter hypocrisy of their worship of Jehovah, boasted of in vv. 4ff., is proved by the idolatry they practiced elsewhere (7:16-20). Jeremiah refutes their objection that the Lord Himself had commanded the outward temple service. He had commanded *obedience to His moral law,* which they were disregarding (7:21-28).

The prophet rebukes, with evident disgust, the abominable nature of their idolatrous worship as proof of their hypocrisy (7:29-34). Retribution will come in the form of complete desecration of their supposedly sacred places. The vale of Hinnom will be a place of slaughter and burial, and unburied corpses of the worshipers shall be food for vultures and ravenous beasts (7:32 to 8:3).

Second Charge (8:4-22)

Jeremiah rebukes the stiff-necked obduracy with which they persist in their perverse course (vv. 4-7). However, they will not admit this, for they claim to be wise. Jeremiah traces their imagined wisdom to the deception of their false teachers (vv. 8,9), and exposes their moral perversion (vv. 10-12).

The prophet pronounces the visitation of judgment—desolation of the land, foreign invasion, captivity—all of which will bring great grief to the people, in which the prophet participates in advance (8:13-22).

Third Charge (chs. 9 and 10)

The prophet exposes the perfidy, deceit, and malicious defamation in every direction which the people of Judah practiced, which will subject them to severe punishment, likened to a fiery melting of ore (9:1-8). This *melting* will be in the form of the desolation of the land and the dispersion of the people (9:9-15). Death is going to take a terrible toll (9:16-22). They might escape, if they would discard their own boasted wisdom and submit to their God, who is full of loving-kindness, justice, and righteousness (9:23,24); but they are "uncircumcised in heart" (9:25,26).

Jeremiah reminds the people in his preaching of the utter vanity, nothingness, and folly of idols (10:1-5) and contrasts them with Jehovah the true and living God (10:6-16). Cf. Isaiah 44:9-20. The prophet visualizes the enemy from "the north country" as already at the gates (10:22), addresses a command to the people to remove into exile (vv. 17,18), laments over the calamity which befalls his people (vv. 19-22), and concludes with a consolatory glance into the future (vv. 23-25).

FOURTH DISCOURSE (CHAPTERS 11 TO 13)

This discourse (as in chs. 7-10) can properly be placed in the early part of Jehoiakim's reign. There seems to be a reference, in this message of Jeremiah, not only to the past general attitude of the nation toward the Mosaic Covenant, but also to their more recent breach thereof after the thoroughgoing reforms of Josiah. This reform, vigorous though it was, did not reach the hearts of the people.

Jeremiah reminds them (11:1-8) of the recent renewal of the covenant between Jehovah and the people, but now there is open conspiracy to break it on the part of the entire people (vv. 9,10); even among the people of Anathoth, Jeremiah's home village (vv. 18-23); and in the prophet's own family (12:1-6). Jehovah says to Jeremiah, "If even the enmity of those at a distance is so intolerable, what will you do when the members of your own family plot to waylay you?" (vv. 5,6). Punishment for this perfidy is announced (11:11-17).

"As the undertakings of the conspirators against the prophet were virtually against the Lord also, so the prophet's action is a symbol of the judgment which the Lord will inflict in larger and severer measure. Therefore what is said in ch. 12:7-11 of abandoning house and heritage applies at the same time to the prophet who leaves his paternal house in Anathoth; and to the Lord who forsakes Israel."— Naegelsbach. The whole land is to be laid waste when the spoiler comes (vv. 12,13).

Surrounding heathen nations, who with Judah have conspired against the covenant of true worship and righteousness, are seen in association with Judah in punishment (v. 14). But common cause in repentance and returning to the Lord will meet with mercy and reestablishment (vv. 15-17).

Message of the Linen Girdle (ch. 13)

Jeremiah is instructed by Jehovah to be participant in a symbolic action, which conveyed an object lesson to the people of Judah. The Hebrew word *Phrath,* translated Euphrates here, is more probably an abbreviation of Ephrath which appears to have been the original name of Bethlehem and its vicinity *(Lange).* The prophet's action, if he had journeyed faraway north to the Euphrates river, would have had no significance to the people of Judah, but nearer at hand it would.

The linen girdle which he is to purchase is representative (because it fits most closely) of the relationship between Israel and the Lord (v. 11). There at Bethlehem-Ephrath he was to hide the girdle in a fissure of some well-known rock in the vicinity. Since the prophet's movements were undoubtedly closely followed, curiosity might call for an explanation of the meaning of his two journeys to Ephrath (cf. Ezekiel 12:3-13). The destruction of the girdle is a picture of the humbling of Judah's pride (vv. 1-11).

Under the figure of jugs filled with wine and dashed to pieces against each other, the prophet depicts the judgment of God upon the royal house, the priests, and the false prophets (vv. 12-14). An admonition to heed the divine warning follows (vv. 15-17), with special address to the king and queen-mother, the heads of the state, to humble themselves (v. 18), for judgment from "the north" (Babylon) is impending—swift, sure, all-encompassing—because of the nation's literal and spiritual lewdness (vv. 18-27).

FIFTH DISCOURSE (CHAPTERS 14:1 TO 17:18)

LANGE'S FIRST MAIN DIVISION (14:1 TO 15:9)

A fearful drought is prevailing in the land at this time (ch. 14). The prophet describes how all classes of the people are keenly suffering (vv. 2-4). "He describes how the terrible thirst conquers even the maternal feeling of the hind (v. 5) and how the wild asses seek the heights in order to obtain some mitigation at least from strange currents of air" (v. 6)—Lange.

The Prophet's First Petition (14:7-9)

The prophet identifies himself with his people and makes acknowledgment of Judah's sins, but petitions the Lord for His own name's sake and for His glory, which is pledged for the sake of the righteous remnant of His people and for the sake of His renown among other nations (cf. Numbers 14:13-16), to act in mitigation of this calamity.

Jehovah's First Refusal (14:10-18)

Jehovah answers that the persistent idolatrous conduct of the people precludes all mercy (v. 10), bids the prophet cease his intercession (v. 11), and the people their hypocritical ceremonies (v. 12). The prophet ventures to interpose that the prophets have sustained the people in their error by false promises (v. 13). Jehovah indicts these false prophets for their lies (v. 14), and pronounces their destruction (v. 15) and that of the people who believe them (v. 16). The wound is incurable (v. 17); and everywhere the prophet goes he meets death and learns that both prophet and priest wander aimlessly with no real consolation for the people (v. 18).

The Prophet's Second Petition (14:19-22)

Out of his deep feeling of pity and compassion for his people, Jeremiah persists in his intercession a second time. He asks the Lord why He has rejected Judah and Zion (v. 19). He sets forth

three reasons why this cannot be: (a) Israel (at least in the prophet
as their representative) acknowledges her sins (v. 20); (b) "Jehovah
must help for His own glory and for the sake of the covenant" (v.
21); (c) "There is no other god who can dispense rain and blessing
than He" (v. 22).

Jehovah's Second Refusal (15:1-9)

The Lord most decisively refuses the prophet's petition. Even
the intercession of a Moses or a Samuel would be of no avail (cf.
Exodus 32:11-14, 1 Samuel 12:16-23). The people are rejected from
the presence of the Lord (v. 1), but not to some place of asylum,
for when the people inquire where they might go, the prophet is
to tell them their destruction will take various forms (vv. 2-4)—a
difficult ministry.

The prophet can declare only that there is no further prospect of
pity or succor for Jerusalem (v. 5). Judah has rejected the Lord. He
has in turn rejected them and can no more retract His purpose of
judgment (v. 6). "Winnowed" out of the country like chaff, Israel
is bereaved of his men and sons and the enemy will come with the
sword after the fugitive remnant (vv. 7-9).

LANGE'S SECOND MAIN DIVISION (15:10 TO 16:9)

The Complaint of the Prophet (15:10-18)

Jeremiah now becomes introspective over the consequences to
him personally of Jehovah's refusal to answer his petitions. He laments his birth to be a man whom all curse (v. 10), but the Lord
assures him of His care and promises that his enemies will be sup-
pliants in the day of affliction (v. 11). However, Jeremiah, along
with his people, will have to be a partaker of the general distress
which a national judgment entails (vv. 12-14).

The prophet continues his plea (vv. 15-18). In effect he says:
"Suffer not that in consequence of the delay of Thy vengeance I be
swept away of mine enemies. It is for Thy sake I have been re-
proached. I have given only Thy word from my innermost heart
and I have identified myself wholly with Thee. I have had no joy
in the society of the idle; I have been lonely and have been in accord
with Thy wrath against the sins of Judah. Why is my situation not
mitigated? Am I not to rely on Thy word?" Rotherham translates
verse 18: "Wilt thou indeed be to me as a brook that disappointeth,
waters that cannot be trusted?"

Jeremiah was obviously discouraged and seemingly ready to give up.

Jehovah's Consolatory Answer (15:19-21)

In verse 19 there is a gentle reproof of the prophet for his depression and doubt of the fidelity and trustworthiness of the Lord (cf. v. 18). So he needs to "return." "Put such thoughts away from you," replies Jehovah, "and you shall continue to be my mouthpiece; your enemies will finally agree with your testimony; I will endue you with resistless firmness, and give you protection and deliverance from all dangers."

Personal Instructions to the Prophet (16:1-9)

Jehovah commands the prophet to forego marriage and the begetting of children, for these would not escape the universal calamity of death (vv. 1-4), and further, for a sign of the imminence of the divine judgment. Jeremiah is commanded not to mourn for the dead, for since God has taken away peace from His people, "only a false consolation could be given" (vv. 5-7). He is also instructed not to engage even in legitimate nuptial merrymaking, for in view of the impending judgment this would be a mockery (vv. 8,9).

LANGE'S THIRD DIVISION (16:10 TO 17:18)

In this final section of the fifth discourse, the prophet gives the reason for the rejection of Judah and a definite announcement of the captivity.

Idolatry the Cause of Exile (16:10-15)

When the people come with an air of injured innocence and inquire the reasons for the divine disfavor (v. 10), Jeremiah is to reaffirm the departure of their fathers from God, and their own worse sin (vv. 11,12), with the consequent punishment of rigorous servitude "day and night" of idol gods in the land of their captivity (v. 13).

On the question of whether verses 14 and 15 belong in this context (they are found in an appropriate context in Jeremiah 23:7,8) expositors disagree. At any rate, in this context they are not consolatory, but sad. They confirm the declaration of the captivity, but provide a gleam of hope for the righteous.

Description of Judah's Removal (16:16-18)

Their removal is likened to fishermen who fish out a lake, or hunters who exterminate wild animals, even from the most effectual cover (v. 16). Just so, Judah's ways are not hid from the Lord and He will render to them "double" retribution by banishing them from their land (vv. 17,18).

Jehovah's Answer to 16:10

To their contention that idolatry along with the temple service to Jehovah is not sin, Jeremiah points out that in the near future the heathen will perceive what Israel has failed to perceive—that idols are folly and that Jehovah is the true God (vv. 19-21).

Judah's sin is certified, recorded ineradicably, even recorded on their own hearts, despite all efforts to deny it (17:1), and desolation and deportation will be their judgment (vv. 2-4).

Retrospect (17:5-13)

In verses 5-13 Jeremiah indicates the most hidden and inward roots of the spiritual and physical corruption of the people—their perverse disposition, which regards not the Lord, but flesh, as the source of all blessing (v. 5). The punishment of this sin is mentioned in verse 6, and the contrast is shown by the blessings mentioned in verses 7,8.

Their hearts were full of perfidy (v. 9), yet the Lord viewed it all (v. 10); their avarice will only bring them to poverty and shame (v. 11), with destruction upon all those who have forsaken Jehovah (vv. 12,13).

Jeremiah's Petition (17:14-18)

The prophet prays for safety and deliverance for himself (v. 14) from the scorners (v. 15), for he had not presumptuously assumed the prophetic office (v. 16). His persecutors, he prays, may have double retribution (vv. 17,18).

Sixth Discourse (chapter 17:19-27)

This brief message—delivered probably under the arch of the city gate, where all classes passed through—is a warning and admonition against profanation of the sabbath (vv. 19-23); with a promise that great material blessing will result to king, city, and temple if they will sanctify the sabbath (vv. 24-26); concluding with a warning of a fiery judgment which will consume the gates and palaces of the city, if they continue to desecrate the sabbath (v. 27).

SEVENTH DISCOURSE (CHAPTERS 18 TO 20)

This discourse deals with symbols of pottery. As these chapters appear under a common superscription of the longer form—" 'The Word which came to Jeremiah from the Lord'—which does not recur until 26:1, they may be regarded as a connected whole."—Naegelsbach.

The Clay and the Potter (ch. 18)

Jeremiah receives the command to go to the potter's house to receive a revelation from the Lord (v. 1). He obeys and witnesses how a piece of work is spoiled on the wheel and how the potter immediately refashions the clay into a new vessel (vv. 1-4). The application is that as the clay is in the hand of the potter, so is Israel in the hands of the Lord (vv. 5,6). Just as the Lord is dissuaded by repentance from visiting judgment, so by evil-doing He may be prevented from performing His gracious promises (vv. 7-10).

Application

The application is obvious. God declares that He is about to "form" calamity against Judah (v. 11). The call to repentance (v. 11) is met with stubborn refusal (v. 12). Because of this unheard-of (v. 13) and unnatural apostasy (vv. 14, 15), desolation, dispersion, and flight before their enemies is decreed (vv. 16,17).

The Rebellious People (18:18)
The Prophet's Petition (18:19-23)

Jeremiah represents to the Lord the personal enmity of the people toward him in answer to his faithful admonitions (18:18); and prays in strong terms that the Lord will avenge him of these adversaries, and not forgive them but overthrow them in His anger (vv. 19-23).

The Broken Vessel (chs. 19 and 20)
The Incident (19:1-13)

The prophet now receives the command to buy an earthenware pitcher from the potter and, in company with the elders of the people and the priests, to go to the valley of Ben-Hinnom, or Tophet, near "the east gate" (vv. 1,2). There he pronounces a terrific judgment upon the vile center of abominable idolatries and cruelty of

Baal worship, which he prophesies will shortly be a shambles (vv. 3-7); he depicts the consequent hunger of the impending siege and the desolation of the city (vv. 8,9).

In the presence of the assembled leaders he breaks the pitcher (v. 10) with the explanation that thus, as easily, Jerusalem and its people will be destroyed (v. 11); and Tophet, now a place of refuse burning, will be a burial place for the corpses of the slain (vv. 12,13).

The Sequel (19:14 to 20:18)

Pashur (19:14 to 20:6)

The prophet returns from Tophet into the temple court and probably repeats there his predictions of dire calamity (19:14,15). For this, Jeremiah is struck by Pashur, the governor of the temple, who commits him to the painful punishment of the stocks in the high gate of Benjamin (20:1,2). On the morrow, upon his release (v. 3) the prophet is inspired to pronounce dire calamity upon Pashur ("Liberation"), whose name is now to be Magor-missabib ("terror on every side"). He is to witness terrible scenes of carnage; Judah is to be carried into captivity; he himself will survive all these horrors, go to Babylon, and die an exile there (vv. 4-6).

This will be the judgment upon him personally for his prophetic deceptions (20:6).

Jeremiah's Discouragement (20:7-18)

The close connection between this passage and the previous passage seems evident from the Hebrew words Magor-missabib in v. 10—"fear on every side," applied by Jeremiah to so prominent a personage as Pashur. If we bear in mind that Jeremiah had just had the most painful torture of a night in the stocks, and that it was the first time he had had to suffer physical ill-treatment, we can readily understand his discouragement and the feelings which called forth this lament.

He calls to mind that he had not assumed the prophetic office. He complains that all he has received has been scorn and derision (vv. 7,8). But when he has been disposed to leave his prophetic vocation, there comes an impulse within which burns like a fire which must find expression (v. 9). And yet his ministry is still fraught with attempts to overthrow him, even from those intimates who should have been better disposed (v. 10).

He is consoled by the fact that God is with him and that his enemies will be put to shame (vv. 11,12). He breaks out into an exhortation to praise the Lord as the deliverer of the needy (v. 13).

Yet another wave of depression seems to overwhelm him. He curses the day of his birth and the man who brought to his father the news of that event (vv. 14-17), for he had come forth to a life of sorrow and shame (v. 18).

The only sensible explanation of all this is that Jeremiah like Elijah was a man "of like passions" to any one of us. Elijah became discouraged and desired to die; so did Jeremiah. He is expressing his own human feelings. Men of God do not cease to be human and subject to human emotions and reflexes.

EIGHTH SECTION (CHAPTERS 21 TO 24)

The King's Question—the Prophet's Answer (21:1-7)

To King Zedekiah's petition that the prophet seek the interposition of the Lord for deliverance from the attacking Chaldeans, Jeremiah gives the answer that not only will they retreat before them, but Jehovah will actually interpose against them with pestilence and will surrender the survivors of the siege to death at the hands of Nebuchadnezzar, including the king and his courtiers.

The Way of Escape (21:8,10)

To the rank and file of the people the prophet announces that the life and death of individuals depends upon surrender to the Chaldeans or otherwise, for the destruction of the city has been irrevocably determined (vv. 8-10).

Exhortation to the House of David (21:11-14)

This message must be older chronologically than the two preceding messages, for at the date to which 21:1-7 belongs such an admonition as this could have no place.

The royal family is cautioned to rule righteously that the anger of the Lord should not burn to ultimate destruction. But their nonfulfillment of this charge is presupposed and judgment is pronounced.

A Divine Alternative (22:1-9)

Chronologically this passage, as evidenced by its language, belongs to the reign of Jehoiakim and before the crisis of the battle of Carchemish, when Pharaoh-necho was defeated by the Babylonians.

There is no mention of the Chaldeans. The warning corresponds to the character of Jehoiakim.

The royal house is exhorted to practice justice and righteousness to the end that David's line should continue in royal splendor. If not, the king's house will be made desolate; destroyers, like the fellers of a forest, will cut it down.

Prophecy Concerning Shallum (22:10-12)

Here is an utterance, probably the oldest in the book, concerning Shallum or Jehoahaz, the son of Josiah. There was universal mourning over Josiah's tragic death at Megiddo and horror at the captivity of his son after only a brief reign of three months. Many might hope, since he was still young, for Jehoahaz' return, but this hope is cut off by Jeremiah, who says that there is more cause to mourn for Jehoahaz than for Josiah. The dead is more fortunate than the living, for Jehoahaz will perish in the suffering and humiliation of captivity.

Prophecy Concerning Jehoiakim and His People (22:13-23)

Jeremiah cries a woe upon Jehoiakim, who unlike his godly father Josiah has been ruling despotically, selfishly, and oppressively to indulge his desire for fine architecture. He even is charged with doing innocent persons to death. Therefore, he will miserably perish, unwept. Dragged and cast out like an ass, his body will be far from the royal city and the tombs of the kings (vv. 13-19).

This prophecy came early in the reign of Jehoiakim.

The people who have harmonized with their pastors (23:1) or rulers in worldly lust and pride must share their fate (ch. 22:20-23).

Prophecy Concerning Jehoiachin (22:24-30)

A solemn word of judgment is pronounced upon King Jehoiachin (Coniah), successor to Jehoiakim. His captivity by Nebuchadnezzar, along with the queen mother, is announced. In Babylon he is to die.

Verses 28-30 were evidently pronounced after the previous prophecy had been fulfilled. Cf. v. 26 (future) with v. 28 (past). No descendant of Jeconiah will ever sit upon the throne of David (v. 30). In this prophecy the truth of the virgin birth of Messiah is safeguarded. Joseph, the foster father of Jesus, was in the succession of Coniah (Matthew 1:11,16). Had Jesus been the actual son of Joseph, He would have no right to the throne, for Coniah's curse would be upon Him; but Jesus does have the right to the throne, since He was the legal son of Joseph, through Joseph's marriage to Mary before Jesus was born.

The Unrighteous Kings and the Righteous King (23:1-8)

In general this passage, as Naegelsbach observes, is suitably connected with the entirety of the previous context, for it represents a comprehensive conclusion. It originally formed a connected whole only with 22:1-9,13-23, since 22:10-12,24-30 must have been inserted afterwards.

The prophet pronounces a woe upon Jehoiakim, the king then reigning, and upon all bad shepherding (vv. 1,2). In glorious contrast to this, the Lord promises to shepherd the faithful remnant Himself and to provide faithful shepherds for them (vv. 3,4).

A scion of the family of David will arise to rule Israel wisely, justly, prosperously, for He is to be Jehovah-Tsidkenu, the Lord our Righteousness—providing righteousness, administering righteousness, fulfilling the covenant promise to restore Israel, the united nation, to their own land from their worldwide dispersion (vv. 5-8).

Against False Prophets (23:9-40)

These blind leaders of the blind are indicted for their profane example. Not only had both prophets and priests desecrated the sanctuary with their crimes and set this horrible example, but they had actually fortified evildoers in their wickedness, so that the nation had become like Sodom and Gomorrah. Therefore, as profaners of the land, they must drink the gall of bitterness (vv. 9-15).

Verses 16-40 constitute the prophet's warning against the deceptions of these false prophets, "who instead of exhorting the people to repentance by warnings of impending judgment [as faithful Jeremiah], were lulling them into a false security with promises of peace and safety." They were criminally mingling man's word and God's Word and were assuming to speak under the "burden" of inspiration as an oracle of God.

The Sign of the Figs (ch. 24)

Under the symbolism of two baskets of figs, one sound and edible, the other rotten and inedible, is seen the future of those Jews who had been taken to Babylon in the first deportation in Jehoiachin's reign, and of those of the final captivity in the reign of Zedekiah (vv. 1-3).

The Lord will recognize the first group as good, and will bring them back to build and plant, and inwardly renew them (vv. 4-7). The second group, those left in Palestine with Zedekiah and those who had migrated to Egypt, will be slain (vv. 8-10).

Professor Graf remarks that those who remained may have triumphed over the others and extolled their own apparent good fortune.

Summary—The Scope of Judgment (ch. 25)

This message was given in the fourth year of Jehoiakim, just as the whole known world was about to be trampled under the feet of Babylon, 604 B.C.

Jeremiah speaks generally to Jerusalem and all Judah, reminding them that for 23 years he and probably Habakkuk, Zephaniah, and Urijah had brought to the nation a call to repentance which had gone unheeded (vv. 1-7). Now comes the specific word that this rising power of Babylon would overwhelm them and surrounding nations, and 70 years later Babylon itself would be destroyed (vv. 8-14).

This broad scope of judgment upon the nations is depicted under the symbol of a "winecup of fury" which Jeremiah, in representative action, causes each nation to drink, beginning with Judah. Babylon herself—"the king of Sheshach"—drinks "after them" (vv. 15-29).

The fulfillment of this symbolic drinking is set forth in verses 30-38.

Lesson 33

Jeremiah 26-52

MORE SPECIFIC MESSAGES OF REBUKE, JUDGMENT, AND RESTORATION

THE PROPHET OF THE LORD AND THE FALSE PROPHETS (CHAPTERS 26 TO 29)

Chapter 26

This series of chapters recounts the conflict of the true prophets of God with the false prophets and with the civil authorities. In the beginning of Jehoiakim's reign Jeremiah is bidden to stand in the fore-court of the temple and to proclaim his revelation to all the Jews who came to the feasts.

In discussing chapters 7-10 we referred to chapter 26 as being the historical account of the experiences of Jeremiah himself when he gave those discourses (chs. 7-10) in the temple area. Dr. Naeglesbach suggests, as a reason chapter 26 does not stand where it properly belongs, "that the series of great discourses [beginning with ch. 7] was not to be interrupted by a long historical section."

After giving his message he was apprehended by the priests and prophets, and the sentence of death was summarily pronounced (vv. 1-8). The princes were apprised of the messages of Jeremiah by the priests and prophets, but after the former had heard their import repeated they took sides against the latter and acquitted the prophet (vv. 9-16).

Certain of the elders, local magistrates, took sides with the princes, who at this early date in Jehoiakim's reign had not yet become filled with blood-thirsty hatred towards Jeremiah, and cited Micah's case as a precedent (vv. 17-19). He had prophesied similarly potent words, but had not been punished by Hezekiah. [Hezekiah was a different king than Jehoiakim, however.]

Verse 20 does not continue the narrative of Jeremiah's friends. Jeremiah probably added the story in order to show how great his danger was in the reign of wicked Jehoiakim (vv. 20-24).

Chapter 27

There is strong critical textual opinion that 27:1 should read "Zedekiah, son of Josiah," instead of Jehoiakim (cf. vv. 3,12,20). The prophet is bidden to prepare wooden yokes, and in a pantomimic action he is to put them upon his neck in the presence of ambassadors to Zedekiah from certain foreign powers. He is to explain to these ambassadors that the yoke represents servitude to Babylon, under which they are all advised to come voluntarily. Each ambassador is to take one of these replicas home and to report this same counsel to his sovereign (vv. 1-4).

The prophet says God has purposed to give Nebuchadnezzar authority over all these nations, Judah included, and their salvation will be to submit to him (vv. 5-13). Jeremiah also challenges the messages of the false prophets who said that the vessels of the temple which had already been taken to Babylon in Jeconiah's reign, would speedily be returned. He puts the lie on this and prophesies that the remaining ones will also go to Babylon, not to be returned until the captivity is ended (vv. 14-22).

Chapter 28

This chapter recounts the open contest between Jeremiah and Hananiah, probably a priest from Gideon, who predicted in the presence of priests and people that the sacred vessels would be returned in two years, because Babylon would be defeated. Hananiah emphasized this publicly by taking a symbolic yoke from Jeremiah's shoulder and breaking it (vv. 1-11).

Jeremiah predicts that all that has been effected by this performance is the substitution of an iron yoke for a wooden one. He says Nebuchadnezzar will put such a yoke upon the nations by divine appointment. Jeremiah pronounces upon Hananiah death within a year, because he misused the name of the Lord (v. 16) and misled the people into a false confidence. Hananiah died in two months.

Chapter 29

Letter to the Exiles in Babylon (vv. 1-23)

Jeremiah takes advantage of an opportunity afforded by an embassy, dispatched by Zedekiah to Babylon (v. 3), to send a letter to those who had been already deported (v. 2), counseling the exiles to humble submission to their lot, to settle down peaceably and contentedly in Babylon, and to await the Lord's deliverance for the nation. He warns them against a false hope of speedy return predicted by false prophets among them (vv. 4-14).

He predicts that their own brethren still remaining in Jerusalem and Judah will be slain (vv. 15-19). He singles out two of these false prophets in Babylon, Ahab and Zedekiah [not the king] and predicts their horrible death for their presumption and blasphemy (vv. 20-23).

Consequences of the Letter (vv. 24-32)

Jeremiah's letter caused great exasperation among the false prophets in Babylon. One of them, Shemaiah, complained in a letter to the overseer of the temple in Jerusalem because he did not act against the mad prophet Jeremiah. The prophet had been apprised of this message by the overseer Zephaniah himself. Jeremiah was commanded by the Lord to announce to Shemaiah that his family would become extinct and that he himself would not see the salvation of Israel.

MESSAGES OF CONSOLATION (CHAPTERS 30 TO 33)

Chapter 30

The message of these chapters was clearly to be committed to writing (vv. 1,2). As to what exact time it was received we have no clear evidence. Unquestionably it was to be laid up for the guidance and encouragement of the godly Israelites for all time.

First, the prophet contemplates Israel's (twelve tribes) return from captivity (vv. 1-3); then he looks further into the future and sees their deliverance from the final Tribulation or "time of Jacob's trouble" in the last days. He says the nation will emerge from these purging fires to the realization of the full blessing of the Davidic Covenant. This will be accomplished through discipline (vv. 4-11).

Verses 12-17 are closely connected to and explain three thoughts in verse 11: Zion is chastised according to her deserts, but not destroyed, while destruction becomes the lot of her enemies. These "lovers" (foreign nations), to whom she has looked for assistance and whose idols she has copied, are pictured as deserting her, but God will in turn punish them and restore health to Zion.

Restored Israel is seen as a flourishing and prosperous commonwealth, blessed materially, with righteous rulers who honor God,
but their enemies shall be chastised and the wicked in the nation
shall have no part in these glories (vv. 18-24).

Chapter 31

Jeremiah addresses himself first to Israel, the northern kingdom
alone (vv. 1-22); then, to Judah alone (vv. 23-26); and finally, to the
whole Israelitish nation (vv. 27-40).

Some of the main themes of this chapter are: the constancy of
God's love for His covenant people (vv. 1-3); promise of joyous,
fruitful restoration to repentant Israel (vv. 4-14); past weeping for
bereavement of children turned to joy (vv. 15-17); Ephraim's backsliding and God's faithful chastening (vv. 18-22); Judah's felicitation
of her sister nation (vv. 23-26); a united nation acknowledging God's
just dealings (vv. 27-30); the new covenant, not of "the letter" [law]
which killeth (2 Corinthians 3:6), but of inward union with God,
producing practical righteousness, and which is to be eternal (vv.
31-37); an enlarged city, hitherto unholy, now sanctified to God (vv.
38-40).

In these chapters we stand "at the most comforting and brightest
point in the prophecies of Jeremiah."

Chapter 32

This chapter embraces one continuous theme. At the time when
the Chaldeans had invested the city of Jerusalem (a siege which
resulted in its final fall) and all hope of deliverance had vanished,
Jeremiah was in prison on account of his prophecy of inevitable ruin.
He received a revelation that his cousin Hanameel (v. 7) would
come to him offering his inheritance in Anathoth for sale, because
of Jeremiah's right of redemption. Hanameel came and Jeremiah,
recognizing the Lord's will, carefully observed all the formalities
and purchased it.

This action seemed utter folly in the light of the pending overthrow of the kingdom of which Jeremiah was fully aware, but it was
done as a sign that "houses, fields, and vineyards shall be possessed
again in this land" (vv. 1-15).

After the transaction with Hanameel had been closed Jeremiah
begins to realize the utter incongruity of purchasing property in the
face of impending captivity, destruction, and desolation. He seeks

God, acknowledging His past faithfulness and power (vv. 16-25) and receives the fresh revelation of God's ability to order events so that property will be valuable and usable (vv. 26,27). Even though the nation must be punished and banished from the land, Jehovah purposes to restore them, and the normal economic life will be resumed (vv. 28-44).

Chapter 33

The prophet, still in the court of the prison, receives a second revelation of consolatory character. In the face of a condition of houses already thrown down in the interest of defense (vv. 4,5) the prophet foretells ultimate healing and peace (v. 6), the return of the exiles (v. 7), and forgiveness of all sin (v. 8). Jerusalem will then be the object of Jehovah's joy, a monument to the nations of the divine faithfulness to the people of Israel (v. 9).

Joyous City Life

Again will be heard the joyous participation of the people of Jerusalem in normal civil and religious life. Sheer delight in the goodness of the Lord will be manifest (vv. 10,11).

Glorious Country Life

Pastoral life with all its beauty and prosperity will be resumed. The landscape will be dotted with contented flocks under the care of the shepherds (vv. 12,13).

Jehovah's Branch

All these blessings will be brought to pass under the righteous rule of the Branch of David. Justice, salvation, and security will be the portion of a city and nation partaking of the very righteousness of their King. David's house shall be perpetuated forever and the priestly tribe of Levi will again stand in holy service before the Lord (vv. 14-18).

Perpetuity

These promised glories shall not cease, according to God's covenants with Abraham and with David, any more than that the recurring days and seasons should cease in God's faithfulness. They shall last forever (vv. 19-26).

HISTORICAL APPENDIX (CHAPTERS 34 TO 39)

These chapters constitute a record of events which took place in the personal life of the prophet having to do with kings Zedekiah and Jehoiakim, as well as historical events of importance in the reigns of these kings. They are the closing days of Judah's history as an independent kingdom. The Babylonian encroachments, begun during Jehoiakim's reign, eventuated in the siege and capture of the city by Nebuchadnezzar in the eleventh year of Zedekiah's reign.

Chapter 34

During the siege (v. 1) Jeremiah receives the command to go and announce to Zedekiah that the city will be given into the hands of the king of Babylon and burned (v. 2). Zedekiah himself will be captured, taken to Babylon, die there, and accorded kingly honors in his interment (vv. 3-5). Jeremiah carries out this commission at a time when the yet unconquered cities of Palestine are all under siege (vv. 6,7).

The people of Jerusalem are denounced for breaking their covenanted word. The law of Moses required that every servant of Hebrew origin was to be released after six years' service (without respect to the Sabbatical year). Cf. Exodus 21:1-11; Leviticus 25:37-41; Deuteronomy 15:2. This command had long been violated. The pressure of the siege, however, aroused the thought that it might be advantageous to obey this law, so the people had signed a covenant to release their slaves. But when Nebuchadnezzar's armies withdrew for a time, and the danger of invasion seemed past, they broke the covenant, revealing the shallowness of their motives.

The judgment pronounced by Jeremiah is that Nebuchadnezzar's armies will return and they who have made slaves of others will themselves become captives (vv. 8-22).

Chapter 35

In this chapter we see the counterpart of the disobedience of the Israelites in the obedience of the Rechabites. These people were descendants of Hobab, Moses' brother-in-law, a branch of the tribe of Kenites, who migrated with Israel to Canaan (Numbers 10:29; Judges 1:16; 4:11-17; 5:24; 1 Samuel 15:6). They had persisted in unwavering loyalty and obedience to their revered ancestor, Jonadab, who had required them to follow rules of simple living.

Their example is held up to the Jews as a rebuke for their stubborn disobedience, despite repeated warnings and admonitions from a faithful God, of every command of His. Therefore, evil has been pronounced and will be fulfilled.

Chapter 36

In the fourth year of Jehoiakim's reign Jeremiah is instructed to commit to writing all his pronouncements from the beginning of his ministry, a period of 23 years. This fourth year of Jehoiakim was a turning point in world history. Nebuchadnezzar had defeated the Egyptians at Carchemish, as previously noted, assumed universal dominion, and became the instrument of judgment "out of the north country," so often predicted by the prophet. The way to Palestine was now open to the Babylonians, and their arrival was predicted after a short interval.

Judah and Jerusalem are now to hear in concentrated form all the messages they had been hearing for 23 years. Baruch, Jeremiah's secretary, wrote them at the prophet's dictation in a scroll. Since Jeremiah was in custody at this time, he instructed Baruch to read them in the temple to the assembled people on a fast day. This Baruch faithfully carried out (vv. 1-10).

Michaiah, son of Gemariah, heard the public reading and gave notice of it to the princes, including his father. Thereupon they summoned Baruch, who brought the roll and read it to the assembled princes. The messaage made a deep impression (v. 16). The princes declared that they must inform the king, inquired as to the circumstances of the writing, and commanded him and also Jeremiah to hide themselves (vv. 17-19).

The princes, after depositing the scroll in the chamber of Elishama, the scribe, reported what had occurred (v. 20). The king had the roll brought and Jehudi read it in the king's winterhouse, in the presence of the king and his princes, before a fire burning on the hearth. The language and construction of the Hebrew original here clearly indicates that the scroll was read entirely, column by column, and then progressively cut up and thrown into the fire until the whole was consumed (vv. 21-24).

Several of the princes pleaded with the king not to burn the roll, but he refused and called for the apprehension of Baruch and Jeremiah. The Lord concealed them (vv. 25,26).

Jehoiakim could, indeed, burn the roll, but could not destroy the living Word of God. He gained nothing by his blasphemous act but greater guilt, intensified judgment, and more prophecies predicting calamity in a new roll (vv. 27-32).

Chapters 37 and 38

The events of these chapters, and also chapter 34, transpired in the tenth and eleventh years of Zedekiah's reign. In reply to an embassage from Zedekiah seeking Jeremiah's intercession to God in behalf of the city (37:1-5), now being besieged by the Chaldeans, he replied that the army of Pharaoh, which had come to his assistance, would return to Egypt, and the army of the Chaldeans, temporarily withdrawn, would resume the siege, capture the city and burn it (vv. 6-8). Were the Egyptians to smite the entire Chaldean army, God would vitalize even the wounded to rise from their tents and burn Jerusalem (vv. 9,10).

Jeremiah's Imprisonment

Jeremiah had wished, during the temporary withdrawal of the Chaldeans, to leave Jerusalem and go to Anathoth on the business of inheritance (37:11,12). He was detained at the gate by the commander of the watch and charged with designs of going over to the enemy (v. 13). Irijah brought him to the princes, who angrily smote the prophet and imprisoned him, where he remained many days (vv. 14-16).

One day Zedekiah secretly had the prophet brought to his palace, undoubtedly after the Chaldeans had returned as Jeremiah had prophesied (v. 8), to inquire if there were any word from the Lord. "Yes," said the prophet, "but the same word that I have already pronounced, that thou shalt be delivered into the hand of the king of Babylon" (v. 17).

Second Stage of Jeremiah's Imprisonment

Jeremiah besought the king that he should not be sent back to the dungeon (vv. 15,16), for he had been innocent of wrongdoing. He reminded the king of the falsity of the messages of his prophets, who had predicted that the king of Babylon would not come against Judah. Zedekiah did not send Jeremiah back to the prison, but had him confined in the court of the guard and scantily supplied with bread (vv. 18-21).

Third Stage of Jeremiah's Imprisonment

In response to the petition of the princes who were irked and angered by Jeremiah's predictions of coming disaster, which they said were lowering the morale of the warriors, the weak Zedekiah gave the prophet up to them. They lowered him into a dungeon-pit in the prison court, where he would have perished had not the Cushite Ebed-melech petitioned the king for his life. Zedekiah, with increasing vacillation and fear as the Babylonians thundered at the walls, remanded Jeremiah to the eunuch, who had him drawn up out of the dungeon and confined in the prison court (38:1-13).

Final Stage of Jeremiah's Imprisonment

Zedekiah again secretly interviewed the prophet, desiring that he disclose the future without reserve, promising with an oath that his life would be spared and protected. Jeremiah laid before the king the alternatives of surrender at once to the Babylonian generals and safety for himself and his household, with a spared city, or destruction of the city, humiliation for the women of his harem, and captivity for himself and his household, if he refused to surrender (vv. 14-23).

Zedekiah released Jeremiah back to the court of the guard where he remained until the city fell. Zedekiah charged him not to reveal the true import of his secret interview to the princes. Apparently the king's visit was known, for the princes came to the prophet inquiring of Zedekiah's purpose, which Jeremiah did not reveal (vv. 24-28).

Chapter 39

This chapter is a record of the capture of Jerusalem, the belated flight of the king, his capture, the slaying of his sons, his own blinding before King Nebuchadnezzar at Riblah, and his removal to Babylon (vv. 1-7).

The account further tells of the burning of the city and the removal of the people that survived the siege. Those of the poorer class of agriculturists were left in the countryside of Judah to carry on their occupation (vv. 8-10).

By explicit personal orders of Nebuchadnezzar Jeremiah was given favor and personal liberty. He might have gone to Babylon in honor (cf. ch. 40:4), but he chose to remain "among the people" (vv. 11-14).

The chapter closes with the record of Jeremiah's assurance to Ebed-melech, while he was still in prison, before the fall of the city. Because the Cushite had befriended the prophet he was to be spared from the vengeance of his enemies, and his life protected wherever he went (vv. 15-18).

MESSAGES AFTER THE FALL OF JERUSALEM (CHAPTERS 40 TO 45)

Chapter 40

It would seem that in the unavoidable confusion following the fall of Jerusalem, Jeremiah, contrary to Nebuchadnezzar's orders (39:11-14), was included among the captives, bound with chains, and taken to Ramah. Here the error was discovered (undoubtedly Nebuchadnezzar was fully aware of Jeremiah's eminent personage and of his prophecies) and the captain of the guard released Jeremiah, after first giving him the opportunity of going in full freedom to Babylon. The prophet returned to Gedaliah, who had been made Palestinian governor, to Mizpah to be with his people (vv. 1-6).

The scattered bands of rovers rallied to Gedaliah, who counseled them to loyalty to the Chaldeans and to settle down to peaceful pursuits in the land (vv. 7-10). Dispersed Jews from other surrounding countries also gathered to Gedaliah's leadership (vv. 11,12). However, reports came that one of these band leaders, Ishmael, the son of Nethaniah, of the royal stock (cf. 36:14; 41:1) had been incited by Baalis, king of the Ammonites, to assassinate Gedaliah.

The rest of the band leaders warned Gedaliah, but he believed them not (ch. 40:13,14). So sure was Johanan of the truth of the rumors, that he secretly offered to rid Gedaliah of this menace, but the governor forbade this, in confidence that the reports were false (vv. 15,16).

Chapter 41

The suspicions against Ishmael were well-founded. He came to Mizpah with 10 men and treacherously slew Gedaliah, as well as all the Jews that were with him and the Chaldeans in his retinue (vv. 1-3). This dastardly deed was not immediately known. Eighty Israelites, who were bringing offerings to the destroyed sanctuary, were met by the dissembling Ishmael, who professed loyalty to Gedaliah. Seventy of them were cold-bloodedly murdered and thrown into a cistern. Ten of the party survived by promising Ishmael supplies (vv. 1-9).

Ishmael then forced the rest of the people in Mizpah to accompany him to Ammon. But he was overtaken by Johanan and other band leaders. The captives immediately left Ishmael and joined Johanan, but Ishmael escaped with eight men to the Ammonites (vv. 10-15). Thereupon the leaders assembled all the people in the neighborhood of Bethlehem, preparatory to a flight to Egypt, for they felt themselves liable to extreme measures at the hands of the Chaldeans, due to Gedaliah's murder (vv. 16-18).

Chapter 42

Under the leadership of Johanan and Jezaniah, all the people requested Jeremiah to inquire of the Lord what should now be done (vv. 1-3). Jeremiah promised to do so (v. 4), and the people solemnly promised to obey the expected revelation, whatever it be (vv. 5,6).

After 10 days the answer came from the Lord, and Jeremiah summoned the people (vv. 7,8). If they remain in the land the Lord will prosper them, Jeremiah says. They need not fear the Chaldeans, for God will dispose the king of Babylon to forward their restoration (vv. 9-12).

But he warns that if, on the contrary, they do not remain in the country but flee to Egypt, they will perish there by the same calamities which they now fear in the land. They will be the objects of God's wrath just as definitely as those who perish in the fall of Jerusalem (vv. 13-18).

The prophet knows of their self-deception and hypocrisy. He knows that before they inquired of the Lord by him, they had already resolved not to obey the Lord's command. He urges them to reconsider, for as surely as they go to Egypt, there will they perish (vv. 19-22).

Chapter 43

These leaders declare that Jeremiah's declaration of the message of God is false and the result of influence from Baruch, his secretary, who is friendly to the Chaldeans (vv. 1-3).

Thereupon the whole mass of remaining population, including Jeremiah and Baruch (who undoubtedly were coerced) start their trek to Egypt, and settle at Tahpanhes (vv. 4-7).

Prophecy

In the presence of the Jews, Jeremiah is bidden by Jehovah to hide great stones in the clay of a brickkiln, opposite an entry-way to Pharaoh's palace grounds in Tahpanhes. This is to indicate to them that the Lord will bring Nebuchadnezzar to Egypt and that he will erect his royal pavilion on these very stones (vv. 8-10). Nebuchadnezzar will visit upon Egypt the terrors of war, burn idol temples, completely subjugate the country, and break in pieces the statues of Bethshemesh (house of the sun). This is a reference possibly to the obelisks of the temple of Heliopolis (city of the sun), of which there were many (vv. 11-13).

Archaeological expeditions have discovered at Tahpanhes, on the border of Egypt, bricks which formed a pavement on which Nebuchadnezzar's throne was set temporarily. These bricks have the name of King Nebuchadnezzar upon them.

Chapter 44
(Jeremiah's Last Message to Judah)

The Word of the Lord to the Israelites dwelling in Egypt is now pronounced by Jeremiah. He reminds them of the idolatry which brought about the fall of Jerusalem and the captivity to Babylon (vv. 1-6). He charges they have not humbled themselves, but have persisted in idolatry and have deliberately disobeyed God's law (vv. 7-10). As a consequence the remnant of Judah in Egypt will be destroyed just as Judah and Jerusalem were, by the sword, famine, and pestilence. Only a small number of fugitives will escape (vv. 11-14).

A group of women, evidently gathered to celebrate a festival in honor of the "queen of heaven," defy the prophet, utterly repudiate the message, and inform him that they will continue to perform their vows and make their offerings to the queen of heaven as they had done in Judah. They ascribe their misfortune to the temporary cessation of sacrifice to her and affirm that they are resuming their vows to her by concurrence of their husbands (vv. 15-19).

Jeremiah refutes their assertions that their misfortunes dated from the cessation of this worship. He declared that it was on account of this very idolatry, which God could no longer abide, that calamity had come upon them (vv. 21-23).

He makes positive announcement of the severest punishment upon their stubborn defiance of the true God. As a sign that He will make good His word, Pharaoh-hophra, king of Egypt, will be given into the hands of Nebuchadnezzar, just as Zedekiah had been. Only a remnant shall escape (vv. 24-30).

Chapter 45
In the fourth year of Jehoiakim when Baruch, Jeremiah's secretary, has finished writing out the prophecies at his dictation (vv. 1,2), the prophet has a comforting word to his friend in answer to his expression of sorrow over prevailing conditions (v.3): The Lord will desolate the whole land (v. 4), but let Baruch consider it a reward for distinguished service, if he is permitted to escape with his life.

PROPHECIES AGAINST FOREIGN NATIONS
(CHAPTERS 46 TO 51)
(These utterances came at different times during Jeremiah's ministry.)

EGYPT (CHAPTER 46)

The great empire of Egypt, despite the rallying of all her military forces and might under Pharaoh-necho, is now to be defeated and turned back by Nebuchadnezzar's armies. This defeat was accomplished at Carchemish on the Euphrates River about 605 B.C. (vv. 1-12). It was on the way to this battle that this Egyptian king encountered and slew Josiah (2 Chronicles 35:20-24).

A second prophecy follows, given at another time, concerning Nebuchadnezzar's invasion of Egypt. The cities of Egypt are seen rallying to her defense, but to no avail (vv. 13-19). Egypt is compared to a fat cow, but a gad-fly (Hebrew text) from the north (Babylon) brings destruction (v. 20). Egypt's mercenary armies are likened to fatted calves which flee away (v. 21), and her people to a forest which is hewn down (vv. 22,23). The great city of Thebes (No) and her vast system of idol vanities is to be destroyed at the hands of Nebuchadnezzar (vv. 24-26).

The last two verses of the prophecy are of the restoration of Israel, possibly given at a different time, although as Dr. Naegelsbach says Jeremiah may have "felt the need of causing the light of Israel to shine brightly on the dark background of their ancient enemy, Egypt" (vv. 27,28).

PHILISTIA AND TYRE (CHAPTER 47)

Israel's implacable enemy, Philistia, along with her sister nation to the north, Phoenicia, or Tyre, are to be completely overwhelmed as by great floodwaters. Such terror will seize the Philistines that fathers will not look back to rescue their children. Their cities of Gaza and Ashkelon will fall.

MOAB (CHAPTER 48)

The cities of Moab are seen falling one by one before invading armies and their idol gods and priests are abolished. Judgment comes for trusting in their wealth and for their worship of Chemosh (v. 7); for living in ease and luxury (v. 11); rejoicing over Israel's misfortunes (v. 27); pride (v. 29); and for magnifying themselves against Jehovah (v. 42).

Their restoration in the last days is predicted (v. 47; cf. Isaiah 16:1-5).

AMMON, EDOM, SYRIA, ARABIA, ELAM (CHAPTER 49)

The prophet in a series of questions alludes to the illegal possession by *Ammon* of the tribe of Gad (cf. Joshua 13:24,25; Amos 1:13) and declares that this will not continue for Israel will repossess it (vv. 1,2). War and desolation of the land will be her punishment (vv. 3-5). Her captivity will eventuate in restoration (v. 6).

Utter destruction is pronounced upon *Edom,* Israel's implacable enemy (vv. 7-22). Cf. Numbers 20:18; Ezekiel 25:12-14; Amos 1:11; Obadiah.

Syria is represented by her capital Damascus. Her northern borders, Hamath and Arpad, will be terrorized by evil tidings (undoubtedly the news of the approach of the Babylonian armies). The armies reach Damascus and in her streets her defenders are slain and the city is destroyed (vv. 23-27).

The roving Bedouin pastoral tribes of Kedar and Hazar, lands of *Arabia,* are to be smitten by Nebuchadnezzar and their flocks of sheep, cattle, and camels carried away as booty. These lands are to be left desolate and denuded of inhabitants (vv. 28-33).

Elam was a province east of Babylonia, a warrior people, noted for their efficient use of the bow and arrows. Their history is closely related to the empires of Assyria, Babylon, and Persia. Jeremiah says they are to fall before their enemies, probably the Babylonians, but will be restored in the "latter days." A partial fulfillment of verse 39 may be found when the magi came to our Lord at Bethlehem; and still more when Parthians, Medes, and Elamites heard the gospel at Pentecost (vv. 34-39).

BABYLON (CHAPTERS 50 AND 51)

Babylon, that great empire which appears so frequently in Jeremiah's utterances, is now seen under Jehovah's hand of judgment. The nation was a scourge of Jehovah upon Judah and the surrounding nations (cf. Jeremiah 27:7). The dealings of God with Babylon are similar to those with Assyria (cf. again Isaiah 10:5-34).

Undoubtedly the fulfillment of 50:1-5 is to be found primarily in the overthrow of the Babylonian Empire by the Medes and Persians in 536 B.C. (see Daniel 5) and by Israel's partial restoration at that time, but the words "perpetual covenant that shall not be forgotten" require the exhaustive fulfillment of the last days, when the final Babylon is destroyed (see Isaiah 13 and 14) and Israel is regathered from her worldwide dispersion.

He says Israel has greatly sinned by her idolatry (v. 6) and has received deserved punishment from her enemies (v. 7). The hour of deliverance is near, because God is sending hosts of nations from the north (Medo-Persia) against Babylon (v. 9). She shall be spoiled, as she has devastated others (v. 10), because she arrogantly and maliciously exceeded her commission (v. 11). Babylon shall be desolated (vv. 12,13). Babylon's enemies are summoned prophetically to attack Babylon, to throw down her walls, to upset her economic life, because of her sin, and as a judgment of Jehovah against her (vv. 14-16).

The people of Israel (the whole nation) have been like frightened sheep, scattered and devoured, first by Assyria and now by Babylonia (v. 17). But Assyria has already been punished and Babylon will follow (v. 18). Israel will again "feed" in her own pasture, for God will forgive the nation's iniquity and preserve it through a faithful remnant (vv. 19,20).

The same general themes prevail throughout chapter 50 to the end.

Then chapter 51 concludes the prophetic forecast concerning the once proud city and empire. The themes of Israel's sin, her chastisement at the hands of Babylon, Babylon's punishment, and Israel's restoration continue throughout.

This entire prophecy (chs. 50 and 51) was transcribed as a single document, and when Zedekiah, in the fourth year of his reign, made a journey to Babylon, Jeremiah committed the prophetic document to Seraiah, the brother of Baruch, the king's marshall, with instructions to read it in Babylon and then, with a prayer, to sink it in the Euphrates River.

This was a sign or symbolic action depicting Babylon's final doom and oblivion. Cf. Revelation 18:21.

CONCLUSION AND RETROSPECT
CHAPTER 52
(Compiled by someone later than Jeremiah)

This chapter is a historical appendix containing a brief survey of the events from the beginning of the reign of Zedekiah to the death of Jehoiachin, his nephew and predecessor, in Babylon.

We are already quite familiar with all the events in this historical sketch, so we will not recapitulate. An interesting brief account is added (vv. 31-34) of the experience of Jehoiachin, who was taken to Babylon in the second deportation (2 Kings 24:10-16). Evil-merodach, son of Nebuchadnezzar, performed this act of grace upon Jehoiachin on his ascendancy to the throne of Babylon. He brought Jehoiachin out of prison, received him graciously, clothed him in garments befitting his station, and exalted him to a place of eminence above the "kings" (probably princes or nobles) in his court (vv. 31-34).

Lesson 34

Lamentations

The book called Lamentations is a series of five poems, recording keen, heartbreaking sorrow over the miseries and desolations of Jerusalem resulting from her siege and destruction. Just as Psalm 119 is a Hebrew acrostic poem consisting of 22 strophes of eight verses each, each strophe (in the Hebrew) beginning with a letter of the Hebrew alphabet in order, so the first, second, and fourth of these acrostic poems consist of 22 verses each, and each verse begins with a letter of the Hebrew alphabet, all in succession. The third poem has three verses to each letter, 66 in all, while the fifth has 22 verses but not in alphabetical order.

Authorship

The authorship of Jeremiah is disputed only by those higher critics who reason that he could not have written it because of the difference in literary style and language between the prophecy and the poem. Examine the writings of any literary genius and one will find marked contrasts when they engage in different kinds of literary composition.

The Septuagint (LXX) version of the Old Testament gives this prefix to the book: "And it came to pass, after Israel was taken captive, and Jerusalem made desolate, that Jeremiah sat weeping, and lamented with this lamentation over Jerusalem, and said . . ." It is thought that this prefix must have been in the Hebrew copy from which the Septuagint translation was made. Evangelical scholars have generally admitted that these poems were written by Jeremiah.

In the Hebrew Old Testament this book does not follow the Book of Jeremiah, as in our Bible, but is in the group called "Hagiographa" or "Holy Writings": Song, Ruth, Lamentations, Ecclesiastes, Esther. Evidently these were on separate rolls because they were read at different feasts. This book (Lamentations) was chanted every Fri-

day at the Wailing Wall in Jerusalem prior to partition and read in
the synagogues throughout the world on the ninth day of the fourth
month (Jeremiah 52:6) in remembrance of the destruction of Jerusalem. As someone has said, it is a hymn of sorrow, "every letter
written with a tear, every word with the sound of a broken heart."

"Jeremiah's Grotto"

"This is the name of the place, just outside the north wall of
Jerusalem, where, tradition says, Jeremiah wept his bitter tears and
composed this sorrowful elegy over the city he had tried so hard to
save. This grotto is under the knoll that is now called 'Golgotha,'
the selfsame hill on which the cross of Jesus stood. Thus the suffering
prophet wept where later the suffering Savior died."—Halley.

Composition of the Book

The book must have been composed between the fall of the city
and Jeremiah's forced departure for Egypt. Probably a number of
copies were made; some taken to Egypt; others sent to Babylon for
the captives to memorize and sing. Cf. Psalm 137 for this emotional
reaction.

First Poem (chapter 1)

The beauty of these poems is spoiled for us in our English version.
Let us put several verses of the first poem, in an English translation,
somewhat in the form they take as poetry. Of course, the Hebrew
words would read from right to left, but we reverse the order.

Aleph.
How sitteth solitary
    The city that was full of people!
She is become as a widow!
    She that was great among the nations,
A Princess over the Provinces,
    Is become tributary.

Beth.
Bitterly she weepeth in the night,
    And her tears are [constantly] upon her cheeks.
She hath no comforter
    From among all her lovers:
All her friends have dealt treacherously with her,
    They have become her enemies.

And so the poem runs through every letter of the Hebrew alphabet—each succeeding verse beginning with the next letter from Aleph to Tau.

In this first poem the prophet visualizes the ideal person or genius of the city, the daughter of Jerusalem, now become a widow, lamenting over the ruin of the city, the nation, and the temple. Sometimes the prophet speaks about her, tells what she is doing, and again he uses the first person and puts the words in her mouth.

The whole picture is of a stunned, dazed, heartbroken person weeping with grief inconsolable.

The words *friends* and *lovers* (vv. 2,19) indicate the human supports on which Jerusalem foolishly and presumptuously believed she could rely, especially all those nations whose friendship she had so often preferred, instead of trusting Jehovah. (Cf. Jeremiah 2:13,18,33,36,37; 22:20,22; Ezekiel 23.) These passages "show, in harmony with history, that the nations toward which Israel felt itself drawn in amorous love, but by which they were not only deserted, but treated even with positive hostility, were especially Assyria, Babylon, and Egypt"—especially the latter in the crises of Assyrian and Babylonian invasion.

Judah's exile (v. 3), the cessation of the solemn feasts (v. 4), the ascendancy of her enemies by divine decree (v. 5), the flight and wandering of the princes (v. 6) are seen. Jerusalem is indicted again for her sins as the reason for her affliction (vv. 7-11).

From the last clause of verse 11 the poet lets the daughter of Jerusalem speak. She invites all who pass (12-14, 18); she laments the death of her heroes under the combined power of the enemy, and weeps inconsolably over her calamity, for she stretched forth her hands in vain for help (vv. 16,17).

The last three verses of the first poem are a prayer that the Lord will regard her misery (v. 20) and bring upon her enemies such a day of vengeance as He had brought upon Zion (vv. 21,22).

SECOND POEM (CHAPTER 2)

Note again how beautifully poetic is this threnody even in an English translation.

Aleph.

How doth the Lord cover with a cloud, in His anger
  The daughter of Zion!

He, from heaven, hath cast down to the ground
   The glory of Israel!
He remembered not His footstool
   In the day of His anger

   Beth.
The Lord swallowed up and spared not
   All the habitation of Jacob:
He demolished in His wrath
   The strongholds of the daughter of Judah:
He cast down to the ground—He polluted
   The kingdom and its princes.

The prominent element in this poem is the Lord's *anger,* His righteous indignation against His rebellious people.

Note verses 1-5, 21, 22 for the above citation. The city of Jerusalem, which Jesus mentioned as being "set on a hill," and surrounded by mountains, was for physical situation the most beautiful city then known, "the perfection of beauty, the joy of the whole earth" (v. 15), even when compared with Babylon, Nineveh, Thebes, and Memphis, which were built on river plains. "Moreover, it was the city of God's special care, chosen of Him for a unique mission, the main channel for God's dealings with men, most favored and highly privileged city in all the world, beloved of God in an exceptional and very special way, and under His special protection. Moreover, it was so well fortified that it was generally believed to be impregnable (4:12). But this City of God had become worse than Sodom (4:6); and impregnable walls are no defense against the anger of God. That the God of infinite and unfathomable love is also a God of terrible wrath toward those who persistently spurn His love, is a teaching that is stated and illustrated again and again and again throughout the Bible."—Halley.

THIRD POEM (CHAPTER 3)

"This Song, which as the third one of the five holds the middle place, is the culmination point of the whole book, and thus affords a strong argument for the opinion that the whole book is constructed on one carefully considered plan. It is the culmination point, both as to its matter and as to its form. As to its matter because we have here the sublimest conceptions of suffering. As to its form, because here the art of the Poet displays itself in full splendor. This appears, first of all, in the alphabetical arrangement. Whilst the other songs have only 22 alphabetically arranged verses, this one contains 66 verses, arranged in triplets, the three verses of each triplet beginning with the same letter. Each verse is a distich [stanza of two lines], composed of a rising and falling inflection. The ternary [arrangement in threes] division is observable not merely in reference to the verses beginning with the same initial letter, but with regard to the arrangement of the whole: for the whole Song is naturally divided into three parts. The first part embraces verses 1-18; the second, verses 19-42; the third, verses 43-66."—Naegelsbach.

Note again the poetic form of the first six verses

Aleph.
I am the man who saw affliction
    By the rod of His wrath.

Aleph.
He led me and brought me
    Into darkness and not light.

Aleph.
Surely against me He turned His hand.
    Again and again the whole day long.

Beth.
He caused my flesh and my skin to waste away,
    He broke my bones.

Beth.
He built around me and encompassed me
    With bitterness and distress.

Beth.
He caused me to dwell in dark places,
    As the dead of old.

This poem contains a description of the personal sorrows of one prominent man. He was distinguished by his position as well as by his sufferings (cf. v. 14). He evidently stood out before all the people.

It is not difficult to recognize Jeremiah in this description. Note that verse 53 refers to what is related in Jeremiah 38.

Part One (vv. 1-18)

Jeremiah seems to be complaining that God has ignored him and his prayers (vv. 8,44). He speaks of God only indefinitely, in the

third person, verses 1-16. In verse 17 he addresses God in the second
person; and in verse 18 he addresses Him distinctly by name. Naegelsbach points out that this is evidently a designed *climax* and is
due to the *art* of the poet, of which this song affords striking evidence.

Jeremiah is speaking for himself, yet in part seems to be person-
ating the nation. Though there is complaint, he justifies God, acknowledging that they deserve worse (v. 22).

The figures of speech in Part One are most striking and vivid,
expressing in the highest degree the bitterness and sorrow of spirit
which he, as the representative of his people, feels over their calamity.

Part Two (vv. 19-42)

In this passage the poet "rises out of the night of sorrow into the
clear day of comfort and hope; yet he allows a morning dawn to
precede (vv. 19-21) and an evening twilight to follow this day (vv.
40-42)." Verses 19-21 are a clear transition from Part 1. Jeremiah
can pray again!

Jeremiah prays that the Lord once more be mindful of him in the
midst of his bitterness, and he expresses hope of this (vv. 19-21).
From verse 22 to 47 the prophet no longer speaks in the first person
singular. "It is as if he felt the necessity, at this culmination point
of the poem, of letting the individual step back behind the sublime
and universal truth which he pronounces."—Naegelsbach.

Note that each triad of verses throughout Part Two, as regards
its sense, is a complete whole. This is peculiarly evident in the
original, but interestingly observable in the English translation.

The whole series of triads (vv. 22-40) is a sublime expression of
the nature of God—His faithfulness, long-suffering, mercy, justice,
and righteousness.

Verse 39 again constitutes a transition to something new. "If there
must be sighing let it be sighing over sin," says this verse. This
exhortation is responded to (vv. 40-42); then follows (vv. 43-47) the
expression of a united people ("we") under the chastening hand of
God for their *sins*.

Part Three (vv. 43-66)

This has been compared to the night returning after the day.
From verse 48 to the end the prophet speaks in the first person

singular, perhaps becoming introspective again after basking in the sunlight on the mountains, as seen (vv. 21-39). The shadows gradually fall until the night of those sufferings with which Israel was punished closes in.

FOURTH POEM (CHAPTER 4)

"The first poem related especially to the city of Jerusalem; the second to Zion and the holy places; the third to the sufferings of the prophet as a representative of the spiritual Israel; this fourth poem to the sufferings of the people generally, embracing all classes."—Hornblower.

Once again note the beauty of form, even in an English translation, of the first four verses.

Aleph.
How doth the gold become dim!
  The choice gold change its color!
The hallowed stones are cast forth
  At the head of every street.

Beth.
The noble sons of Zion,
  Who are equal in value to the purest gold,
How are they esteemed as earthen pitchers
  The work of the hands of the potter!

Gimel.
Even jackals drew out the breasts,
  They suckled their whelps.
The daughter of my people became cruel,
  Like ostriches in the wilderness.

Daleth.
The tongue of the sucking babe cleaved
  To the roof of his mouth for thirst:
Young children asked bread.
  There was none to break to them.

Part One (vv. 1-6)

Verses 1, 2 describe the sad fate of the sons of Zion, "scions of the noblest lineage" (Jeremiah 2:21). [There is something very noble, virile, and inspiring about the modern "sons of Zion," the Chalutzim (pioneers), the young people (despite their rejection of Christ) who have gone from good positions in the United States and other lands to break stone for road making, to drain swamps, plant trees, etc., in the remaking of Israel.]

Verses 3-5 describe the harrowing grief caused by the sufferings of little children, which could not possibly be relieved, and verse 6 depicts the sin of Zion as being even greater than Sodom's, judging by Zion's punishment.

Part Two (vv. 7-11)

This part of Poem Four begins, much like verses 1-6, with what the Nazarites (better, "nobles" or "princes," by Hebrew text) of Zion had to suffer. So great was the altering of their appearance through the sufferings of the siege that they could not be recognized on the streets (vv. 7-9). Verse 10 is a tragic picture of the lengths to which mothers could go in the straitness of the siege. Verse 11 corresponds to verse 6 of Part One. Here is a statement that these tragic conditions measured the divine wrath against Zion.

Part Three (vv. 12-16)

Jeremiah concurs in what seemed to be current opinion among all the nations that Jerusalem was impregnable, either because of its reputed theocratic administration or because of its situation (v. 12). The explanation of its fall is that its leaders, especially the prophets and priests, had corrupted themselves so far (vv. 13,14) that the people (sinful though they were) had to repudiate them (v. 15), and God must reject and scatter them (v. 16).

Part Four (vv. 17-22)

They in Jerusalem had pinned their last hope upon the Egyptian king, but he had failed them (v. 17). Jeremiah graphically pictures the last hours of the city (v. 18) and the flight, pursuit, and capture of King Zedekiah (vv. 19,20). Their last hope that they might live under his shadow, even in a foreign land, was dashed to pieces (v. 20).

In conclusion the poet addresses a threatening word to Edom for her perfidy. He says that Edom rejoiced maliciously in the destruction of Jerusalem, and even contributed towards it (v. 21). Cf. Psalm 137:7. A word of comfort is addressed to Zion (v. 22).

FIFTH POEM (CHAPTER 5)

This chapter is not a Hebrew acrostic. Nevertheless "it is evident from the agreement in the number of the verses with the number of letters in the Hebrew alphabet, that the chapter should be regarded as belonging to the four preceding ones as a member of the same family. The acrostic is wanting, because the contents are in prose."—Naegelsbach.

We feel with other expositors that Dr. Naegelsbach is wrong in the statement that "the contents are in prose." It is true that there is no acrostic here, but there are distinct poetic characteristics in this chapter, which even the acrostic poems do not possess. Dr. W. H. Hornblower points out some of these characteristics:

1. It has that unfailing mark of Hebrew poetry . . . parallelisms of thought, one half of the verses exactly and beautifully corresponding in its sentiment and form of construction to the preceding half.

2. The language is so unmistakably rhythmical as to be almost metrical.

3. There are also clear evidences of resemblance in sound, which cannot be accidental and could only be allowed in poetry.

4. In spirit as well as in form, this chapter is poetry of the highest order.

Analysis

The poem is divided into an introduction (v. 1), two principal parts (vv. 2-7, 8-16) and a conclusion (vv. 17-22).

Introduction

The first verse contains the prayer that Jehovah will be mindful of the affliction and reproach that has come upon Zion, some features of which the prophet recounts in what follows. It is really the introductory sentence to the whole prayer.

Part One (vv. 2-7)

All their possessions, fixed and movable, are seized by the enemy (v. 2). Families are scattered, fathers have disappeared, mothers are widowed (v. 3). They must buy what they need; they are driven beyond their strength (vv. 4,5). They have made themselves subservient both to Egypt and to Assyria to prolong their lives (v. 6). Their misfortune is caused by the sins of the fathers, the consequences of which now their posterity have to bear (v. 7).

Part Two (vv. 8-16)

Some are suffering under the rigorous bondage imposed by slave-drivers, while others are exposed to the peril of robbers in the wilderness (vv. 8,9). All are hungry (v. 10). Their women have been dishonored (v. 11). Their nobles have been hung up or treated outrageously (v. 12). Their young men have been compelled to carry heavy hand mills, the boys to carry heavy loads of wood (v. 13). All the old expressions of fellowship and joy have ceased (vv. 14,15). Their debasement has come, not merely because their fathers sinned, but because they themselves have sinned (v. 16).

Conclusion (vv. 17-22)

Verses 17 and 18 introduce the closing prayer (vv. 19-22). The desolation of the holy mountain can but bring deep pain to a true Israelite (vv. 17,18). But consolation is found in the stability of God's throne forever (v. 19). Then follows a sad recognition in the form of a question that God has forsaken them (v. 20); but that inspires a prayer for His renewed favor and their reestablishment (v. 21). The last verse in the margin is in the form of a question and represents the import of the original text—"For hast thou utterly rejected us and art exceedingly angry with us?"

The answer must be in the negative, for God "keepeth not His anger forever." "His mercy endureth forever" and "the gifts and calling of God (to Israel) are without repentance" (Romans 11:29).

Lesson 35

Habakkuk and Obadiah

HABAKKUK
Background

This prophecy was given on the eve of Judah's captivity to Babylon, as the "great day of the Lord," spoken of by Zephaniah, was about to break. Assyria, a great world power, was fading fast under the blows of the rising Babylonian might. The Babylonian power was sweeping westward like a flood (1:5-11), but had not yet reached Judah (3:16).

Habakkuk, also, may have been saddened by the tragic death of good King Josiah, at Megiddo, where he engaged in a vain attempt to frustrate the plans of Pharaoh-Necho of Egypt. (See 2 Chronicles 35:20-34.)

The duel between Chaldea and Egypt was about to come to an end at the great battle of Carchemish, north of Palestine, near the Euphrates River in 605 B.C.

Mighty upheavals were taking place in world history. Habakkuk was in the midst of them, felt their impact, and was greatly perplexed. He probably belongs to the period between 625 and 600 B.C. during the reigns of Jehoahaz and Jehoiakim.

The Man Habakkuk

Little is known of the prophet personally. Many legends were current among the Jews respecting him, but they shed no light upon his career. From 3:1 and 3:19 we gather that he may have been a Levite participating in the music of the Temple.

But he was a man with deep perplexities. He has been called the "freethinker among the prophets," and the "father of Israel's religious doubt," but "he was a man of clear faith and powerful hold upon God." He could not at first square his belief with the tre-

153

mendous facts of life as he so vividly saw them. He was troubled
with the "Why?" of the apparent prosperity of the wicked (1:12-16).

"He could not get his questions answered. A man of reverent
spirit, with keen, sensitive, highly developed faculties, he was more
seriously troubled than any other man in the kingdom."—Yates.

He was undoubtedly familiar with the words and works of Amos,
Hosea, Micah, and Isaiah. He knew the precepts and promises of
the Law of Moses. "In addition he was a careful student of life and
experience of men. It was at this point that his most serious problems
arose, for he had great difficulty in harmonizing the rich promises
and the dire threats of God with the actual happenings of his daily
observation."—Yates.

But he knew where to take his perplexities. He went to the Lord
who quickly dispelled them and "who presented a solution to his
problems summed up in a statement which is the heart of the book—
'The just shall live by his faith' " (2:4).

In all this mystery and perplexity, true to his name ("to embrace,"
"to cling," "to wrestle,") he clung to God and, pouring out his
difficulties to Him in prayer, waited patiently (2:1) for the divine
explanation.

The Book

It is said that Benjamin Franklin read Habakkuk to a literary circle
in Paris, winning their unanimous tribute of admiration for an author
of whom not one of them had ever heard before.

The book may have been a favorite with Paul. He quotes 1:5 in
his warning to the unbelieving Jews at Antioch (Acts 13:41), and the
famous statement of 2:4 he quotes three times (Romans 1:17; Ga-
latians 3:11; Hebrews 10:38).

Habakkuk is *conversational.* Two-thirds of it is conversation or
dialogue between the prophet and the Lord.

FIRST CONVERSATION

Habakkuk's First Complaint (ch. 1:1-4)

Habakkuk is perplexed with the silence and forbearance of God
permitting evil to continue, and pours out his soul to God. He is
in perplexity: (1) at the seeming neglect of his prayer (v. 2); and (2)
at the Lord's seeming indifference to sin and suffering (vv. 3,4).

Why, he asks, does God allow the wicked and lawless men of
Judah to continue unpunished? How long will God allow the injustice, the brutality, the wrong to go on in Jerusalem?

Jehovah's First Answer (ch. 1:5-11)

God answers by stating that His silence does not mean ignorance nor indifference. He is not inattentive nor inactive, but He is about to bring punishment upon sinful Judah.

God's reply challenges Habakkuk to look beyond the limited borders of Judah. The prophet was aware of some of the events already transpiring in Nahum's "great day of the Lord." He knew of the death of the Assyrian Empire and of the rising power of Babylon.

God's reply revealed that He—

(1) Is about to do something incredible (v. 5).

(2) Will use these Chaldeans to chastise Judah for her sin (v. 6).

(3) Has chosen them as terrible and dreadful instruments who will cause an awful scourge to sweep over the land. Judgment will come upon Judah.

SECOND CONVERSATION

Habakkuk's Second Complaint (ch. 1:12-17)

Jehovah's answer to the prophet's first protest, though it solved one difficulty, raised another, posing a difficult moral problem; namely, how could God use such a means to chastise Judah—the Chaldeans, a nation far worse than themselves? How could He, the eternal holy God, let punishment come upon the people of Judah, even though sinful, by a people more sinful? (vv. 12,13). How could God reconcile the cruelty and inhumanity of the enemy with His own purity and holiness? How could He permit them to catch men as fishes (vv. 14,15), when they glorify themselves? (vv. 16,17).

An Important Decision (ch. 2:1)

Apparently the prophet does not receive an immediate answer to this second perplexity and Jehovah subjects him to the discipline of delay. He had pretty boldly challenged God to defend His actions and, it would seem, a little presumptuously:

Thou art of purer eyes than to behold evil, and thou canst not look on perverseness; wherefore dost thou look upon them that deal treacherously, and holdest thy peace when the wicked swallow up the man who is more righteous than he? (1:13)

Now the Lord lets him wait. Habakkuk "finds the solution only when he obediently takes his place on the watchtower to wait expectantly for the true revelation from God. The world is in ruins about him and the hosts of Chaldea are coming to destroy what is left, but he is finding the one source of solution to his problems. Reverently and expectantly he watches for the answer from God."— Yates.

Jehovah's Second Reply (ch. 2:2-20)

In due course the reply comes. God is not unmindful of the wickedness of the Chaldeans, but declares in 2:5ff that "they will perish by the very explosive power of evil" within their own perverted hearts (v. 4).

Jehovah instructs the prophet—

(1) To write very plainly what He was about to say (v. 2).

(2) That the divine purpose is moving inexorably to certain fulfillment. "The present situation requires patience. God does not feel any need for hurry" (v. 3).

> *Though the mills of God grind slowly,*
> *Yet they grind exceeding small:*
> *Though with patience He stands waiting,*
> *With exactness grinds He all.*
> —Longfellow, in *Retribution*

(3) That righteousness must triumph—"The just shall *live* by his faith." Those counted righteous through their faith would be preserved, certainly in the ultimate eternity, from the sorrows of earth (v. 4).

"No matter how gloomy the outlook and how triumphant evil may seem, the just man must not judge by appearances, but rather by God's Word; though the wicked may live and prosper in their wickedness and the righteous suffer, the latter are to live a life of faithfulness and trustfulness. The prophet learned this lesson well, for, whereas his prophecy begins with mystery, questioning and doubt, it ends with certainty, affirmation, and faith."

(4) That a series of five woes will come upon the Chaldeans:

a. The haughtiness, arrogance, greed, and sadism of the conqueror is described and condemned—a terrific indictment (vv. 5-8).

b. The lust for land and possessions will meet with retribution (vv. 9-11).

c. The oppression and murder that destroys cities and rebuilds them with blood is judged (vv. 12-14).

d. The godless revelries, where God is dishonored in drunkenness and as a result of which people suffer, will receive retribution (vv. 15-17).

e. The folly of idol worship is disclosed. It is utterly irrational and must meet with condemnation from the true and holy God (vv. 18-20).

Note the ultimate purpose of God, despite the woes and injustices of earth, to fill all the world with His glory (v. 14).

HABAKKUK'S HYMN AND DOXOLOGY (CHAPTER 3)

Pindar, a Greek poet of the fourth century B.C., was a great *lyric* poet, noted for the beauty and grandeur of his style. Habakkuk's poem in the Hebrew (ch. 3) has been called Habakkuk's Pindaric Ode, in recognition of its magnificence.

Habakkuk's fervent prayer is rewarded by a revelation of God himself. If all the details were known, Habakkuk's experience would doubtless be similar to that of Job (Job 42:5,6) when God's majesty and power were revealed to him (vv. 2,16).

The prophet's cry is that Jehovah will work again in behalf of His people as of old (v. 2). He recognizes that God has met His people in every crisis by the display of His mighty power. As he looks he sees and understands the import of God's resistless onward march through the centuries, as He uses sometimes the forces of nature to accomplish His purposes. He understands more clearly now that Jehovah is in *active* control of all things great and small, of the nations and their restless surgings.

The last three verses are a sublime picture of faith. Though disaster and ruin may await him and his people, he "comes to realize that he can implicitly trust in Jehovah. He sees that only a small part of God's plan is visible at the time and that God would have him wait patiently for the fuller revelation."—Yates.

OBADIAH

The prophecy of Obadiah is the shortest book of the Old Testament. It is clearly seen that it is directed against Edom, a country to the south and east of the Dead Sea.

The Edomites

The Edomites were descendants of Jacob's twin brother Esau. The personal antagonism between them was perpetuated seemingly in the very blood of their descendants. The Edomites were as different from the Israelites in genius and character as their ancestors were. Like Esau, they were fleshly minded. They lived for material possessions, for spoil and rapine.

Their capital city was Sela, or Petra, and their fortified strongholds were Teman and Bozrah. History records their forays upon neighboring peoples. They would attack and then retreat to these strongholds which were well-nigh impregnable, especially Petra. Note 1:3.

Petra is today a magnificent example of ancient architectural beauty. Its temples, houses, and storage rooms, carved out of and extending into the perpendicular cliffs of solid rock, are today one of the wonders of the world.

Many students of prophecy feel that the rock-hewn city will be the refuge from Antichrist for the faithful remnant of Jews in the closing days of the Great Tribulation.

Their Biblical History

The Edomites refused to allow the Israelites passage through their territory at the time of the exodus from Egypt (Numbers 20:14-21; 21:4). They were a proud, bitter, resentful people and took advantage of every opportunity to harm Jacob's descendants. Israel and Edom were perpetually at war.

In the battle for the conquest of Palestine they fought against Israel. David subdued Edom, and Solomon continued to hold it in subjection, but they took advantage of every opportunity to rebel. They did so in the reign of Ahaz. When Nebuchadnezzar captured Jerusalem (587 B.C.) Edom rejoiced over Judah's downfall and cruelly took part in the plundering and massacre (Psalm 137:7).

In days gone by God had commanded Israel to treat them kindly (Deuteronomy 23:7) but now their cup of iniquity was full and God's sentence of annihilation was pronounced by Obadiah against them.

This word was not fulfilled all at once, but rather in progressive stages. In 582 Edom was invaded and practically destroyed by the Babylonians whom they had aided against Jerusalem. Those who were left continued as active enemies of the Jews. After Israel's restoration, Cyrus, king of Persia, overcame them. Judas Maccabaeus drove them out of southern Judah in 164 B.C. and John Hyrcanus later forced them to submit to circumcision and to accept Judaism.

They became the hated Idumeans of New Testament days. The Herodian family, Edomites (Idumeans), were placed by the Romans in control of Judah in 63 B.C. Herod the Great, an Idumean, was the one who gave the Jews the temple of Jesus' day and who sought to kill the infant Jesus. He died an awful death shortly afterward.

Herod Antipas, his son, was tetrarch of Galilee under Roman suzerainty. To him Christ was sent by Pilate, but Jesus spoke not a word to him (Luke 23:9). With the destruction of Jerusalem by the Romans in A.D. 70 the Edomites disappeared from history.

Obadiah the Man

Nothing whatsoever is known of the personal life of this prophet beyond what his words in these 21 verses reveal. We do not know where he was when he uttered and recorded this prophecy. The name means "worshiper of Jehovah" or "servant of Jehovah," according to the vocalization of the word.

"We know from the temper of his book that he was a pious, patriotic, sensitive resident of Judah who dared put into words something of the flaming indignation of his soul. He was hurt by the serious lack of ordinary decency displayed by his neighbors. In biting words he denounced these proud sinners who deserved all the punishment that God was about to heap upon them. He seemed to be thoroughly willing to wait for God to take His own time in destroying the old strongholds, for he had faith to believe that Yahweh would bring about a glorious victory and that right would triumph over wrong."—Yates.

The Theme

The theme is the utter destruction of Edom. Nothing shall save this guilty nation. "Rock fortresses [v. 3], impregnable cities, narrow mountain gorges, proud warriors cannot avail, for Jehovah has already decreed her destruction."

THE SIN OF EDOM (vv. 1-14)

Their pride in their rock-hewn fortress of Sela (vv. 3,4) and in their wise and mighty men (vv. 7-9) is uncovered. But their greatest sin was their perpetual violence against Judah in the day of her calamity (vv. 10-14). They had manifested an inhuman spirit toward the people of Judah when disaster had struck (vv. 11,12). They took fiendish delight in their "brother's" misfortune. They helped capture fleeing Israelites, treated them cruelly, and sold them as slaves (v. 14), and shared in the loot when the city was captured (v. 16).

EDOM'S PUNISHMENT (VV. 15-21)

Retribution of the same kind which Edom had meted out to others would be visited upon her. As they looted and spoiled in Jerusalem, so should they with other heathen nations be despoiled (vv. 15,16).

In the hour of judgment Edom will be ruined, while the remnant of Israel will be restored and blessed. Edom's territory will be occupied by other peoples, but salvation will be in Mt. Zion, where God's kingdom will be established (vv. 17-21).

Lesson 36

Daniel 1-5

Political and Historical Background
The period of Daniel's life and of his ministry as prophet and statesman is coterminous with the rise and fall of the Second Babylonian Empire. During his life the whole period of Judah's servitude to Babylon ran its course—605-536 B.C.

Judgments upon Judah
1. Judah was in servitude to Babylon for 70 years. This chastisement would have doubtless proven sufficient had Judah been loyal in her vassalage to Babylon, but King Jehoiakim, after being released by Nebuchadnezzar, revolted to Egypt. The Babylonians had taken some of the sacred vessels and certain of the nobles and princes of the land. Among these were Daniel and his three companions (2 Chronicles 36:4-8; 2 Kings 23:34 to 24:6).

2. The captivity to Babylon took place in 597 B.C. when, after the ignominious death of Jehoiakim (Jeremiah 22:18,19; 2 Chronicles 36:8) his successor, Jehoiachin, was taken captive to Babylon together with his household, "the strength and flower of his kingdom," and more of the sacred vessels (2 Chronicles 36:8-10; 2 Kings 24:8-16). Jehoiachin's uncle, Mattaniah, was placed on the throne by Nebuchadnezzar, but like Jehoiakim proved treacherous, on account of which the third blow fell (2 Kings 24:17 to 25:7).

3. The desolations of Jerusalem lasted 70 years from the fall of the city (about 586-516) to the completion of the second temple (2 Kings 25:8-21; Ezra 6:15).

4. The poor people of the land had been left by Nebuchadnezzar to till the ground, and they came from all parts to the protection of Gedaliah, whom the King had appointed governor (2 Kings 25:22-24). After the assassination of Gedaliah by Ishmael (2 Kings 25:25,26),

the remnant of the people still persisted in their rebellion, and in spite of the warnings of Jeremiah (Jeremiah 44:1-8) went down to Egypt where the Lord utterly destroyed them and the nation was dispersed to the four corners of the earth (2 Kings 25:26).

The Man Daniel

"It was as Prince Royal that Nebuchadnezzar first took Jerusalem, his reign as king beginning the next year (605 B.C.). So that it was in the second year (604-603 B.C.) that the Hebrew youths, after a period of three years' Chaldean tuition, were presented at court. We may safely say from the degree of maturity, as well as signal ability, required by Nebuchadnezzar in selecting these youths for deportation that Daniel may have been deported at about the age of 19."—Stevens. (The word *children* in verse 4 is "youths.")

This would make the date of his birth about 624 B.C., the very year of the rise of the second Babylonian Empire. Thus his long life of more than 90 years spanned the whole history of that empire.

GREAT MORAL AND RELIGIOUS DECISION (CHAPTER 1)
(See 2 Chronicles 34)

"We cannot believe that Daniel was a purposeless young man when he passed through the gates of the new, ambitious capital of the world. A very interesting and profitable study may be made right here into the circumstances of Daniel's earlier years, in order to form an approximate idea of the process under which this rare character was developed for so high a destiny.

"We cannot doubt that so intelligent, observant and favored a youth had taken a keen and profitable interest in the momentous events which, as we have noted, were in progress in the course of Gentile empire. But of far stronger influence upon him would be the stirring contemporaneous events in the history of his native land. From 1:3 we may infer that he was a child of the royal house or of the highest nobility and, therefore, reared in close touch with the highest personages of the nation. First among these stood the good king Josiah."

Assuming that Daniel was 19 when taken to Babylon "in the third year of Jehoiakim," this would carry his birth back to the fifteenth year (624 B.C.) of Josiah's reign of 31 years (2 Chronicles 34:1). Next, perhaps, to David himself, Josiah was dearer to the heart of God and of the people than any other king. "He did that which was right in the sight of the Lord, and walked in the ways of David his father, and declined neither to the right hand, nor to the left" (34:2). At 16 years of age "he began to seek after the God of David his father" (34:3). For four years he so grew in the knowledge and zeal of God that at 20 years of age he set resolutely about the task of extirpating the extreme system of idolatry which his predecessors, Manasseh and Amon, during 57 years of shameless rule, had established and perpetuated throughout the land. This occupied him for six years. "And when he had broken down the altars and the groves, and had beaten the graven images into powder, and cut down all the idols throughout all the land of Israel, he returned to Jerusalem" (34:7). Now Daniel would have become old enough to catch the inspiration of this holy achievement.

Then Josiah immediately took up vigorously the task of renovating the neglected temple, which was full of rubbish and sadly out of repair (34:8-13). There turned up amidst the rubbish a copy of the law of Moses. Manasseh had evidently taken pains to wipe out even the written law from the land! How remarkable that Josiah could have gained such intimate acquaintance with God and such holy, intelligent zeal, without a copy of the Scriptures to aid him. The discovery of this copy of the Law led, upon its being read before the king, to the utmost apprehension of the extreme judgment of God, and to the most anxious appeal to God for mercy, which was promised for Josiah's days (34:14-28). Thereupon Josiah had the nation assembled to hear the Law, and swore all to the most faithful observance of the same (34:29-33).

It is to be noted that, from the next year after Josiah commenced all these public reforms, he had had the association and assistance of Jeremiah, who, according to Jeremiah 1:2, was called just at this juncture and almost as a youth to his great prophetic office. His was the task of the internal, spiritual reform; while Josiah's was that of external, conventional reform. Jeremiah's work was to tear away the mask from the hollow-hearted reformation of the people.

Josiah's epoch of reform was crowned with a most glorious passover (2 Chronicles 35:1-19). "And there was no passover like to that kept in Israel from the days of Samuel the prophet: neither did all the kings of Israel keep such a passover as Josiah kept" (35:18). Now we can see that, under such leaders of affairs in Judah and under such influences, critical and stirring, Daniel's young heart must have received an unusual molding for good. Back of all there lay, most likely, a godly parental care, which subsidized and supplemented these circumstances for the best ends.

"But we are called now to note particularly the change of conditions affecting Daniel's training of character, which occurred when he was supposedly 16 years of age. At that time a tragedy hitherto unparalleled befell Judah in the untimely death of Josiah, in the prime of life and success, on account of apparently the one and only misstep of his life; namely, his misguided and foolish interference with Egypt's attempt to gain supremacy over the decaying power of Assyria. The sad story and its profound effect is told in 2 Chronicles 35:20-25.

"The impressionable heart of the lad Daniel must have been affected profoundly and indelibly by this whole affair. Yet, all the more critical must have been this period of his life, because of the sudden and extreme contrast now introduced into his political and moral surroundings and influences. The son of Josiah, Jehoahaz (also called Shallum in Jeremiah 22:11,12), took not up his father's mantle, but that of his wicked predecessors; and after a reign of only three months he was taken away captive for the rest of his life by the Egyptian king, Pharaoh-Necho, on his return from his defeat in the East (2 Kings 23:31-34). Jehoiakim, another son of Josiah, then took up the reins of government; but, as we have seen, only to undo as rapidly as possible all the good which Josiah had accomplished. Now that the kingdom was reeling along dizzily in abandoned wickedness, wanton idolatry and reckless violation of political obligation, every worldly inducement to a prince in the morning of life would urge Daniel to forsake the memories of Josiah, spurn the relentless jeremiads of the prophet, and conform to the morals and politics of the day. These very conditions, however, impelled a soul like Daniel's to root itself in the deepest fastnesses of the national faith. He girded himself to withstand, rather than drift with, the current of his times.

"With some such previous moral training, Daniel met the supreme demand upon his personal decision which was occasioned by the new and testing surroundings and temptations of the imperial court, the capital not only of Gentile power but also of heathen idolatry. Daniel had to decide, at the risk alike of forfeiting the most dazzling earthly prospects and of provoking the murderous wrath of the irresponsible young autocrat, that he would not be of Babylon although in it, that he would be as out and out for God in Babylon as in Jerusalem, that, while politically under the feet of Babylon, yet morally and spiritually he would put Babylon under his feet."— Seiss.

Daniel's courtesy is seen in the record (1:11-14), for he *requested* that they be allowed to eat the simpler fare. (He did not make a peremptory *demand* upon his superiors.) Not only did Daniel have the supernatural endowment of ability to understand all visions and dreams but he was intellectually endowed as well (1:17,20). The Lord made use of both to further His purposes in Babylon politically, as well as to reveal to the prophet the great scope of world-empire lasting to the end of Gentile dominion.

THE BOOK ITSELF

The book consists of two distinct parts distinguished by the language in which each is written. Chapter 1 is an introductory chapter recounting the initiation of the "four Hebrew children" to the Babylonian court. This chapter is in Hebrew as is 2:1-3. Chapters 2:4 to 7:28 are written in Aramaic or Chaldee, the language of Babylon, while chapters 8 to 12 are written in Hebrew. This language division is appropriate, for chapters 2-7 have to do with the "times of the Gentiles," world-empire down to the end of the age. They give a comprehensive view of the long period during which the Jews are subordinated to Gentile rule; namely, from the time of Nebuchadnezzar to the coming of Messiah, their deliverer. Chapters 8-12 have to do peculiarly with the fortunes of the Jews, as related to these empires.

NEBUCHADNEZZAR'S DREAM OF THE GREAT IMAGE
(CHAPTER 2)

The second chapter of Daniel has been called the A B C of prophecy. It contains the most complete and yet the most simple prophetic picture which we have in the whole Word of God.

The time of this chapter is 603 B.C., the second year of the actual reign of Nebuchadnezzar as king. He was ruler over the greater part of the civilized world known at this time (although portions of the world—the northern shores of the Mediterranean, portions of southern Egypt, and the regions beyond—were outside the borders of his dominion).

Israel had been unfaithful to God and the title to rule over the nations had been given definitely by God to Nebuchadnezzar. A remarkable word to this effect is to be found in Jeremiah 27:5-9. "I have made the earth, the man and the beast that are upon the ground, by my great power and by my outstretched arm, and have given it unto whom it seemed meet unto me. And now have I given all these lands into the hand of Nebuchadnezzar the king of Babylon, my servant; and the beasts of the field have I given him also to serve him. And all nations shall serve him, and his son, and his son's son, until the very time of his land come: and then many nations and great kings shall serve themselves of him. And it shall come to pass, that the nation and kingdom which will not serve the same Nebuchadnezzar the king of Babylon, and that will not put their neck under the yoke of the king of Babylon, that nation will I punish, saith the Lord, with the sword, and with the famine, and with the pestilence, until I have consumed them by his hand. Therefore hearken not ye to your prophets, nor to your diviners, nor to your dreamers, nor to your enchanters, nor to your sorcerers, which speak unto you, saying, Ye shall not serve the king of Babylon." For some reason, after dreaming a vivid dream, the king's spirit was greatly agitated and he became sleepless. He was the greatest monarch the world had ever known, with absolute power over his subjects. He probably began to ponder what might come to pass in after years.

The Magicians

He summoned all the masters of the sacred wisdom into his presence and demanded that they recall the dream to his recollection. "It was the custom of ancient monarchs to gather around them the best representatives of science and learning that could be found. It helped to dignify their thrones. Babylon especially had her orders of wise men, priests, magicians, etc., supported by the state and held in high honor. It would be useless to try to define the particular office, pretension, or sphere of duty of these several classes. It is enough to know that they were the recognized keepers of the highest wisdom, the skilled dealers in all learned things, the men set to ascertain and interpret the messages and will of the gods. They professed to know the mind of the gods, to read fortunes and events from the stars, to obtain oracles from the unseen powers, to explain dreams, visions, and omens, to charm spirits, cure diseases, and procure supernatural interferences and aids. The libraries of such practitioners at Ephesus—which upon their conversion by the preaching of the apostle Paul, they publicly burned—were valued at 50,000 pieces of silver."—From Seiss, *Voices from Babylon.*

These men protested to the king the impossibility of recalling the dream, but the king was adamant and ordered their execution. Evidently Daniel and his three friends were included in this classification of wise men. Daniel with tact and wisdom sought a reprieve through Arioch, the captain of the guard, and was granted a short time by the king to bring him the interpretation.

Prayer for Light and Guidance

He went to Shadrach, Meshach, and Abed-nego and together they sought the Lord in prayer that they should not perish with the rest of the wise men of Babylon. The secret was revealed to Daniel and, after a profound expression of thanks and worship to God for His mercies, they went to Arioch again and were brought into the king's presence by him. Daniel then made known the dream and its interpretation.

The dream and its interpretation, as far as Nebuchadnezzar was concerned, were ordained of God to show the king that He was the supreme Deity and omniscient (2:47). Through the ability of Daniel to give the interpretation, he was exalted with his friends to a prominent place in imperial affairs, revealing God's purpose to have men of sterling character, wisdom, and ability in control of affairs.

Dispensational Fulfillments

The dispensational character of Gentile times is also revealed by this chapter. Four successive empires were shown to be appointed by God to rule the earth until He establishes His own theocratic kingdom at the advent of Him "whose right it is," as King of kings and Lord of lords, and as King of the Jews.

These four empires are:

1. Babylon (2:37,38)
2. Medo-Persia (2:39)
3. Greece (2:39)
4. Rome (2:40)

(Chapter 8 gives us a further prophecy concerning Medo-Persia and Greece under the symbolisms of the ram and the he-goat.)

Profane history amply tells what this second kingdom was, but we need not go beyond the records of the Bible to identify it.

(Remember that this is a prophecy. Cf. 2 Chronicles 36:20.) In the
account of the overthrow of Babylon on the night of Belshazzar's
impious feast, this same power is referred to as of "the Medes and
Persians" (ch. 5).

The latter is still unfinished. This succession of empires is represented by the parts of the body from the head downward to the
feet. Each metal is seen to be relatively inferior in value, weight,
and specific gravity (the ratio between the weight of a body and the
weight of an equal volume of water).

"The first empire only is a perfect unity as well as being of the
finest quality. The last is not only the most inferior in character,
but is divided (legs, and feet, and toes). It also has an entirely alien
and fragile admixture. Herein lies the secret that Gentile rule can
endure only on the principle of absolute monarchy, a single absolute
ruling head, which head shall be personally accountable to God.
Constitutionalism, republicanism, democracy are all alien and weak-
ening elements, actually disintegrating to true government, like clay
to the iron."—Stevens.

The Toes

In explanation of the toes of the statue, Daniel said: "And as the
toes of the feet were part of iron, and part of clay, so the kingdom
[the fourth] shall be partly strong, and partly broken [*brittle,* margin].
And whereas thou sawest iron mixed with miry clay, they [the toes,
i.e., the kings of the ten kingdoms; comparison with Daniel 7:7,8,24,
and Revelation 13:1; 17:12 will confirm the significance of the toes]
shall mingle themselves with the seed of men [the mass of humanity
within their domain]: but they shall not cleave one to another [po-
litical treaties and alliances will be broken], even as iron is not mixed
with clay. And in the days of these kings shall the God of heaven
set up a kingdom, which shall never be destroyed: and the kingdom
shall not be left to other people, but it shall break in pieces and
consume all these kingdoms, and it shall stand for ever" (2:42-44).
(The stone is the most important figure in the whole picture.)

End-Time Fulfillment

Dr. Nathaniel West sums up verses 42-44 in the following language: "Among the secrets of the future, the prophet reveals (1) the
total destruction . . . of the politically organized Gentile power and
the substitution of the kingdom of God in the stead of all earthly

kingdoms forever, and (2) that the time of the world-crisis is 'here-after,' even in 'the days of those kings,' the toes, therefore in the last days of the kings who are the heads of the separate and con-temporaneous kingdoms into which the fourth . . . empire will be divided. By the iron he means the hard and strong imperial, and by the clay, the weaker more plastic and popular elements in human governments, seeking vainly to combine and to cohere in political unity; absolutism repelling popular freedom and constitutionalism, and reversely, the latter repelling the former; mixed monarchies, where the popular will wars against the imperialism of crowns and defies the will of the crown; a state of political instability and in-security. . . . By the Stone cut out of the mountain without hands and falling upon the toes of the statue, is meant the descent of Jesus Christ from heaven in judgment to smite the kings of the earth and to dash the nations in pieces. By the fall of the statue, the destruction of the whole world-power is meant; and by the stone becoming a mountain and filling the whole earth is meant the world-embracing, universal, indestructible, and everlasting kingdom of Christ set up in victory on this present earth on the ruins of all existing govern-ments, in the last days of the last kingdoms into which the Roman territory will be divided." Cf. Revelation 19:15.

First Advent Not Involved

That the setting up of the Messianic kingdom was not fulfilled in the first advent of Christ, can be proven in several ways: (1) If, as we believe, the division of the two legs represents the eastern and western empires of Rome, this separation did not occur until the fourth century after Christ's first coming. (2) The spread of the gospel, leavening—so interpreted—the world is not the kingdom which, according to the chapter under consideration and other Scrip-ture, is set up by the sudden appearing of the "sign of the Son of man" in the heavens. (3) Gentile rule was not manifested in the form pictured for us here, as 10 confederated kingdoms. (4) Gentile supremacy was not ended at the first advent.

Present-Day Application

The meaning of this passage is clearly that in the last days Gentile rule will be consummated in a final manifestation of the Roman dominion (only four great kingdoms are possible) in the form of 10 confederated nations, occupying the territory of the original Roman dominion. Someone may ask, "Why does Scripture pass over in silence all the intervening centuries since the first advent of Christ?" The answer is that God, since Calvary, has been dealing with the world in grace. Judgment fell upon the Jewish nation in A.D. 70 for their final rejection both of Christ himself and of the Holy Spirit after the Day of Pentecost. God's prophetic clock ceases to keep time when the Jews are out of the land and are not constituted as a sovereign nation. Effort has been made by historical interpreters of Daniel and Revelation to find in history 10 kingdoms which would fulfill the requirements of Daniel 2 and 7 and Revelation 13, but the many and varying opinions would indicate that these are not to be clearly identified until the last days just before the coming of the Lord.

We have reached the stage today of the mixture of the iron of imperial strength and the clay of popular freedoms and constitutionalism. There was a time when *vox populi vox dei* (the voice of the people is accepted *as* the voice of God), but today the leaders of the radical, socialistic, communistic parties claim that the voice of the people *is* the voice of God, for they recognize no other god but the people. This spirit is preparing the way for the deification of humanity in the final great superman, the Antichrist of the last days. The once proud monarchies of ancient history and of more recent years have all fallen, and practically every country on the globe has either some form of democratic government, or, if it has a king, his power is only nominal and is limited by the popular assembly. Herein lies the weakness of democracy—the unstable, fickle, changing, popular whim or opinion. This condition is being intensified as the standards and restraints of both God's law and man's are being disallowed and repudiated by the mass of humanity. Men are clamoring for freedom of thought and speech and listening to the voice of science (often falsely so called) in place of the voice of revelation. In the name of this better (?) voice the poison of the evolutionary theory is being injected into the minds of the youth of this generation. Why is this so terrible? Because this theory, if believed, banishes forever from the mind the presence and activity of a personal God as the Creator and upholder of the universe. If there is no personal God exercising His moral government, then human responsibility ceases and every man does "that which is right in his own eyes." Result—anarchy, chaos, and confusion.

PRESERVED FROM FIERY DEATH (CHAPTER 3)

It is to this incident that the writer of the Book of Hebrews refers in chapter 11 when he speaks of those who through faith "quenched the violence [power] of fire" (v. 34).

Nebuchadnezzar had led Babylonia in the first of a series of triumphs over the power of Egypt at the battle of Carchemish, 605 B.C. Pharaoh-necho was sent reeling back to the Nile and Egypt's dream of world dominion was over. Nebuchadnezzar was, indeed, "a king of kings" (2:37). He had reached the pinnacle of human greatness and power and undoubtedly became lifted up in pride.

It has been suggested that the image was of Nebuchadnezzar's god Bel-Merodach, but it seems more likely that it was of himself. A number of reasons might explain the erection of this great image of gold, 90 feet high (probably including the pedestal) and nine feet wide, in the broad plain of Dura, where a multitude could gather:

1. Out of pride and vanity over his successes in battle (cf. also 4:29,30) and in line with Daniel's interpretation of his dream—"Thou art this head of gold." It may have been to set forth the glory and stability of his monarchy. In other words, his kingdom was to be *all* gold, with no succession by another nation. Was he implying to contradict the dream of the image in chapter 2?

2. To purge himself of the jealousies of his subjects, especially of his officials, given impulse by his praise of the God of Israel and the promotion of the Jews (cf. 2:46-49).

3. On the advice of his nobles to bring about uniformity of religion in the kingdom.

4. Out of ingratitude and of jealousy of Daniel to lay a snare for him and his companions (hardly likely).

5. To memorialize Jehovah with a heathen conception (again hardly likely).

6. To honor himself with his own image. If this event occurred after 586 B.C., the date of Jerusalem's fall to Nebuchadnezzar, we can see how that event might give impulse to self-exaltation. He may have imagined himself now victor over Jehovah.

Chapter 3 is so familiar to most of us, and the story in the text so clear, that extended comment is hardly necessary.

Note the progression through the Book of Daniel in Nebuchadnezzar's religious experience—"a God *of* gods, a Lord of kings (2:47);

"Blessed be the God of Shadrach, Meshach, and Abed-nego" (3:28); "the high God" (4:2); "the King of heaven, all whose works are truth, and his ways judgment: and those that walk in pride he is able to abase" (4:37).

A PROUD KING DEBASED (CHAPTER 4)

It is probable that this incident took place about the year 574 B.C., or even later, toward the close of Nebuchadnezzar's reign of 43 years.

Note that what is recorded here is evidently copied by Daniel from an original document from the archives of Babylon. It is clearly a royal proclamation (cf. 4:1) issued by the king himself and is, in its main account, in the first person. Nebuchadnezzar is describing his own personal experience of the dealings of Jehovah with him.

His Dream (vv. 4-18)

The king dreamed "when he was at rest in his house and flourishing in his palace" (v. 4). All was tranquil in his dominions. His wars were over; his enemies had been subdued; he had finished his great public works involving the city itself, and the Hanging Gardens (considered a wonder of the world then) were completed.

The king's dream filled him with terror, probably because of some premonition that it concerned him personally. The court magicians, astrologers, etc., were summoned, but were baffled as to the import of the dream. Daniel then came into the king's presence and Nebuchadnezzar related to him the dream:

The Great Tree

Strong, lofty, universally visible;

Leaves fair, much fruit, beasts and fowls sheltered and fed thereby;

Cut down, stripped, despoiled by a heavenly being;

A stump left, bound with bands of brass and iron.

A personalized application was then given to all this in verses 15,16.

The great king recognized that the dream, whatever its meaning, was definitely related to the sovereignty of "heaven" (vv. 13,17), and that the "most High" is active in the affairs of human government, and promotes whom He wills (v. 17).

Nebuchadnezzar recognized the inability of his "wise men" to interpret the dream, but from his previous experience with Daniel (ch. 2) he knew his ability and that he was endued with supernatural power (4:18).

Daniel apparently was considerably agitated in his own spirit, knowing now that the dream concerned Nebuchadnezzar himself and that it would mean a most humbling experience to the proud king. Consequently he hesitated to give it immediately, but was commanded to proceed.

The Interpretation
    The Tree—
    Nebuchadnezzar, the sovereign of a great empire, universal in
        extent.
    The Felling of the Tree—
        The humiliation of the king;
        The dementia accompanying it.
    The Band Around the Stump—
        The continuance of the empire;
        The security of the king's throne to him;
        His restoration.

Daniel now uncompromisingly counseled the king to open the way to escape the dire consequences outlined in the dream, by breaking off his sins. He intimated that if he did there might be a prolonging of his prosperity (v. 27).

"Daniel's advice is to imitate those two great attributes of God which are the theme of the whole Old Testament, justice and mercy. Oppression and injustice were almost inseparable from heathen despotism. Daniel's advice implies that Nebuchadnezzar had fallen into them."—Gortner.

The Sequel
The circumstances of the fulfillment of the dream a year later are recorded in this court document (vv. 28-37). It is evident that the king's pride overruled any disposition toward a change of conduct in the affairs of the empire. He is seen boastfully laying claim for himself to all the glory, achievement, and progress of the city and empire. It may be that he was strolling the ramparts of his palace or walking along the lofty city wall surveying the great city, when the divine sentence was executed.

The cuneiform inscriptions that the archaeologist has discovered, and which have been deciphered by scholars, give considerable interesting information concerning the kings of Babylon and their achievements. Nebuchadnezzar apparently tried to outdo all who preceded him or who might follow him.

Nebuchadnezzar completed some important public works which his father Nabopolassar commenced. He finished the great double wall of the city, constructed a reservoir, fortified the city, established flood control, accumulated stores of silver and gold, and built the Hanging Gardens for his Median wife.

From the description given (v. 33) of the king's malady it may be gathered that he suffered from a form of insanity called lycanthropy, in which the victim imagines himself a wolf or other animal. "It is likely that while afflicted, he was conscious of his identity as Nebuchadnezzar, and this fact may have greatly aggravated his mental torture."

At the end of "seven times" (v. 25), undoubtedly seven years here, his reason began to return, and he recognized that this judgment had come upon him because he had assumed glory that did not belong to him. He lifted up his eyes to heaven and "blessed the most High" (v. 34). He acknowledged the eternal sovereignty of God—that He is supreme in the heavenlies and upon earth (v. 35). He was restored to his kingdom, reascended his throne, and assumed a degree of majestic dignity not previously manifested in him (v. 36).

History records that Nebuchadnezzar was "a man of peculiarly religious character." Undoubtedly a heathen at first, his conceptions of God underwent a radical transformation as this Scripture record reveals, in large measure due to his contact with the great man of God, Daniel.

Was Nebuchadnezzar "converted" as we would modernly say? Nobody knows, but that progressive change to a recognition of God as the supreme ruler of the universe, "whose works are truth, and his ways judgment [justice]," is evident (4:37).

A GREAT EMPIRE ENDS (CHAPTER 5)

Babylon was the first of the Gentile empires symbolized by the image of chapter 2. It was to be succeeded by a second "inferior" kingdom, which proved to be Medo-Persia. The time had now come to transfer the sovereignty from the "head of gold" to the "breast and arms of silver."

Archaeological Evidence

Profane historians up until 1854 were agreed that the Biblical record of Daniel was unreliable in referring to Belshazzar as the last king of Babylon, for they said that "Nabonidus was king at the time Babylon fell, that he was outside of the city at the head of his army, that he was met and worsted in battle by Cyrus, that he was taken prisoner, his life spared, and that he was treated with kindness and consideration by the conqueror." However, both are true. Discoveries of clay cylinders by the archaeologist, Sir Henry Rawlinson, in 1854 among the ruins of Babylon, evidence that Nabonidus was the last king of Babylon, but that he had a son named Belshazzar, or Belsharuzzar, who was associated with his father in the government of the empire at the time Babylon fell.

Belshazzar had been left at the head of affairs in the city, while Nabonidus did battle with Cyrus outside the city. Thus we can see the appropriateness of Belshazzar's offer to make Daniel the "third ruler in the kingdom" (v. 16).

There seems to be some evidence that Nabonidus married a daughter of Nebuchadnezzar or of Evil-merodach, his son, and that when Nergalsharezer, who succeeded Evil-merodach, died, Nabonidus seized the throne. Of this marriage Belshazzar was born, so that Nebuchadnezzar was his grandfather or great-grandfather. Every male ancestor is spoken of in Chaldea as "father," thus the reference to "Nebuchadnezzar thy father" (v. 11).

The Feast (vv. 1-4)

The feast of Belshazzar was an undisguised, impious insult to Jehovah, the God of Israel, in the fact of the revelers drinking from the sacred vessels of the temple, which Nebuchadnezzar had brought from Jerusalem. Their use intimated that Jehovah must have been weak, because He could not protect His own, and that Babylonian gods were stronger and gave the victory over the Jews.

The Mysterious Hand (vv. 5-9)

"Over against the candlestick," where the light shone upon the wall, there appeared "the fingers of a man's hand" and wrote. Dr. Albert Barnes makes the suggestion that this candlestick was the one from the temple of Solomon, and that the nearness of the writing to it may have intimated that the rebuke was directed against the sacrilege of the banquet.

Is it any wonder that the king was terrified in the midst of the drunken revelry (v. 6). In the prophecy of Isaiah 45:1 concerning Cyrus there is a forecast of this very detail—"I will loose the loins of kings, to open before him the two-leaved gates." This prophecy was written over a century before Cyrus was born. The Greek tourist, Herodotus, records that the great two-leaved gates in the walls along the banks of the Euphrates, which flowed through the midst of Babylon, were left open carelessly or in fancied self-security on that night, and Cyrus and his men marched into the city streets unchallenged. They had already entered the dry bed of the river, whose waters they had diverted into another channel around the city, through the outer city walls. The records of Cyrus do not agree with this, however, but indicate the people opened the gates.

Belshazzar *cried aloud* in his terror to bring the "wise men" and offered great honor and reward to any one of them who could interpret the mystery, but none could. The king was left "greatly upset, and he changed color; and his lords were thrown into consternation."—Gordon. Moffatt renders v. 9: "At this king Belshazzar was greatly alarmed, his color paled, and his lords were at their wit's end."

The Queen (vv. 10-12)

The queen of verse 10 was not Belshazzar's wife, but undoubtedly the queen-mother. Dr. Joseph A. Seiss comments: "The queen-mother was in the palace. She had taken no part in the banquet. Her royal husband was a prisoner in Borsippa, and she was the daughter of Nebuchadnezzar. She had most likely advised against this whole demonstration. She knew what her father had experienced in his lifetime, and to what sort of doctrines he had been converted before he died. She had respect for his memory, for the convictions he had so fully pronounced, for the God he had learned to fear and honor, and for the noble men whom he was pleased to favor for their holy services to him; and she could look with no favor upon this ill-timed and impious behavior of her licentious son."

Her words to Belshazzar (vv. 11,12) clearly evidence her personal acquaintance with Daniel, who was undoubtedly in obscurity in the kingdom at this time.

Other expositors think that she was the queen-dowager, the widow of Evil-merodach, the daughter-in-law of Nebuchadnezzar, the famous Nitrocris, who is mentioned by Herodotus as a "woman of extraordinary prudence." This is surely borne out by the commendable conduct of this queen on this occasion.

Daniel (vv. 13-23)

Daniel was summoned and Belshazzar, possibly in flattery (for he had had nothing to do with Daniel previously) expressed confidence in the report he had heard of him and offered him great reward for the interpretation of the mysterious handwriting (vv. 13-16).

Rewards meant nothing to Daniel. He had set "his affections on things above" (v. 17). After recalling to Belshazzar's memory some of the personal history and experiences of his grandfather Nebuchadnezzar, Daniel fearlessly rebuked Belshazzar for his pride— "thou hast not humbled thyself" (v. 22); for his blasphemy—"thou hast lifted up thyself against the Lord of heaven"; for his sacrilege— "thou and thy lords . . . have drunk wine" in the "vessels of his house"; for his idolatry—"thou hast praised the gods of silver, and gold . . . which see not, nor hear, nor know"; for his ungodliness— "the God in whose hand thy breath is . . . hast thou not glorified" (v. 23).

The climax of all this impiety was the sending by Jehovah of this mysterious hand to arrest the king and to pronounce judgment upon him, whose cup of iniquity was full.

The Interpretation (vv. 24-29)

Daniel proceeded, then, to interpret the writing:
"MENE, MENE, TEKEL, UPHARSIN."

MENE: Literally, "There is number [or numbering]" which being interpreted would mean, "Thy kingdom is numbered" or "God hath numbered thy kingdom and finished it." This word is repeated for emphasis.

TEKEL: Literally, "He hath weighed." This word is applied to the act of the goldsmith, who weighs the gold and ascertains the amount of alloy, that he may separate it from the pure metal.

UPHARSIN: Literally, "Is divided." This word is simply the plural of the word *Peres* in verse 28.

Daniel then added, by way of explanation, in the prophetic spirit, "Thy kingdom is divided and given to the Medes and Persians."

The word *Peres* has the same consonants as the word *Persians*. "Numbered, numbered, weighed, divided" is the literal rendering of the words, and Daniel interprets their significance to Belshazzar as follows:

"The years of your kingdom have run their course; you yourself have been weighed in the divine scales and are found wanting (short weight); and your kingdom is now about to be divided among the Medes and Persians, the enemies now thundering at your gates."

Belshazzar at least honorably rewarded Daniel as he had promised, but it must have been in disbelief of his words and in utter disregard of the significance of his father Nabonidus' defeat and of the presence of the Medo-Persian hosts surrounding the city.

Lesson 37

Daniel 6-12

A WICKED PLOT AND ITS FAILURE (CHAPTER 6)

The Medo-Persian Empire superseded the Babylonian, and Darius the Median (5:31) ascended the throne of world empire. The sovereignty, in the symbolism of chapter 2, has now shifted to the "breast and arms of silver."

Daniel was undoubtedly well known to Darius, for he had visited Shushan, the capital of Persia, in the third year of Belshazzar's reign (cf. 8:1,2). This Darius was king of Babylonia, but not of Media or Persia. Among all the possibilities, the name of Gobryas (Gubaru) seems to be a translation of Darius. There is strong historical evidence that Cyrus appointed him subking over Babylonia, Syria, Phoenicia, and Palestine, and that he reigned as king over this territory for 14 years until 525 B.C. Cyrus himself did not make Babylon his headquarters but ruled from Ecbatana in Media and from Pasargadae in ancient Persia.

Darius' kingdom was now organized into provinces and over each he set a provincial governor, or "prince," or satrap. Over these satraps the king set three presidents, and the chief of these three was Daniel (6:1,2).

Daniel was a man distinguished for his wisdom and statesmanship, a man richly endowed by God. Darius recognized his ability and purposed to make him next to himself "over the whole realm," probably as premier (or prime minister).

Jealous, Murderous Associates (vv. 4-9)

The envy and jealousy of Daniel's political associates was aroused by his promotion over them—he, a foreigner, a Jew! His consistently righteous and just conduct in a heathen court that was given to scheming, bribery, etc., was a rebuke to their consciences, and his

179

worship of the true God put the lie upon their heathen idolatry.
"Why should the king pass us by and exalt this foreigner?" (v. 4).

"For one so long at the front politically, and the favorite at the
hated Babylonian court, to be still preeminent in the victor's palace;
and, besides, for that one—now in his 'dotage' and so 'superannu-
ated,' as his rivals no doubt argued—to be displacing 'young blood,'
was intolerable to these rivals of Machiavelian principles and ambitions. They were, therefore, determined to displace him by any
means fair or foul."—W. C. Stevens.

They did have confidence in Daniel's religious integrity and knew
he would disobey any law that ran counter to the law of Jehovah
and his responsibility to Him (v. 5).

They deliberately lied in stating to the king the agreement of the
governors and presidents to petition the king, for Daniel had no
knowledge of this. It seems strange that the king did not notice
Daniel's absence and did not inquire as to Daniel's concurrence in
the request (vv. 6-9).

The Faithful Daniel (vv. 10,11)

Daniel, as chief of the presidents, had access to the king and soon
became aware of this newly signed decree and of its implications as
far as he was concerned, but it deterred him not for a moment from
his daily devotions (vv. 10,11; cf. 1 Kings 8:46-49). "He might have
desisted from this practice, or he might have closed the windows
and drawn the shades down; or he might have gone to a secluded
spot, a secret place, to pray; but to have done so would have been
to deny God, or at least to have given God a subordinate place in
his daily program. Daniel was not a man who would do this."—
Gortner.

Temporary Success (vv. 11-18)

As they expected, these plotters found Daniel engaged in petition
to God and immediately reported to Darius the violation of the
decree. He was forced by his own decree, against his will, to order
the execution of the sentence against Daniel. The king seemed to
have some confidence that Jehovah would deliver Daniel (v. 16).
Note that the lions' den was doubly sealed, with the king's signet
and with that of his lords. This was done so that neither could release
Daniel without the consent of the other, and it was certain the
nobles desired to tie the king's hands (v. 17).

The king passed a restless, sleepless night and had none of his customary diversions to try to induce sleep. His whole emotional nature was expressing itself in sorrow and regret over the tragic fate of his prime minister (v. 18).

Miraculous Preservation (vv. 19-23)

Reference to Daniel's faith in God for deliverance from apparently sure death is found in Hebrews 11:33—"stopped [literally, *sealed*] the mouths of lions." It was an achievement of faith.

The Tables Turned (vv. 24-28)

Proverbs 11:8—*"The righteous is delivered out of trouble, and the wicked cometh in his stead"*—expresses the principle here illustrated. Daniel escaped and these plotters experienced the very horrible death they had designed for him (vv. 24-27).

Josephus, the Jewish historian, describes what followed Daniel's deliverance: "Now when his enemies saw that Daniel had suffered nothing which was terrible, they would not own that he was preserved by God, and by His providence; but they said that the lions had been filled full with food, and on that account it was, as they supposed, that the lions would not touch Daniel, nor come to him; and this they alleged to the king: but the king, out of abhorrence of their wickedness, gave order, that they should throw in a great deal of flesh to the lions; and when they had filled themselves, he gave further orders that Daniel's enemies should be cast into the den, that he might learn if the lions, now that they were full, would touch them or not. And it appeared plain to Darius, after the princes had been cast to the wild beasts, that it was God who preserved Daniel, for the lions spared none of them, but tore them all to pieces, as if they had been very hungry, and wanted food."

The chapter closes with a statement concerning Daniel's prosperity through the reign of Darius and into the reign of Cyrus (v. 28).

BEAST-VISION OF GENTILE TIMES (CHAPTER 7)

The first six chapters of Daniel (ch. 2 excepted) are largely the historical part, related to the personal history of the prophet, while the last six are a collection of Daniel's prophetic visions, not arranged chronologically, received at different times and explained by divine power.

In chapter 2 we have what is called the image-vision; in chapter 7 the beast-vision of "the times of the Gentiles." Nebuchadnezzar, the king, saw world empires from the standpont of a worldly monarch, its pomp and glory. Daniel, the prophet of God, saw the same thing from the divine standpoint, as ravenous beasts devouring each other. In both chapters the chronological scope is from Nebuchadnezzar to the setting up of Messiah's kingdom.

Political Turmoil (vv. 1-3)

The vision of chapter 7 was received in the first year of Belshazzar, about 541 B.C., five years before Israel's release from captivity. Daniel saw a "great sea," probably the Mediterranean, which is often so designated. The winds of heaven were fiercely rushing upon it from contrary directions, tossing up the waves and spume. This commotion seems to be the cause of the emergence of "four great beasts," not all at once but in succession. They are all unnatural, hybrid creatures.

What is the significance of the striving of the winds upon the great sea? Waters in agitation are clearly in Scripture a symbol of fallen humanity in its restless surgings—*"The wicked are like the troubled sea, when it cannot rest, whose waters cast up mire and dirt"* (Isaiah 57:20); *"the waters which thou sawest, where the whore sitteth, are peoples, and multitudes, and nations, and tongues"* (Revelation 17:15).

The striving of the winds can correctly be the influence of Satanic power—"the prince of the power of the air" (Ephesians 2:2)—causing political and economic turmoil among men which produces changes in governmental form and succession. Satan is the "god of this world" (2 Corinthians 4:4) and he dominates the kingdoms and empires.

Beast Like a Lion (v. 4)

The Smith-Goodspeed translation of this verse reads: "The first was like a lion, with the wings of an eagle: I watched till its wings were plucked off and it was raised from the earth, and made to stand on two feet like a man, while the *mind* of a man was given to it." Note the word *mind* which is a better rendering than "heart."

There has been little question among interpreters that this first beast symbolizes the Babylonian Empire, which reached its zenith during Nebuchadnezzar's reign. The prophet Jeremiah (Jeremiah

4:7,13) used the lion and the eagle symbolism to refer to Babylon (cf. also Ezekiel 17:3,12). It was also during the reign of this powerful king that disintegrating forces began to work. "Aggression flagged, its eagle-wings were plucked and its conquest stopped." The empire was humbled representatively in the mental madness of Nebuchadnezzar. It is to this humiliation and restoration that reference is made in the latter half of verse 4, according to the best expositors (see Daniel 4). The beast like a lion corresponds to the head of gold of the image in chapter 2.

Beast Like a Bear (v. 5)

It is not difficult to identify the second beast with the Medo-Persian Empire which conquered Babylon and succeeded it. The burly bear corresponds to the heavy chest of Nebuchadnezzar's image. The two sides, one higher and stronger than the other, fit the dual composition of this empire, Persia becoming the dominant portion. The three ribs in the mouth of the bear are generally agreed to mean Lydia, Babylon, and Egypt, which were seized and held by Medo-Persia.

The bear symbolism itself—a lumbering, heavy beast, which overcomes by its weight—and the bidding to "devour much flesh" are pictures of the Medo-Persian conquests won by sheer weight of numbers, and of the tremendous waste of human life which characterized these ponderous aggressions.

We are told that the Medo-Persian armies, even on moderate expeditions, ranged from a third to a full million men. Darius marched through the desolate regions of Scythia with 700,000 men. Xerxes came against Greece with 2,500,000 fighting men.

They never displayed the speed and agility of a winged lion, nor of the winged leopard which followed.

Beast Like a Leopard (v. 6)

Again the identity of this empire is not difficult to establish. Medo-Persia was succeeded by the Graeco-Macedonian Empire established by the conquests of Alexander the Great. The leopard belongs more to the lion order than the bear. Cruel and fierce, it is noted for its watchful lying in wait for its prey and for its swift, sudden attack. This symbolic leopard had the additional assistance to swiftness of four wings. It corresponds to the belly and thighs of the image.

All this is preeminently characteristic of Alexander's conquests. It is written of him that "he was impetuous and fierce in his warlike expeditions, as a panther after his prey, and came on his enemies with that speed as if he flew with a double pair of wings."

He began his wars at the age of 20 and at 32 the whole known world was under his dominion. "Nations were his playthings, thrones were his toys. And in a most emphatic and special sense dominion was *given* to him."

But note that this leopard had four heads. Alexander did not live to enjoy his conquests nor to crystallize his empire. He died at 32 as a result of a drunken debauch. The empire was swiftly divided among four of his generals. It was the same dominion, but exercised from four points under four sovereigns—Lysimachus for Thrace and Asia Minor; Seleucus for Syria and the East; Ptolemy Soter for Egypt; and Cassander for Macedonia. All was ultimately swallowed up by Rome.

Daniel prophesied all this exact foreshadowing long before Alexander's father, Philip of Macedon, was born.

The Nondescript Beast (v. 7)

It was the fourth beast, most of all, that arrested Daniel's attention and whose career and end he was most concerned to understand. That it represents an empire, world dominion or rule, is clear from the interpretation given him by an angelic interpreter—"These . . . beasts, which are four, are four kings" (dynasties or empires) and "the fourth beast shall be the fourth kingdom upon earth" (vv. 17,23). It is completely successive to the preceding forms of political administration. It is not a fragment of coexistent governments. It is a great universal dominion. And it continues "substantially, in one form or another, to the end time—to the coming of the Son of man as the appointed King and Judge of the world. In other words, it is the only great world power from the termination of the four-headed Macedonian Empire to the end of all mere earthly political rule."— Seiss.

As you study Old Testament prophecy, try to dismiss from your mind the church period in which we now are and which is nearing its end. If you are able to do so, you will save yourself from hopeless confusion. Church truth is a revelation, as Paul says, "which in other ages *was not made known* to the sons of men, as it is NOW revealed unto his holy apostles and prophets by the Spirit" (Ephesians 3:5).

The prophets viewed future events leading to the final setting up of the kingdom of God as one series of successive events, without taking into account time gaps, of which we are now cognizant. This is prophetic perspective.

Where is the difficulty in identifying the empire that succeeded Alexander's dominion? There is no history apart from the mighty, iron-imbued, long-lived empire, "the most decisively marked of all political power which ever controlled our world"—the Roman Empire. How complete is the symbolic summation of verse 7 of what history records of Rome!

"It did not sweep over the world like a tornado ravaging, extorting submission and receiving tribute, without molding things to itself; but it relentlessly consolidated all its materials into a settled and abiding order of common law which still holds its place in living force after the lapse of more than two thousand years. All the governments on earth are still essentially Roman, and in their laws and codes Roman empire still holds the sway of the world, and must as long as human government exists. This fourth beast cannot, therefore, stand for anything other than the Roman dominion and rule."—Seiss.

The Ten Horns and a Little Horn

The "ten horns" of this last beast and "the little horn" which came up among them attracts Daniel's interest most (vv. 8,19,20). Verse 24 explains that these ten horns represent "ten kings" or kingdoms which shall arise from this empire, and the "little horn" represents another "king" which shall come up among them and succeed them in power by subduing three of the ten.

The question naturally arises, Have these ten kings or kingdoms already appeared or are they yet to appear? It cannot be clearly shown that just so many divisions of the Roman dominion have occurred, either contemporaneously or successively, in the past. That they belong to a future period is clear from the fact that these ten kings and the "little horn" king, who gains the ascendancy over them, continue until the setting up of the kingdom of God upon earth (vv. 9-14,26,27).

That there will be a ten-kingdomed confederacy in the last days presided over by another king is clear from the Book of Revelation (Revelation 13:1; 17:12,13). That they were still future to John's day (A.D. 96) is clear from Revelation 17:12—"have received no kingdom as yet."

From the human elements introduced into the symbolic picture (7:8)—"eyes like the eyes of man, and a mouth speaking great things"—it is clear that the "little horn" represents a powerful king of the last days, who will arise from a political condition of ten kings, constituting a final form of the Roman Empire. This political set-up will probably be in evidence in the area of the "great sea" (7:2), the Mediterranean.

It was the ambition of the late dictator Mussolini to reestablish the ancient glory of Rome. While his program failed and he met an ignominious death, that is not to dispose of the matter finally. It can well be revived by a future ruler, for political conditions change like a kaleidoscope, and what we now observe will be superseded by other political alignments.

Antichrist

The Scriptures everywhere speak of this final Satanically inspired, anti-Christian power. The Church fathers from the days of the apostle John onward anticipated such. They called it the "Antichrist of the last days, who should pervert . . . everything in the world and press his awful domination for three and a half years, until suddenly overwhelmed by the revelation of Jesus Christ in the great day of judgment."—Seiss.

The Messianic Kingdom

Verses 9-14 are the revelation to Daniel of a heavenly scene in which the glorious majesty of the Divine Father and His throne appear. The Son of Man (v. 13), our Lord Jesus Christ, is brought before this august throne where He is invested with kingly authority and universal dominion, and His kingdom is set up on the earth. This follows the destruction of the last form of Gentile rule under the "little horn" (vv. 11,22,26).

This final Antichrist or beast-king is seen to be a blasphemer, a persecutor of Israel, a dictator (vv. 21,25). The word "saints" (v. 21) does not apply here to New Testament saints, but is used in its generic sense as referring to those "separated unto God" as was Israel by covenant relation.

The beast vision (ch. 7) corresponds in its succession of empires to the image vision (ch. 2). The fourth beast corresponds to the legs of iron and the "feet of iron and clay," the kingdom which is superseded by the dominion of Christ represented by the "stone cut out of the mountain without hands" (ch. 2) which smote the image of Gentile rule and reduced it to chaff.

THE WORLD POWERS AND ISRAEL

THE RAM AND THE HE-GOAT (CHAPTER 8)

This vision was received by Daniel in the third and last year of King Belshazzar. The ram and the he-goat symbolize two of the kingdoms of the beast vision (ch. 7) and the two of the image vision represented by the breast and arms of silver and the belly and thighs of brass; namely, Medo-Persia and Graeco-Macedonia.

The question naturally presents itself, Why are the same prophecies presented in different forms? There are several reasons:

1. That additional details might be given.

2. That the truth set forth may be indelibly impressed upon minds and hearts.

3. That their importance might be emphasized and appreciated.

4. That the truth presented might be viewed from different angles.

5. That smaller geographical limits might be defined from which the "little horn" (ch. 7) will come.

Messianic prophecy, for example, is presented in different forms and from different viewpoints, and in relation to differing backgrounds.

The Symbolic Ram (vv. 3,4)

Daniel himself was in Shushan, the city where the Persian kings had their winter residence. It is altogether possible that he was there on a diplomatic mission from Babylon. In vision he was on the bank of the river Ulai. There he saw first the ram described by him in verses 3,4.

The two horns of this ram symbolize the two nations of which this empire (the beast symbol in Scripture consistently means a king or kingdom) is made up. "Media was an independent kingdom long before Persia was anything but a province, but when Cyrus came to the throne the Persian part became much the greater of the two. This was foreshown in the vision in that the horn which sprang up last became much higher than the other."

Daniel beheld this ram "pushing"—thrusting violently with its head, denoting military aggression—toward the west, north, and south. The east is not mentioned, for the Persians made no conquests in that direction. To the westward, however, they conquered Babylon, Syria, and Asia Minor; to the northward Armenia and the Caspian countries; and to the South, Egypt, Libya, etc.

The history of the Medo-Persian Empire is one of great expansion and conquest over a period of 200 years. It truly did "become great" or "magnified" itself (ASV).

The He-Goat (vv. 5-8)

There can be no question that this goat represents the Graeco-Macedonian Empire and its conspicuous horn, Alexander the Great. The interpreting angel said so in clear language (8:21). Even the escutcheon of this empire bore this figure, and the figure of a goat with a single horn are found on Macedonian monuments.

Special Reference to This Symbolic Goat

As a world power in general it had the savage qualities of a leopard (ch. 7) but "in relation to the Jews it was a mild and fostering power rather than a beast of prey."

Josephus, the Jewish historian, records that on his eastern expeditions Alexander came to Palestine with all the pride of a victorious conqueror and was about to turn his armies loose upon Jerusalem, but was arrested by a dream. At the same time the Jewish high priest had a dream involving Alexander, and through these dreams a friendly conference resulted. "Then the great conqueror met the high priest, and when he saw upon his golden miter the great name of Jehovah he bowed down before it and gave the high priest his right hand. Having come into Jerusalem, he had sacrifices offered for him, while the priests brought to him this very Book of Daniel and pointed out to him this very chapter in which the holy prophet had recorded the coming of a Greek conqueror who should vanquish and destroy the Persian dominion." Alexander granted the Jews great favors and concessions.

The symbolic items and the history of Graeco-Macedonia fit like lock and key. It originated in the "west," the far west from Persia (v. 5). It came with marvelous velocity and determination—"touched not the ground." It struck the Medo-Persian ram, shattered both his horns, trod him down, and took his dominion (v. 7). It required several battles to accomplish this, but it was done as history records. Graeco-Macedonia became great, but only for a brief time as a unit.

In the midst of the greatest power and triumph of this "goat," its great horn was broken, not in battle, but by the early and unexpected death of Alexander, due to unbridled excesses over his victories and to a fever. He died in Babylon in the thirty-third year of his age. His son never came to the throne. The military chieftains whom Alexander had placed over the conquered countries fought with each other for years, until finally, upon the death of Antigonus, king of Macedonia, 239 B.C., the empire settled into four monarchies, answering to the four heads of the leopard (ch. 7) and the "four notable horns" of this goat (v. 8).

Lysimachus took Thrace and Asia Minor; Cassander took Greece; Ptolemy Soter became king of Egypt; and Seleucus gained control of Syria and the East.

The "Little Horn" (vv. 9-14)

Out of one of these four sections of the Macedonian Empire Daniel beheld a "little horn" springing up—"a sprig of one of the four"—which grew great toward the south, east, and "the glorious land" (Palestine), even to the "host of heaven"—the hierarchy of the temple—some of whom it cast down and trampled upon, magnifying itself even against the "Prince of the host" (God Himself or the High Priest), abolishing the daily sacrifice, polluting the temple, setting up its own "host" over against the heavenly order, and enacting the most murderous and blasphemous scenes against Jehovah, His truth and His people.

Antiochus Epiphanes

Expositors quite generally interpret this as Antiochus Epiphanes, the eighth king of the Seleucid dynasty, who reigned 175-164 B.C. He was, indeed, a devil incarnate. He came into power toward the close of the Syrian dynasty, when it already had begun to come under the growing power of Rome. He got the kingdom by deceit and flatteries. The writings of Josephus and the Books of the Maccabees tell the story of his doings.

"This vile man conceived the idea of establishing throughout his kingdom, inclusive of Palestine, the worship of Jupiter Olympus, identifying himself with that god, and intent on making his own worship universal. With infatuated zeal and stubbornness he tried to extirpate every other worship, and particularly the worship of Jehovah at Jerusalem. Among the Jews themselves he found many

faithless ones ready to enter into his plans and to help on his idolatrous designs. He bought up these traitors, sold out the high priesthood to the highest bidders, ejected one and another from it for a
price, and rifled the temple again and again of all the gold, silver,
and treasures in any way connected with it, dealing out slaughter
and death to those who dared to remonstrate. With the most shame-
ful perfidy and deceit he got possession of Jerusalem, fell upon its
inhabitants, destroyed the lives of multitudes in cold blood, robbed
and destroyed the houses, carried off women and children into
slavery, made a military stronghold of the city, put the worst of men
into it to watch for and slay every earnest believer in the God of
Abraham who might come thither to do homage to Jehovah, polluted
the sanctuary on all sides with innocent blood, prohibited circumcision on pain of death, abolished the temple services and kept it
vacated till the weeds grew up in the passageways of God's house,
set the image of his own idol on the Almighty's altar, offered swine's
flesh in sacrifice in special defiance of the God of Israel, and forced
all Jews who would remain faithful to the religion of their fathers
to hide themselves in the mountains and desolate places in order
to save their lives. Thus did he practice and prosper, and destroy
the holy people, slaughtering them by thousands, magnifying himself against the God of Israel, calling to his aid every treacherous
craft, casting down the rightful priests, burning the sacred books,
determined to abolish both the law and the prophets and to sub-
merge the Jews and their religion in the vilest heathen abomination."—Seiss.

Duration of This Sacrilege

The duration of the treading down of the sanctuary by this vile
king is given by the angel as "two thousand and three hundred"—
not "days," as our version says, but "evening [and] morning; then
shall the sanctuary be cleansed," or 2,300 evening mornings. This
reference is not to the evening and morning which make up a day,
but to the sacrifice interrupted, which was offered each morning
and each evening. Twenty-three hundred of these evening-morning
interruptions would cover eleven hundred and fifty days, or three
years and a portion thereof.

According to the records in the Book of Maccabees it was a little
over three years, 168-165 B.C., from the day the first idolatrous
sacrifice was made upon the altar of God under Antiochus until the

true offering was reinstituted. If the period be taken as so many "days," that is, a little more than six years, we have the length of time from the first denudation of the temple by Antiochus to the righting of it again under the Maccabean heroes.

Antiochus and Antichrist (vv. 15-26)

Some expositors say that the fulfillment of the passage about the little horn of chapter 8 was exhausted by the Greek Antichrist, Antiochus Epiphanes. But while he did fulfill much of this description, there are certain time elements in the chapter which he failed to fulfill. Certain expressions used in describing the "little horn" identify him as coming into power at the end of the "times of the Gentiles"; namely, "the time of the end" (v. 17), "in the last end of the indignation" (8:19), "when the transgressors are come to the full" (8:23), "He shall stand up against the Prince of princes" (8:25), and "many days" (8:26). The phrase "the time of the end" is an expression in prophecy which includes both a near and a far horizon of fulfillment.*

The "indignation" in prophecy denotes God's judicial wrath against Israel for their transgression of His covenant, and "the last end of the indignation" is that final stroke of God's judgment upon restoration. "Indignation" has fallen upon them many times, but the final act of the drama will be when they make their covenant with Antichrist in the last days and fill up the measure of their apostasy. "When the transgressors are come to the full" indicates the consummation of lawlessness or transgression both of Jew and of Gentile upon whom will be visited the vials of God's wrath in the last days just before the coming of the Lord. "He shall stand up against the Prince of princes" can mean no other than the final act of blasphemous self-exaltation of Antichrist against the Lord Jesus Christ, the

---

*For examples of this double (or near and far horizon) fulfillment of prophecy, compare John the Baptist with Elijah (Malachi 4:5,6; John 1:19-21; Matthew 17:10-12; Matthew 11:14; Luke 1:17); Sennacherib, the Assyrian invader of Palestine in the reign of Hezekiah, with the final Assyrian of the last days (Isaiah 10:5,12; Micah 5:2-5). Isaiah prophesied the invasion of Palestine by the king of Babylon also (Isaiah 13:1-6), but lying in the background of this passage of Isaiah 13 and 14 there is seen a future king of Babylon (Isaiah 14:1-14) against whom Israel shall take up a proverb when the Lord shall give them rest from their sorrow and from their fear and from their hard bondage wherein they were made to serve. This rest must still be future; consequently the deduction is that Isaiah referred to a final king of Babylon of whom the former was a shadow or type.

King of kings and Lord of lords, at the battle of Armageddon (cf. Revelation, ch. 19).

Import of These Time Elements

These time elements doubtless belong to the time of the Great Tribulation, the final stage of God's prolonged chastisement of His people and of Israel's disobedience. This, of course, implies their return in unbelief to Palestine, the rebuilding of the temple, the setting up of the temple sacrifices again, and finally of the visible sign of Christ's presence in the sky as the object of Antichrist's defiance (Matthew 24:30). Antiochus Epiphanes was indeed a true picture and foreshadowing of the final Antichrist, whose Satanic hatred of the Jews will be as intense as the historical facts quoted above concerning Antiochus depict.

If the exegesis of the foregoing paragraphs is sound—and we believe it rests upon sound principles—we must look for a revival in the last days of the four kingdoms into which Alexander's Graeco-Macedonian kingdom was divided, and out of one of which the final "little horn"—Antichrist—will arise. One of the purposes of the revelation to Daniel in ch. 8 seems to be to narrow down the locality from which the final "little horn" arises, from one of ten kingdoms (ch. 7) to one of four kingdoms (ch. 8). "The question may arise, How can these little horns be identical, seeing one is prophesied to be a king out of the final ten kingdoms of the Roman Empire, and the other is to be a king out of one of the four divisions of the Greek Empire of Alexander the Great? This may quite easily be done by assuming that these four kingdoms will constitute geographically four of the ten final kingdoms of the Roman Empire (in its eastern half). This is entirely legitimate, seeing that in all these successions of empire, individual kingdoms have to a large extent passed without material change ethnically or geographically from one supremacy to another."—Stevens.

Prophecy and History

What, then, were the boundaries of the four divisions of Alexander's empire? As we have already seen, Alexander the "notable horn" (Daniel 8:5,8,21), first king of the Graeco-Macedonian Empire, after a rapid conquest of Medo-Persia in a series of battles 334-323 B.C., died at 32 years of age after a drunken debauch. He ended his short career with no successor. No one could be agreed upon

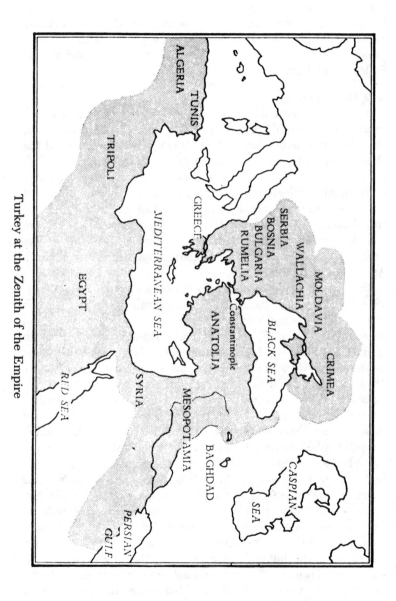

Turkey at the Zenith of the Empire

to rule over the whole territory, so four of his generals—Cassander, Lysimachus, Seleucus, and Ptolemy—partitioned the domain among themselves. Cassander took Greece; Lysimachus, Thrace and Asia Minor; Seleucus, Syria and the hinterland of Mesopotamia; and Ptolemy took Egypt.

Asia Minor-Turkey

It would require much space and a lengthy tracing of the changes in sovereignty in this part of the world through the centuries to show how the "latter time of their kingdom" *is now here* and has already begun. In modern history this tracing involves the Turkish Empire from the zenith of its extent and power (see map, page 192) in the middle of the fifteenth century to the present day. From that point of greatest extent under Osman, the Turkish Empire gradually shrank under the impact of attacks by Russia, England, and France, and the regaining of their independence by smaller nations, like Serbia, Greece, Romania, and Bulgaria, along with most of North Africa, except Egypt.

This brings our history down to the beginning of World War I, 1914-1918 (see map, page 194). Turkey fought in that war on the side of Germany and was completely defeated. Egypt was freed from any semblance of Turkish influence; Palestine and the Arabian countries of Syria and Mesopotamia were taken away. Turkey was apparently prostrate and the Paris Peace Conference began January 18, 1919. Allied rivalries were here most apparent. The Italian delegates withdrew on account of President Wilson's proposal regarding the transfer of the port of Fiume to Yugoslavia. France and England rushed Greek troops to Smyrna to forestall Italy, which had landed troops at Adalia in Asia Minor. Greek imperialistic ambitions enraged Turkey and gave impetus to the Nationalistic Movement headed by Mustapha Kemal Pasha. On April 24, 1920, the Turkish National Assembly met at Angora and repudiated the Constantinople government. On August 10, 1920, the Treaty of Sevres, which reduced Turkey from a nation of 613,500 square miles and 20,000,000 inhabitants to one of 75,000 square miles and 8,000,000 inhabitants, was signed by the Sultan at Constantinople. The Turkish Nationalists had to be reckoned with and would not consent to its terms. In the meantime, the Greeks had advanced half across Anatolia, but were finally repulsed by the newly organized Nationalist army under the leadership of Mustapha Kemal.

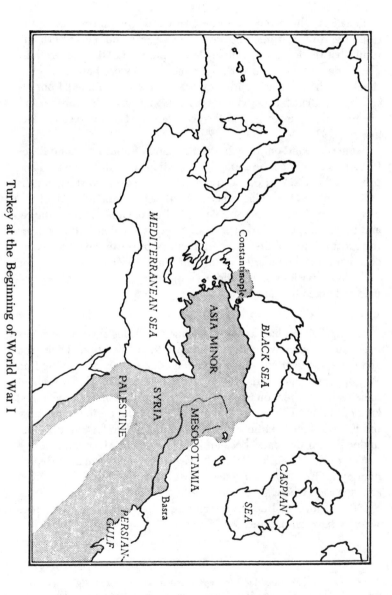

Turkey at the Beginning of World War I

Then came the London Conference of February 21, 1921. Great Britain was backing the Greeks, and France and Italy the Turkish Nationalists. The divergence of interest and opinion resulted in the resumption of hostilities between the Greeks and Turks with the result that the former had finally to abandon Asia Minor altogether. The Nationalists, elated with their successes, were hard to hold in check by their leaders and they were hardly restrained from attacking the British occupying forces in Constantinople. Sober counsels prevailed, however, and the armistice of Mudania resulted October 1, 1922.

From this point on through the First and Second Lausanne Peace Conferences we see the anomaly of a nation absolutely defeated and prostrated in the World War treating with the great western nations as an equal and receiving practically all of her demands. All of this was because of the covetousness and rivalries of Great Britain, France, and Italy. Thus was *Turkey* reconstituted as a nation, reduced from the great empire of the sixteenth century but, wonderful to relate, occupying the boundaries of *the old kingdom of Lysimachus*, one of the four divisions of Alexander's empire, even including the province of Thrace in Europe.

Syria

The Arabs who had fought alongside the Allies against Germany believed that they were about to secure their liberation. Their plan and hope was to attain a federated kingdom, closely associating Iraq (Mesopotamia) and Syria, to include Palestine also. This was about to be realized when, on March 11, 1920, Emir Feisal was proclaimed king of Syria at Damascus. But after a very brief period of fighting, the French deposed him and took over a mandate for Syria. Feisal, under British mandate, became king of Iraq, or Mesopotamia.

As a result of World War II, however, we now have an independent Syria, free from all French control. There seems to be a power struggle as to who will be ruler over a greater Syria, including Iraq, Syria, and Jordan. But the interesting thing is that after centuries *we now have an independent Syria.*

---

*Fuad's son, Farouk, ruled for a few years, but he was deposed. Egypt and Syria combined to form the United Arab Republic, ruled by President Abdel Gamel Nasser, but Syria withdrew in 1961.

Egypt

Egypt was lost to Turkey in 1866. British influence was predominant for many years. At the opening of World War I, Britain proclaimed a protectorate over Egypt. On August 19, 1920, the independence and sovereign status of Egypt was recognized, and Faud II ascended the throne as king. On February 28, 1922, the British protectorate was fully terminated.*

Greece

In 1829, through the intervention of France, England, and Russia, Greece regained her independence from Turkey and has continued a sovereign nation to the present day.

Summary

Thus has come about according to the Word of the Lord through Daniel, "the latter time of their kingdom," as we see today before our very eyes, *an independent Greece, once ruled by Cassander; an independent Turkey* reduced through the centuries to the extent of the former kingdom of Lysimachus, who ruled over Thrace and Asia Minor; *an independent Egypt,* with its own president and parliament, once ruled by *Ptolemy;* and an *independent Syria.*

What does it all portend? We believe that politically the stage is nearly set for the appearance of Antichrist, the "little horn" of Daniel 8, who is to come from one of these four reconstituted kingdoms, "when the transgressors are come to the full." That is, when lawlessness has reached its consummation.

Effect upon the Prophet (v. 27)

Daniel "fainted and was sick certain days," for he saw the terrible suffering his own people were to endure in the distant future. They were then in exile, but this vision foretold a time, after restoration, when they would again apostatize and have to be purged by judgment.

DANIEL'S PRAYER (CHAPTER 9:1-19)

A prophetic date of critical importance was near in relation to Daniel's people, the Jews. Daniel was reading the sacred records. He was studying the Book of Jeremiah and ran across the prediction we now know as Jeremiah 25:11,12, in which the 70 years' desolation of Judah and the judgment of God upon Babylon were foretold.

This period had just about run its course, and it gave Daniel great concern as to the outcome of the current events of his day. So he gave himself to prayer and fasting before the Lord.

To Whom Addressed (v. 4)

There is an unusual combination of the names of God in Daniel's address to the divine Being: "I prayed unto *Jehovah* my *Elohim*, and made my confession, and said, O *Adonai*, the great and revered [or awful] *El*, keeping the covenant and mercy to them that love Him and to them that keep His commandments." He recognized God as the covenant-keeping Jehovah of His people Israel, the great triune Creator and Sustainer of the universe, the Sovereign Lord and Master of all created intelligences, the one God to be revered.

Daniel's Confession (vv. 5-10)

Daniel began by acknowledging his own unworthiness and then graciously identified himself with his people and with their sin. He did not pray at them, "O Lord, they did this and that," but—"we have sinned." Daniel was now close to 90 years of age. He had spent most of his life a captive in a foreign land. He loved his people and the land of his fathers, and longed for their restoration and the fulfillment of their final glorious destiny as revealed in their sacred Scriptures.

God's Justice Acknowledged (vv. 11-15)

Daniel recognized that God's dealings with His people had been justly in accord with His pronouncements of warning and admonition to them (cf. Leviticus 26:14-39; Deuteronomy 28:47-51). He reminded the Lord of His grace and power that constituted them a people when He brought them supernaturally out of Egyptian bondage.

Daniel Pleads for His People (vv. 16-19)

He entreated upon the basis of Jehovah's righteousness and His covenant relationship with them, and to vindicate His own name and purpose in calling them out from the nations, that He turn again in mercy toward them, restore His desolate city and sanctuary, and forgive their sins. He asked Jehovah to act now in accord with His word, because the city of Jerusalem and Israel bore His name.

PROPHECY OF THE SEVENTY WEEKS (CHAPTER 9:20-27)

Dispensationally this is the most important prophecy in the Old Testament. It is actually the key to all prophecy, as many able expositors agree. Upon a clear understanding of it depends a sane, intelligent, symmetrical interpretation of other prophetic Scriptures, especially the Book of Revelation. The chronological periods—"time, times, and half a time," "42 months," "1,260 days," "1,290 days," "1,335 days"—of Daniel and Revelation are incomprehensible apart from a positive grasp of this passage.

Introduction (vv. 20-23)

While Daniel was praying in behalf of his people, about the time of the evening oblation, there appeared to him the angel Gabriel, who announced that he had been dispatched at the beginning of Daniel's supplications to enlighten Daniel, who was a man "greatly beloved" or "delighted in" (Rotherham) in heaven. This must have brought deep satisfaction and gladness to Daniel's heart. Gabriel exhorted him to give special attention to the revelation which was to follow.

The Seventy Weeks (vv. 24-27)

Let us establish the fundamental points of this passage that we may understand it:

1. It concerns exclusively the Jewish people and Jerusalem, their capital city, destined one day to be the world capital. See Isaiah 2:2-4.

If we can once and for all clear our minds of the thought that the Old Testament has any revelation of the Church, as we now understand it, or of a Church dispensation, except in rather veiled references, we will save ourselves endless confusion in Scripture interpretation. See again Ephesians 3:4-6.

This revelation is not concerning the Gentiles, except in a secondary sense, where Antichrist is introduced, nor is it concerning the Church. Verse 24 clearly establishes this—"upon thy [Daniel's] people," the Jews and "upon thy [Daniel's] holy city," Jerusalem.

2. These "weeks" are weeks (or sevens) of years, and not of days. The Hebrew word *shavu'im* and its Greek equivalent *hebdomades* mean simply "sevens." There is nothing in this passage itself to indicate whether these sevens are hours, days, weeks, months, years, or centuries. The bare statement of verse 24 is "Seventy *sevens* are determined [or divided] upon thy people," etc. However, there are keys to the unit of measurement. The answer is found in the fact that Daniel had been thinking not only in terms of *years* (v. 2), but

also in a definite multiple of "sevens" (10x7) of years. Daniel knew that the captivity had been based on Jewish violations of the divine law of the sabbatic year. Since, according to 2 Chronicles 36:21, the Jews had been removed from off the land so that it might rest for 70 years, it is evident that the sabbatic (or seventh) year (Leviticus 25:4) had been violated over a period of 490 years, or exactly 70 "sevens" of years.

3. These 70 sevens of years, or 490 in all, were determined (divided, set apart, cut off) to accomplish a sixfold purpose:

a. *"To finish the transgression."* Whose transgression? Israel's, of course. This refers to Israel's national sin of disobedience of the Mosaic Covenant, their apostasy, and ungodliness. Paul refers to this in Romans 11:25,26. Ungodliness shall be turned away from Jacob, and they will apprehend "a fountain opened to the house of David and to the inhabitants of Jerusalem for sin and for uncleanness" (Zechariah 13:1).

b. *"To make an end of sins."* The same root word in the Hebrew as is used here—"to make an end of"—is used later in the verse—"seal up." The whole thought is to bring to an end, to finish, to finally dispose of, to seal up, as in prison, so that they will never break forth again. Note that this whole series of purposes are *finalities* as far as Israel is concerned. Glorious day for them and for the world!

c. *"To make reconciliation for iniquity"*—literally "to cover iniquity," that is, to make atonement for it, to expiate it by adequate satisfaction, blot it out, hide it forever.

d. *"To bring in everlasting righteousness"*—"to put in normal relations with God, to set human life into thorough accord with Jehovah's will and law, induce a condition of moral rectitude, which thence-forward shall never again be interrupted, but endured for all the ages"—Seiss.

e. *"To seal up the vision and prophecy"*—authenticate and vindicate by fulfillment, make good and finish out in fact and deed all that "God hath spoken by the mouth of all his holy prophets since the world began."

f. *"To anoint the Most Holy"*—"to consecrate and put into place and effectiveness a 'holiness of holinesses' " (literal sense of the words in the last phrase). "It can refer to nothing less than the completed outcome of the redemptive administrations as a whole—

the ultimate result and crown of grace and providence, of which all the prophets speak. Zechariah sings of this 'holiness of holinesses' where he says, 'In that day shall there be upon the bells [or bridles] of the horses, Holiness unto the Lord; and the pots in the Lord's house shall be like the bowls before the altar. Yea, every pot in Jerusalem and in Judah shall be holiness unto the Lord of hosts' (Zechariah 14:20,21; cf. Isaiah 11:4-9). It is not the consecration of a person, an altar, or a house, but the consecration of the whole nation and of everything pertaining to its people. Everything promised, prophesied or ever to be hoped for Israel, is thus summed up in which these 70 sevens are to bring."—Seiss.

This exact expression is used to describe the Holy of Holies, that compartment in the tabernacle and temple where the divine presence was manifested. Consequently, some expositors disagree with Dr. Seiss' abstract interpretation and apply the language to the cleansing of the temple at the time of the end, because it will have been polluted by Antichrist. "It needed cleansing after it had been polluted by Antiochus Epiphanes and it will need cleansing before the millennial age can begin."

4. Two different princes are mentioned who should not be confused: the first named "Messiah the Prince" (v. 25) and the second "the prince that shall come" (v. 26).

5. The entire time period of 70 "sevens" is divided into three lesser periods: first, a period of *seven* "sevens"; after that, a period of *threescore and two* (62) "sevens"; and a final period of *one* "seven" (vv. 25,27).

6. The beginning time of this total period is "the going forth of the commandment to restore and to build Jerusalem" (v. 25). There is only one decree in Old Testament history which can possibly be identified as this commandment. Read carefully Nehemiah 1:1-11; 2:1-8. It was the ruined condition of his beloved city, Jerusalem, that moved Nehemiah's heart to tears and his countenance to sadness in the presence of the Persian king. This all led to the grace of the king toward his cupbearer, and the issuing of the decree in the month Nisan in the twentieth year of Artaxerxes the king (Nehemiah 2:1).

---

*Bullinger fixes this date as 454 B.C. and computes on the basis of solar years to A.D. 29, the year of Messiah's "cutting off."

The twentieth year of Artaxerxes' reign, according to the *Encyclopedia Britannica*, was 445 B.C. Nisan, the first day, would be on our calendar March 14, 445 B.C.*

7. The terminus of the seven "sevens" (49 years) plus the 62 "sevens" (434 years) will be marked by the appearance of Messiah as the "Prince" of Israel (v. 25).

The first period of seven sevens, or 49 years, was consumed in the work of reconstruction in Jerusalem—"the street shall be built again, and the wall, even in troublous times." These "troublous times" are recounted in the Books of Nehemiah and Ezra.

Then, the additional period of 62 sevens (434 years), making 69 sevens or 483 years in all, brings us to Messiah the Prince at the time of His triumphal entry into Jerusalem.

The question naturally arises, If these weeks (or sevens) are composed of years, what is to be the length of the year? The evidence is supplied by the Word of God, which reveals these years to be of 360 days duration. In the account of the Flood, comparing Genesis 7:11 and 8:4, we discern that it lasted "five months." The length of this period is given in Genesis 7:24 and 8:3 as "one hundred fifty days." Thus the earliest known month of Biblical history was 30 days in length. Twelve months of this length would give us a 360-day year.

There is further evidence in Revelation 12:6,13,14 and 13:4-7 to the same fact.

8. The total of 69 sevens of 483 years of 360 days each, make a grand total of 173,880 days. "From March 14, 445 B.C., this number of days reaches to April 6, A.D. 32.* Thus that date is fixed as the end of the era of the 69 weeks. It should mark the day of Messiah's manifestation as Prince of Israel. Sir Robert Anderson, for many years head of England's Scotland Yard, corresponding to the American FBI, and a devout Christian, gives us his conclusion in his book, *The Coming Prince*, that April 6, A.D. 32,* was the tenth of Nisan, the momentous day on which Christ rode into Jerusalem on the 'foal of an ass' and offered Himself to the populace as the prince and king of Israel (Zechariah 9:9; Luke 19:28-44; Matthew 21:1-11)."

The importance of that "day" is seen in that while Christ had previously forbidden His disciples to make Him known as Messiah,

---

*See p. 34, *Prophetic Light*, 1988 edition.

He now rebuked the Pharisees' objections and commended the disciples' shout (Luke 19:39,40). And when He lamented over the city, because He knew of His coming rejection, He sadly referred to "this thy day" and the "time of thy visitation," evidently as the day God had fixed in Daniel's prophecy, the day on which the Messiah would manifest himself as "prince" to Israel. "The things which belong unto thy [Israel's] peace" (Luke 19:42) were distinctly foretold in Daniel 9:24, but they rejected the King and crucified Him. Consequently, their "house [temple] was left unto them desolate" (Matthew 23:37,38).

9. Returning now to Daniel 9:26 we note that "Messiah shall be cut off." This was fulfilled by His crucifixion and rejection by religious leaders and people of Israel. We read in Isaiah 53:8: "He was taken from prison and from judgment: and who shall declare his generation? for he was *cut off* out of the land of the living: for the transgression of my people was he stricken."

"But not for himself" (v. 26). The literal meaning of the Hebrew, thus translated here, is "nothing to him," which might be variously interpreted. (a) It has been translated—"But not for himself," which could be interpreted that it was not for His own sins that He was cut off, but for the sins of others. This was literally true—"For the transgression of my people was he stricken" (Isaiah 53:8). (b) It has been translated—"And shall have nothing," or "there shall be none belonging to him." In this case the meaning is that He shall have no kingdom as yet, for "He came unto his own things and his own people received him not" (John 1:11, literal). His lament over the city of Jerusalem, as He sat on Olivet, was, "O Jerusalem, Jerusalem, . . . how often would I have gathered thy children together, even as a hen gathereth her chickens under her wings, and ye would not!" (Matthew 23:37).

10. Following the cutting off of Messiah is to come the destruction of the city of Jerusalem and the sanctuary (the temple) as a consequence of their cutting off of their proper Prince. This was to be fulfilled by "the people of the prince that shall come." Daniel from previous revelations was apprised already of the coming of a prince or king from the last empire of the succession in chapter 7, the Roman, under the symbolism of the little horn. He was to be a Roman prince. "The people" of a Roman prince would be the Roman people and it was by them, under the generalship of Vespasian and

Titus, that the city and temple were completely desolated in A.D. 70. Jesus spoke of this in Matthew 24:2.

Some would have us believe that the "prince" of verse 26 refers to the Messiah. If this were true, the Christians must have destroyed the city and the sanctuary. There were very few, if any, of them in Jerusalem at the time of its destruction. In fact, the Christians, heeding the warning of Jesus in Luke 21:20,21, fled the city, during a temporary withdrawal of the hostile army, and reached the mountains at Pella.

11. The last two clauses of verse 26 are difficult to translate from the Hebrew, as is seen by the variant translations which scholars have made. But the American Standard Version reads: "And the end thereof [possibly referring here to the city] shall be with a flood [or 'overflowing,' as translated by others], and even unto the end shall be war: desolations are determined." The Smith-Goodspeed rendering is: "And the end shall come in a flood, with war raging to the end," the reference to the end being to the end of the age.

These renderings are in accord with Christ's own prophecy of the course and end of this age. He prophesied that following the destruction of the temple the age would be characterized by warfare (Matthew 24:6,7) and that famines, pestilences, earthquakes [surely these are "desolations"] would occur to the end of this age (Matthew 24:7).

The Seventieth Week

The "seventieth" or last "seven" of the total period comes in verse 27. Some interpreters have regarded the events described here as immediately following verse 26. There is a sense, if the last part of verse 26 be correctly interpreted, that this is true. But the 69 weeks ended with the first advent of Christ, specifically at His triumphal entry. Such interpreters do not take into account the parenthesis of the Church Age, not revealed in the Old Testament. Acts 15:14-18 reveals God's purpose for this present age—"to gather out a people for his name" from the Gentiles, following which will be Israel's restoration.

Daniel's seventieth "week" will be that period of which we commonly speak as the Great Tribulation, the last half of which will be the "time of Jacob's trouble" (Jeremiah 30:4-7). This period of three and one-half years is variously referred to in the Book of Revelation by John, as being future to his day and belonging to the age, as

"1,260 days" (Revelation 11:3; 12:6); "time, times, and half a time" (Revelation 12:14); "42 months" (Revelation 11:2).

Note this paraphrase of verse 27 of the ASV text: "And he [the prince that shall come] shall make a firm covenant with many [of the Jews] for one week [seven years]: and in the midst of the week he shall cause the sacrifice and the oblation to cease; and upon the wing [or pinnacle] of abominations shall come one that maketh desolate; and even unto the full end, and that determined, shall wrath be poured out upon the desolate [the desolator]."

This would convey to us that in the end of this age "the prince," the Antichrist, will make a covenant with apostate Jews, involving the resumption of the ancient sacrificial worship in a rebuilt temple. (See 2 Thessalonians 2:4; Revelation 11:2.) In the middle of this "week," or after three and one-half years, he will break this covenant and cause a cessation of the sacrifices, probably superseding them by forced worship of himself or of his image. (See Revelation, ch. 13, and refer back in your thinking to Antiochus Epiphanes, the Greek Antichrist.)

But the end of Antichrist is determined by God. His wrath shall be poured upon the desolator. He shall be destroyed by the "brightness of his coming" (2 Thessalonians 2:8) and shall be consigned with the "false prophet" to the lake of fire (Revelation 19:19,20).

Then the six-point consummation of verse 24 will be fully realized for Israel through a faithful remnant, the "wisehearted" who have prepared their hearts for their returning Messiah (see Daniel 12:10-12).

DANIEL'S FINAL VISION (CHAPTERS 10 TO 12)

These three chapters comprise Daniel's final vision. The series is most remarkable from the fact that it is so minute in much of its detail that many unbelievers maintain it is not to be regarded as prophecy (particularly ch. 11), but history, and that it must have been written after the events took place. Porphyry, a Greek philosopher and loyal Roman, wrote 15 books against the Christian faith, which in his day (third century A.D.) was rapidly winning adherents. Thousands in the Roman Empire were becoming Christian martyrs, and persecution was ineffective in stamping it out.

He directed his assaults especially against the Book of Daniel, because the book foretold many important events in the political world which came to pass. It seemed to him to predict the coming of Christ and the overthrow of the Roman Empire, which he or any other patriotic Roman did not desire. If he could show that forecasts concerning Babylon, Persia, Greek dominion and its Syrian successors, were written after the events took place, the book would be unreliable. The Empire's future would then be safe. He attacked Daniel 11 particularly and ascribed the book to an unknown Jew living in 163 B.C.

Time of the Vision
Daniel was probably 92 years old at this time, the third year of Cyrus king of Persia, the Cyrus of 2 Chronicles 36:22,23; Isaiah 44:28; 45:1. He is believed by some expositors to be the son of Ahasuerus (Darius the Median, Daniel 5:31) and Esther.

Daniel in Prayer (ch. 10:2-4)
We may easily conceive the reason why the aged saint gave himself to this extraordinary season of prayer and fasting before God. He had no doubt heard how few of the exiles had been inclined to return, in what a comparative mean way the new foundations of the temple had been laid, and how sorely malicious enemies were hindering the work and threatening to have it altogether arrested. After 21 days of soul-travail there appeared to him by the Tigris this radiant, angelic visitor, whose voice put Daniel's attendants to flight, though they saw not the vision. As for Daniel, it was with much difficulty that his bodily strength and mental poise could be recovered sufficiently to receive the communication.

Main Scope of the Vision (ch. 10:1)
Instead of reading, as in the King James Version, "the thing was true and the time appointed was long" the Revised Version accords with the context: "The thing was true, even a great warfare." Young renders it: "The thing is true, and the warfare is great." Moffatt translates: "A true revelation of a great conflict." The warfare was, indeed, to last a long time. This is implied in the original text, hence we have the A.V. rendering.

Division of Chapters 10 to 12
The whole of Daniel's vision naturally falls into three divisions from our English Bible:

1. Daniel's personal experience. Revelation of the conflict in the heavenlies (ch. 10:1 to 11:1).
2. The fortunes of the chosen people. Wars between Syria and Egypt (11:2-35), emphasizing the times of Antiochus Epiphanes (vv. 21-35).
3. Events of the end time. Wars between "the king of the north" and "the king of the south." The tribulation period (11:36 to 12:13).

DANIEL'S PERSONAL EXPERIENCE AND REVELATION (CHAPTERS 10:1 TO 11:1)

Vision of the "Man Clothed in Linen" (ch. 10:4-6)

Some expositors see in this passage Daniel's vision only of an august angelic being, but the details reveal a being of such transcendent dignity, majesty, and glory as to indicate that to this man, "greatly beloved" in heaven, was vouchsafed a revelation of the One we now know as the Lord Jesus Christ, known to Daniel as "Messiah the Prince."

The description answers so fully to the appearance of the glorified Saviour to John on the Isle of Patmos, that one can hardly fail to see the Son of Man in a preincarnate revelation, as the One in whom and through whom all the tremendous events of the future were to be ordered and fulfilled, our mighty Kinsman-Redeemer.

As did John the Revelator, Daniel made use of words that describe natural striking phenomena to depict what he saw in the spiritual realm.

Effect of the Vision upon Daniel (ch. 10:7-11)

Daniel was completely overwhelmed by the suddenness and transcendent glory of the vision. The men with him did not see the vision, but undoubtedly the very atmosphere must have been charged with divine energy, and they were greatly agitated and fled, leaving Daniel alone—"a great quaking fell upon them, so that they fled to hide themselves."

Daniel did not flee, but was greatly affected by the vision (v. 8). Like Isaiah and like John, there remained no natural strength in him. All his human excellencies collapsed, and he sank prostrate into a state close to death. Nor could he rise until touched by the hand of another heavenly visitant who told him to stand upright. Even when he regained his feet he "stood trembling."

We say "another heavenly visitant" touched him and brought the subsequent revelations, for this being later states that he had been in conflict with a Satanic "prince." The Son of God needed not to fight directly with the powers of darkness. This activity could appropriately and with success be delegated to angelic authority. The Son of God would need no assistance from Michael (v. 13).

Mission of the Angel to Daniel (ch. 10:11,12)

The angel was sent specifically to Daniel and in answer to his intense supplications and soul-travail (vv. 11,12). This was undoubtedly related to the divine purpose for Israel, Daniel's people. Note that the angel had evidently been dispatched at the beginning of Daniel's prayer (v. 12), but three weeks had gone by during which no intimation of any answer to his prayer came. But after "three weeks" he arrived and brought to Daniel a tremendous revelation of the offices and dominion of angels, both fallen and unfallen. He explained that the conflict with a Satanic archon, the prince of the kingdom of Persia, was so severe it required assistance and caused the delay. It would certainly seem true that these Satanic powers recognized the importance of the revelations already given to Daniel, and the eminence of Daniel himself as a mouthpiece of God on earth, so they would seek to hinder any angelic ministry to him.

Warfare in the Heavenlies (chs. 10:13 to 11:1)

Daniel's angelic visitant (it may have been Gabriel; cf. 9:21) brought a revelation of tremendous import concerning the spirit world and its relation to earthly kingdoms and events. From this passage it is clear that events in world history have a background of spiritual agencies. These agencies are seen to be both good and bad. The conflict of Christians is against "principalities, against the powers, against the world-rulers of this darkness, against the spiritual hosts of wickedness in the heavenly places" (Ephesians 6:12, ASV).

We are here shown in Daniel that individual evil angels stand at the head of individual kingdoms ("prince of the kingdom of Persia," "prince of Grecia") and in opposition to them, at the head of the Israelitish theocracy, Michael, one of the first or highest princes (see 10:13,20,21; 12:1; Revelation 12:7ff.) who received assistance from and gave it to the angel who came to Daniel.

The great truth behind all this is: (1) that the course of empire is ordained of God (cf. Daniel 4:35) in fulfillment of His redemptive purposes for Israel and through them to the nations of the earth; (2) that Satan ("the god of this age") endeavors to thwart the divine purpose and has set over the affairs of the nations powerful angelic archons who endeavor to influence political events; (3) that there are divinely appointed good angels, whose mission is to oppose these sinister powers and to cause political events to fulfill the divine will.

The angel sent to Daniel needed help. Michael came to his assistance—"Michael, one of the chief princes, came to help me; and I remained there with the kings of Persia." The R.V. margin has, "I was not needed there." Rotherham renders it, "I left him there," which corresponds with the Septuagint, "I left him there with the chief of the kingdom of the Persians." The meaning is clear that a conflict went on for some time; that Michael came to render assistance; that the messenger, being relieved, left Michael to continue the conflict, while he proceeded to deliver his message to Daniel.

Verses 15-19 have further reference to Daniel's personal experiences with these heavenly powers. The angel then informs Daniel that on his return he will again meet in conflict this Satanic "prince of the Persians" (LXX),* following which the Satanic "prince of the Greeks" (LXX) would figure in the contest. Verse 21 signifies clearly that in heaven there is a written record of divinely ordained events— "the Scripture of truth"—which were in part now to be revealed to Daniel. That these events are related to God's redemptive purposes for the world through Israel is clear from verse 21—"Michael your prince" (cf. Daniel 21:1).

That 11:1 belongs, in the continuity of the story, to chapter 10 is clear. It reveals that just before this time "in the first year of Darius" the angel had "stood to confirm and strengthen him." Does "him" mean Michael or Darius? Expositors differ, but the date contributes to the meaning or significance, for it was the time of the change of sovereignty from Babylon to Medo-Persia, the time of Israel's return to Palestine. Michael, as "prince which standeth for the children of thy [Daniel's] people," would perhaps need assistance to further the divine purpose for Israel at this crisis time against the opposition of Satan. Cyrus, who assumed the title of Darius II, would need

---

*Symbol for *The Septuagint,* a translation of the Old Testament into Greek by approximately 70 Jewish scholars.

"confirmation and strength" to hold unswervingly to his purpose to free Israel, possibly against contrary counsel of his courtiers, inspired by Satan.

THE FORTUNES OF THE CHOSEN PEOPLE
(CHAPTER 11:2-35)

This historic foreview which follows is an unfolding of the theme given by the angel—"What shall befall thy [Daniel's] people in the latter days" (10:14). Chapter 11:2-35 depicts the fortunes of the chosen people as related to two divisions of the Grecian Empire, Syria and Egypt, especially Syria.

Persia Wanes (v. 2)

Smith-Goodspeed's rendering of verse 2 is illuminating: "There shall arise three more kings in Persia, then a fourth, who shall be far richer than all of them; and when he has grown strong through his riches, he shall set his forces in motion against the kingdom of Greece."

The identity of the fourth king is clearly established by the description in the text as Xerxes. Following backward to Cyrus (10:1) the successors to Cyrus would be Cambyses, son of Cyrus; Pseudo-Smerdis; and Darius Hystaspis, father of Xerxes.

Darius Hystaspis was the Persian monarch at the time the battle of Marathon was fought. The Greek army under Miltiades numbered 11,000 while the Persian host numbered 100,000. This struggle between Eastern and Western civilization resulted in a blow to Persian supremacy from which that proud empire never recovered.

Darius Hystaspis died before renewed preparations for this struggle had been completed. His son Xerxes equipped an immense army of 1,700,000 fighting men, with a navy of one hundred ships. But Xerxes was defeated at the battle of Thermopylae and in the naval battle of Salamis. This was Persia's last attempt aggressively against Greece. In the next war she was on the defensive against the "mighty king" (v. 3), Alexander the Great.

Greece Arises and Wanes (vv. 3,4)

That the mighty king of verse 3 is Alexander is conceded by all interpreters. We have seen in our study of chapter 8 that his empire was divided among four of his generals toward the four points of the compass. Alexander's posterity did not inherit it and the divided kingdoms did not retain the power with which he ruled (v. 4).

Syria and Egypt (vv. 5-20)

We now meet a foreview in quite minute detail of the struggles between those successors of Alexander who gained control of Syria and those who controlled Egypt—"the king of the north" and "the king of the south." The importance of this detailed forecast is seen in the fact that the fortunes of Israel were vitally involved in the constant clashes over a period of 150 years between Syria and Egypt. Israel was like the grain between the upper and nether millstones.

It might be of interest to you to follow through the verses of chapter 11:5-20, comparing them with the brief historical fulfillment presented below. The striking agreement in detail between prophecy and fulfillment will be obvious. We append Dr. W. C. Stevens' remarks on this parallelism and his historical sketch of those early times:

"It seems very clear that verses 5-35 trace in vision a continuous history of the rivalry between the northern divisions of the quaternate empire already introduced. If so, we should find that the history of Egypt and Syria, subsequent to Alexander the Great's death, answered perfectly to this panorama. Is such the case? The parallelism is so perfect that rationalism early assailed the authenticity of Daniel on the very ground that such a replica of the history of Egypt and Syria in relation to one another—from their first emergence as divisions of the Grecian Empire down to and including the reign of Antiochus Epiphanes, about a century and a half in all— could not have been foreseen and foreshown by any mind. And the same type of rationalism, called Higher Criticism—a traitor in the very camp of the saints—audaciously and insistently dates the authorship of Daniel in the second century B.C., and subsequent to the reign of Antiochus Epiphanes. But we will now reproduce this prediction from the authentic pages of its historic fulfillment.

"Ptolemy Soter was the first one of Alexander's captains to gain control of a partition of the empire. He was the first king of the south, Egypt (v. 5). Seleucus Nicator, "one of his princes"—who was first made prince of the province of Babylonia and then ousted from it—proved strong enough to acquire the dominion of Babylon; from thence he stretched westward and founded for himself the great kingdom of Syria. These two kingdoms sought to establish an affinity (v. 6) by means of a scandalous marriage of Berenice, the daughter of Ptolemy Philadelphus, the second king of Egypt, with Antiochus Theos, king of Syria, who put away Laodice his wife for this purpose. But the issue of this hideous affair was bloody and endless conflict. Berenice lost her place and was poisoned, as was also her offspring. Laodice was taken back.

"A successor to the Egyptian throne, probably Ptolemy Euergetes, a brother of Berenice, invaded the northern kingdom, took the royal fortress, and prevailed everywhere, carrying away "4,000 talents of gold, 40,000 talents of silver, and 2,500 idols and idolatrous vessels" (vv. 7,8). After this, conflict ceased for some years. An ineffectual attempt to retaliate was made by Seleucus II (v. 9). After his death, however, one of his two sons rose to such power and prowess as to assail successfully Egypt's fortress Gaza (v. 10).

"This at last aroused Philopator, the easy-going king of Egypt, to intense indignation (v. 11). A momentous engagement ensued between him and Antiochus III, or the Great, with signal defeat to the latter. This decisive battle was fought near Gaza but, because of Philopator's love of ease, history says, he failed to follow up his advantage (v. 12). After some years of conspicuous progress in the north and of decay in the south, Antiochus of Syria made another and more formidable invasion of Egypt (v. 13). He was assisted by general revolts against Egypt (v. 14). Here was the point where seditious Jews intermeddled. They apostatized from their obligations to Egypt and to God, revolted to the standards of Antiochus as a fine piece of policy which, of course, would be doomed by God to failure (v. 14).

"Antiochus then successfully besieged the well-fortified and stubbornly defended city of Sidon, which was Egypt's most prized northern stronghold (v. 15). Antiochus swept on southward and was welcomed in the Holy Land; but he carried concealed in his hand the castigation of the Jews (v. 16). The next year he renewed his conquest with increased preparation and with extra success (v. 17); but because of Roman interference he changed his warlike purpose to one of diplomacy, and he offered his young daughter Cleopatra in marriage to the new Ptolemy, a mere lad in years. The object of this crafty arrangement was to engage her in intrigue in favor of Syria; but she failed her father in this policy (v. 17).

"In revenge Antiochus then turned his conquests against the isles of the Mediterranean Sea (v. 18) and seized many of them. This, however, brought vigorous resistance from Rome; an able general, Scipio Asiaticus, rebuked the indignity of Antiochus and turned it decisively back upon his impudent head (v. 18). Antiochus fled from one fortress to another (v. 19); but he was brought to a halt and put under heavy terms of tribute. In attempting to plunder a temple he was slain (v. 19).

"Seleucus Philopator, the successor to the throne of Syria, inherited the heavy burden of tribute, and in endeavoring to meet it he sent 'an exactor' to confiscate the treasures of the Jewish temple; but he was soon mysteriously put out of the way (v. 20)."

Antiochus Epiphanes (vv. 21-35)

This passage returns us to further consideration of that vile character, Antiochus Epiphanes, the Greek Antichrist, the little horn, whom we met in chapter 8. Some additional prophetic facts, fulfilled in detail, are given us. Let Dr. Stevens trace them for us:

"The successor to Seleucus Philopator was not the lawful heir, as there was a son of Seleucus Philopator; and another person, a son of Cleopatra and grandson of Antiochus the Great, was strongly supported as claimant. But, owing to intrigue and political favor, the younger brother of Seleucus was accorded the throne, though without its honors (v. 21).

"This person was Antiochus Epiphanes (175-164 B.C.), the 'contemptible' as history denominates him. 'He was given up to the most degraded and unnatural passions; he was unscrupulous, cruel, and of a savage temper; he delighted in the company of the lowest and basest of men, and was most uncertain in his conduct; but yet he was deficient neither in courage, nor in cunning ability.' By means of allies he swept resistance from before him (v. 22), and very early dealt his first malignant blow upon God's people by deposing the High Priest Onias, who was also murdered and succeeded by a mercenary and heathenizing high priest, named Jason. By truce-breaking measures Antiochus advanced his strength (v. 23), although with small resources of his own. He went on to appropriate peaceably neighboring provinces by exhibiting an unprecedented generosity in dispensing his easily gotten riches (v. 24). This was all to the end of reaching the strongholds of his Egyptian rival (v. 24).

"In due time Antiochus exerted a great effort to conquer Egypt (v. 25). Although the king of the south made a most formidable resistance, yet largely owing to the treachery of his most intimate and trusted associates, he succumbed to Antiochus (v. 26). Ptolemy fell into the hands of Antiochus, who made politic and lying terms with him (v. 27), which by divine appointment failed of their purpose. Returning northward laden with spoils of Egypt, Antiochus turned aside on some pretext and 'assailed Jerusalem; he slew 40,000 of the inhabitants, sold as many more for slaves, and plundered the temple, carrying off treasures to the value of 1800 talents'; after which he completed his homeward journey (v. 28). Antiochus later renewed hs plans of conquest against Egypt (v. 29). Although he prospered, history tells us, up to the point of arriving without hindrance within four miles of the city of Alexandria, yet disappointment awaited him; for there he was met by the admiral of a Roman fleet (v. 30) and was compelled to retire. This was in 168 B.C. Antiochus had to bow in discouragement before the tokens of the approach of a new empire of the world, the fourth in Daniel's series. It was a century yet before the token was fulfilled and Rome became mistress of the imperial world.

"In returning northward Antiochus made Jerusalem the victim of his rage and chagrin. He left there armed forces to massacre, humiliate, and horrify the Jews to the utmost (v. 31). 'The king is said to have issued a decree to his whole kingdom, commanding that all his subjects should be one people, with one religion and with the same laws. And, in order to enforce this upon the Jews, their sanctuary was profaned; the offerings and sacrifices were prohibited; and an idol-altar was built over the altar of Jehovah, upon which swine's flesh was sacrificed, presumably to an image placed above the altar. This was the abomination of desolation, the signal that great wrath was upon Israel. Idol-chapels were set up in all the cities of Judea, and the inhabitants were commanded to sacrifice and to burn incense to the gods of Greece. Whoever refused, and whoever was found with the book of the Law in his possession or endeavoring to keep the Law, was put to death without mercy.'

"All this caused many of the Jews to apostatize. But it was the occasion also for the rise of heroes of faith and valor never excelled in Jewish history. This abject degradation of Judea under Antiochus really led to a fuller liberation of the land, and to a long period of greater independence, than had been enjoyed since Nebuchadnezzar's first capture of Jerusalem in 605 B.C.

"It came about in this wise. Mattathias, an old man of the priestly house of Asmon, contemptuously rejected splendid offers which an officer of Antiochus made to him on condition of his joining the unholy crusade. The brave patriot flew at a renegade Jew who was in the act of sacrificing on the heathen altar; he slew both the Jew and the king's commissioner and pulled down the heathen altar. As he fled he raised the standard of revolt with the cry, 'Let all who are zealous for the Law follow me!'" The deeds of this old hero and of his five sons—especially of Judas, surnamed Maccabaeus—by which the Jewish commonwealth was restored until the Roman domination intervened, constitute the most heroic page of Jewish history.

"Something more important, however, than these facts of daring was needed to maintain a seed of adequate vitality for the future. This was found in a class of pious and learned men, called Maskilim— the understanding ones. They were such as spiritually understood and expounded the prophets. What a light in that 'dark place' must this part of Daniel's vision have been! But these devoted teachers also brought out into fresh light the great messianic promises; and by them they nursed a seed who should keep on waiting in fastings and prayers, like Simeon and Anna, for the coming of the greater and truer 'consolation of Israel.'

"It is the illustrious ministry and success of these spiritual luminaries of the Maccabaean days that vv. 33-35 emphasize. They are shown to be the connecting link with the latter days—'the time of the end.' In Antiochus Epiphanes appeared a striking prototype of the 'king of fierce countenance,' whom ch. 8 predicted should come up—'in the latter time of their kingdom'—out of one of the four kingdoms of the old Grecian Empire which Antiochus tyrannized. And God's use of the last great persecutor of Israel, in sifting out the final remnant, was illustrated in the creation of the class of believers of those former days, who were purged from admixture and alloy in the fiery heat of murderous oppression, and who were forged into the finest temper on the anvil of alternate flattery and defection on the part of trusted supporters."

Transition

At this point think again of the law of prophetic perspective—
future events presented as if transpiring in immediate sequence,
time gaps between not clearly appearing.

Verse 35 clearly indicates that the testing of Israel in the fires of
persecution and oppression, in order to purge out a faithful remnant,
will continue right up to "the time of the end." In every period of
their long history there has been this faithful remnant. They were
present in Elijah's day—"I have left me seven thousand in Israel,
all the knees which have not bowed unto Baal" (1 Kings 19:18);
Ezekiel sees in vision those "that sigh and cry for all the abominations
that be done in the midst thereof"—in Jerusalem (Ezekiel 9:4); in
this present dispensation there is the "remnant according to the
election of grace" (Romans 11:5).

Applying the principle of prophetic perspective, the transition
evident in the language of verse 35 is from the times of the Maccabees through the centuries to "the time of end," where we meet
Israel's final arch-persecutor, Antichrist—"the king" (v. 36). This
interpretation can be clearly proved by a reverse process of reading
backward from 12:1, where Israel's final tribulation is predicted.
We can trace this "king" right back to verse 36, where the prediction
concerning him, his activities, his wars, etc., begins.

EVENTS OF THE END TIME (CHAPTERS 11:36 TO 12:13)

Last and Supreme Persecutor of Israel (ch. 11:36-39)

Since the mission of the angel (10:10) to Daniel was to make him
understand what should befall his people "in the latter days" (10:14),
our minds are prepared for the revelation beginning at verse 36 to
the end of the book. Again, the picture of the "vile person," Antiochus Epiphanes, has also projected our minds forward to his antitype. Furthermore, the correct insight into verse 35 points "in
perspective from the Maccabees to their antitype, the separated,
purified, and saved Israelitish remnant of the last days."

This "king" does "according to his will." "Until his time no hater,
no persecutor of Israel shall have been allowed by God to execute
all his malignant will against Israel. Until that day no persecutor
shall have had the power of Satan sufficiently in his hands to be able
to wreak upon Israel the whole impulse of his wicked heart."—
Stevens.

He is the very paragon of self-exaltation and self-deification (cf. 2 Thessalonians 2:4); he is a blasphemer of Almighty God; but he prospers, only "till the indignation"—God's fierce wrath upon Israel—"be accomplished." This king is but the instrument for carrying out the determinate purpose of God to "purify unto himself a peculiar people [the Jewish remnant in this context] zealous of good works" (v. 36).

This "king" is an atheist, except toward himself. The expression, "Neither shall he regard the God of his fathers," leads some to believe that Antichrist will be an apostate Jew, or a descendant of Ishmael, "who will lead and coerce impenitent Israelites to renounce the God of their fathers." "The desire of women," which he repudiates, may be the pious desire of all Jewish womanhood to have the honor of bearing the Messiah (v. 37).

Although an atheist, in the sense of disavowing all hitherto known gods, nevertheless, "in his [God's] estate [place] he will have his god, one never before worshiped." The meaning of verses 38,39 seems to be that this king's god "will give him unparalleled power and authority in the realm of all 'forces.' " This god is undoubtedly *Satan*—"whose coming is according to the working of *Satan* with all power and signs and wonders of falsehood." Satan is just waiting "for the competent man who shall, on condition of worshiping him supremely and alone, receive and exercise all his power and authority before the world" (see Revelation 13:2; 2 Thessalonians 2:4,8, ASV). Verse 39 seems to indicate "that Antichrist will set high in rule those who best meet his religious demands, and give them free rein to rule and to despoil those who refuse to meet these demands, especially loyal Jews."

Whence Shall Antichrist Arise? (ch. 11:40)

Verse 40 definitely supplements what we have already seen from chapter 8 (see 8:9,23) that Antichrist is to arise from one of the four reconstituted kingdoms of the old Grecian Empire, i.e., out of Turkey, Greece, Greater Syria, or Egypt. It is most difficult to determine exactly the antecedents of the pronouns in this verse, consequently to assert a dogmatic conclusion is impossible. But the writer gives his view, as follows:

Since the sequence of chapter 11:5-45 through past history and on into the future is of conflicts between "the king of the north"

(Syria) and "the king of the south" (Egypt), it would seem logical to consider "the king" as a "king of the north" and to understand the sense of verse 40: "And at the time of the end shall the king of the south push at him [the king, v. 36]; and the king of the north shall come against him [the king of the south]." It is clear from verse 43 that Egypt is to come under the power of this final king, along with Ethiopia and Libya.

Furthermore, the fact that Antiochus Epiphanes, the type of the final Antichrist, arose in Syria might lend weight to the view that the antitype will arise from there. We have made mention of a desire on the part of certain Arab leaders to form a Greater Syria, including Mesopotamia (modern Iraq), and Jordan. If this be realized, then the territory of ancient Assyria will be incorporated into this greater Syria. This would then make possible the fulfillment of the prophetic detail that Christ will be the peace, when "the Assyrian" comes into Israel (Micah 5:5).

Antichrist's Conquests (ch. 11:41-43)
Israel will come under his control but Edom, Moab, and the children of Ammon will not be overrun. According to Isaiah 11:14 these three will be incorporated into the domain of Israel at the setting up of Messiah's kingdom. Refer to the discussion of Isaiah 16 and 63 for reasons why they escape "the king."

The Last Roar of the Beast (ch. 11:44,45)
Startling tidings from north and east excite Antichrist to deeds of destructive fury (v. 44). The "many" here, in accord with the general scheme of prophecy, we would understand to refer to Israel against whom his hatred is most intensely directed. This will be his final point of centralized power and where he eventually meets his doom. These tidings may be of the Russian advance upon the land of Israel (Ezekiel 38,39); and the invasion of the "kings of the east" (Revelation 16:12-14). That there will be a converging of the armies of the nations against Israel in the last days is clear from Zechariah 14:1-4.

The Great Tribulation—Salvation of a
Remnant of Israel (ch. 12)
Only a careless, cursory, or biased reader of the Scriptures could fail to see that God's final purpose for the kingdom of God upon

earth involves a repentant, restored, exalted Israel among participating nations, who will enjoy her blessings with her. God has made "a full end" of other proud empires, but He has not made a full end of Israel (Jeremiah 30:11). He has punished her for her stiff-necked unbelief through the centuries, but has kept her a separated people. The fires of the final tribulation will purify a holy remnant who will be the nucleus of the new millennial nation (cf. Isaiah 4:2-4; 60:21; Romans 11:26,27).

Dr. W. C. Stevens in *The Book of Daniel* gives a striking summation of this great truth of a restored Israel:

"We have already detected that the light of this last vision of Daniel converges upon the purified remnant of Israel, who shall constitute the seed that shall inherit the everlasting kingdom of the earth under their Messiah, the Most Holy Son of Man. This kingdom is the theme of the Book of Daniel from first to last. It is the radiant gem set in the ring of the whole prophecy. The exquisite beauty of this gem is created by the composite radiance of five divinely cut facets of latter-day truth:

"1. The coming of the Shepherd, the Stone of Israel, to supersede all earthly rule. Nebuchadnezzar's dream of the great image.

"2. The possession of this kingdom with Him by the saints of Israel. Vision of the four beasts.

"3. The conclusive judgment of God upon the ripened transgressions of Israel. Vision of ram and he-goat.

"4. The galaxy of spiritual consummations to which the Jewish state finally succeeds. The 70 weeks.

"These four cluster about and converge to the capital facet.

"5. The final holy seed of living Israelites who 'shall be named the priests of the Lord.' "

The Marvelous Deliverance (v. 1)

The opening words of this chapter, "And at that time," conclusively prove that 11:36-45 belongs to the last days to which the things of 12:1 belong. Here is a great climactic moment for Israel, when Michael, Israel's angelic defender, arises for the deliverance of Israel from all her enemies earthly and heavenly (cf. Revelation 12).

This will be the time of the Great Tribulation of which our Lord spoke in Matthew 24:15,21—the time of Jacob's trouble (Jeremiah

30:7)—but "he shall be saved out of it." This deliverance is of "every one that shall be found written in the book," that is, a "holy seed." "Ever before, the deliverances of Israel had left a leaven unremoved which soon leavened again the whole lump," but the final tribulation will "purely [thoroughly] purge away [Israel's] dross" (cf. Isaiah 1:25-27).

Resurrected Israelites (v. 2)

"This verse serves as a further earmark of all these things. It is the time of the resurrection of 'them that are Christ's at his coming.' It cannot be, however, the resurrection of all saints at Christ's coming that is here denoted, but only that of the Israelitish portion thereof, especially the Old Testament portion. This is the only construction that is germane to the connection of thought. The blessed revelation of these words to Daniel was that Israel's pious, faithful dead should behold and participate in this glorious consummation. Not that resurrected Israelites shall be a part of the earthly population in the Millennium, any more than resurrected Gentile believers shall be. But they shall arise at this time, and shall have the celestial fruition of all their old-time hopes as believing Israelites. Daniel needed this knowledge, set forth even more emphatically and explicitly than it had ever been before. His people through all the centuries after were to need it; and especially in the approaching day of tribulation will they need it. And we need to realize and rejoice that the resurrection-wife of Jesus Christ will include the Old Testament saints. It is the Saviour's declaration not only that the 12 apostles shall sit on 12 (celestial) thrones judging the 12 tribes of restored Israel in the millennial days, but also that 'many shall come from the east and west, and sit down with Abraham, and Isaac, and Jacob, in the kingdom,' 'when ye shall see Abraham, and Isaac, and Jacob, and all the prophets in the kingdom of God.' "—Stevens.

This resurrection at this time is not to be entire as regards Israel, but partial. This statement is similar to one made by our Lord in John 5:28,29: "All that are in the graves . . . shall come forth; they that have done good, unto the resurrection of life; and they that have done evil, unto the resurrection of damnation." But we know from Revelation 20:5,6 that a thousand years elapses between the resurrection of the blessed and holy and that of the rest of the dead.

So we are logical in exegesis when we paraphrase verse 2: "And many of them that sleep in the dust of the earth shall awake, some [those that are resurrected at that time] to everlasting life, and some [those left for the second resurrection] to shame and everlasting contempt."

The Maskilim (v. 3)

"They that be wise," the Maskilim (Hebrew) or wisehearted, are those understanding ones of Israel in that day of unparalleled darkness and trouble. They are the latter-day counterpart of the "Maskilim" in the days of Antiochus, the Maccabees and their followers, who resisted his attempts to corrupt their worship of the true and living God. These end-time Maskilim will shine out "on the background of tribulation and apostasy in spiritual prominence and steadying power" amidst the abominations of Antichrist; and their testimony and example will "turn many to righteousness" and to expectation of the immediate intervention of their Messiah.

A Sealed Book (v. 4)

Again we have a reference to "the time of the end," when "many shall run to and fro, and knowledge shall be increased." The "time of the end" is the epoch in which Daniel's prophecies and all others will be fulfilled, including those of Revelation up to the beginning of the millennial age. Note from 12:5-8 that Daniel was curious as to events of the end time, but was given no detailed revelations. To John on Patmos were revealed many of the strokes of inspired revelation which fill in the picture of the end time—the Tribulation and the glorious return of the Lord. Could Revelation 5:1,2 have any reference to Daniel 12:4?

In prediction "many shall run to and fro, and knowledge shall be increased," there may be a reference to the unprecedented movement of the world's peoples by increasingly rapid means of transportation, especially by air, which has tended to bring all countries closer together as one world. Isolationism is an outmoded concept today. Knowledge, too, in every field of science, has reached proportions and applications to human need and desire which are astounding and breathtaking in these latter days.

But there is another application of these words that is just as logical. This may be knowledge concerning events of the last days. During the last half a century there has been a more intensive study of prophecy than ever before, "a remarkable increase in knowledge concerning eschatalogical [dealing with last or final things] themes."

Dr. Stevens, on excellent grounds, says verse 4 refers to the availability of Daniel's prophecy to inquiring Israelites, besieging their enlightened teachers, running to and fro through the pages of this book with zest for knowledge of end-time events; and saving "knowledge shall be increased" to them.

An Angelic Interview (vv. 5-7)

Daniel is now included only as an observer and listener. There appeared in his vision two angels and "the man clothed in linen" [Messiah; see 10:5]. The latter's position was in the air "upon" ["above" (Moffatt), "over" (LXX)] the bosom of the Hiddekel (Tigris, see 10:4). The two accompanying angels were seen situated one on each bank of the river. One angel asked the man clothed in linen, "How long shall it be *to the end* of these wonders?" The answer (v. 7) clearly shows that the matter of elapsed time to the "end" was not the real content of the question and that most translators have missed the point. Our English version, if we leave out the italicized words, has the literal thought—*"How long the end of these wonders?"* Rotherham caught the real thought in his rendering: "How long shall be the end of the wonders?"

The point of interest in all the context of chapter 12 is *the end time*. The sense of the question is, "How long will be the end time of these wonders?"

The "man clothed in linen," who was poised in the vision above the waters of the Tigris, gives the answer. Note the similarity of the act of the "man clothed in linen" here and Revelation 10:1-6.

The length of the end time is "time, times, and an half" or three and one-half times, or three and one-half years, the last half of the seventieth "week" of Daniel (ch. 9:27) divided into two parts by the breaking of a covenant made with "many" of the apostate Jews by "the prince that shall come." It is the time when God, using Antichrist, "shall have accomplished to scatter the power of the holy people." This expresses the negative side of God's purpose in "these wonders." "It is only an utterly powerless, helpless Israel—caught in an inextricable net and in hopeless extremity—that God can save for His kingdom."

An Inquiring Prophet (vv. 8,9)

As a listener to this colloquy in the vision Daniel was unable to comprehend all of its significance, so he asked for further light. The reply indicates that he should be satisfied with what had been revealed. His long faithful ministry was about closed, and he was to rest for a season, but will resume his place of glorified activity in these events in the end time as God has ordained as his reward (vv. 9,13).

A Final Revelation (vv. 10-12)

Verse 10 repeats one vital factor of this final vision (chs. 10-12) of Daniel, that a certain class of Israelites, as in all their history and peculiarly as in the days of the Maccabean conflict with Antiochus Epiphanes, will come "through the fires of the final tribulation separated, renovated, and tempered to kingdom-perfection, while the rest will all be forever cut off from kingdom-hope."

The Tribulation, which will melt the wisehearted and cause them to seek the Lord, and whom He will then illumine and enlighten with the glow of revelation from the Word by the Spirit, will only harden the "wicked," the foolish-hearted, and ripen them, like Pharaoh of old, for judgment (v. 10).

Two time measurements are introduced (vv. 11,12) extending from the taking away of "the daily sacrifice" and the setting up of "the abomination that maketh desolate." This returns our thought to 9:27 and forward to Revelation 11:2,3; 12:6,14; and 13:5; where we find that period of three and one-half years or 1,260 days, the last half of Daniel's seventieth "week." Our Lord Himself mentioned this same "abomination of desolation, spoken of by Daniel the prophet" in Matthew 24:15.

Just what significant events will take place at these terminal points of 30 days and 75 days beyond the end of that seventieth week, or 7 years, is not revealed, but this seems clear that the wisehearted Israelite "that shall endure unto the end" (Matthew 24:13) in repudiation of the Antichrist and in loyalty to his Messiah, will find himself over the border in the glorious initial days of the kingdom of God on earth—the full-orbed day of the "Sun of righteousness" (Malachi 4:2).

Lesson 38

Ezekiel 1-24

To refresh your mind concerning the historical background of this book, read 2 Kings 23:30 to 25:30.

The Prophet

Ezekiel's name means "God will strengthen" or "prevail." Like Jeremiah he was a priest as well as a prophet. He doubtless exercised the office of priest in Jerusalem before his exile. He was taken to Babylon with the great company of exiles deported with King Jehoiachin, 597 B.C., 11 years before the destruction of the city of Jerusalem. These captives were distributed throughout Babylonia in little settlements, with freedom for each individual to worship in his "little sanctuary." The better class of the people were deported at this time (2 Kings 24:11-16).

Ezekiel's call to the prophetic office came when he was 30 years of age, in the fifth year of Jehoiachin's captivity, 592 B.C. (1:1,2). He had settled with a company of captives near the river Chebar (1:1; 3:15), a large canal flowing into the Euphrates near Carcesium. This locality was probably the place later identified as Telabib.

The Times

"Jeremiah had already fulfilled 34 years of prophesying and overlaps Ezekiel six years and a half. Daniel had been taken as a youth into captivity during Jehoiakim's reign, eight years before Ezekiel went forth from Jerusalem, and he had attained a high reputation for spiritual life and power, although his prophecies come later than Ezekiel's, circling about the restoration from Babylon, together with more distant developments."—Stevens.

When Ezekiel began his ministry, the fall of Jerusalem was impending. After the exile of Jehoiachin, Nebuchadnezzar had placed Mattaniah, brother of Jehoiakim, upon the throne. Mattaniah's name had been changed to Zedekiah. These early exiles were exposed to conflicting sentiments, varying counsels, and even false prophecies. They did not know whether to settle down for a long period of exile. Some were expecting deliverance through alliance with Egypt, and it was the prophet's mission to disenchant them. This ministry was a hard one, because it was largely to a "rebellious house" (3:27). Ezekiel's life was further saddened by the death of his wife (24:18). Tradition says that she was put to death by one of his fellow exiles, a leader among them, against whom he had prophesied for his idolatry. Ezekiel spoke directly to the exiles before him, and indirectly to those classes remaining still in Jerusalem.

The Book

"Ezekiel's messages were largely communicated to him through symbolic visions, and are, on that account, more difficult to understand. In this respect, as well as others, he is like Daniel and John the Revelator. See 1:1, 'The heavens were opened.' Cf. Revelation 4:1."—Stevens.

The book divides itself into three main divisions:

1. Prophecies delivered before the siege of Jerusalem, foretelling its overthrow, chapters 1-24. These correspond to Jeremiah's message in general character.

2. Prophecies delivered during the period of the siege, chapters 25-32. These are directed chiefly against the surrounding Gentile nations.

3. Prophecies delivered after the downfall of the city, chapters 33-48. These deal with restoration entirely and, like the latter chapters of Isaiah, are designed to comfort and hearten the believing few among the incorrigible apostates among the people.

"The key to the book is the oft-repeated expression: 'They shall know in that day that I am the Lord,' namely, by the fulfillment of the thing prophesied in the same connection. It is also noteworthy that Ezekiel is always addressed, 'Son of man'; it may be as a type of Christ."—Stevens.

INTRODUCTION TO FIRST DIVISION (CHAPTERS 1 TO 24)

As we have seen, the standpoint is the impending doom of Jerusalem. Jehoiachin, with many of the princes and influential people, had been taken captive. Zedekiah was on the throne in Jerusalem. Before the king and the nobles was the message of Isaiah; and Jeremiah was prophesying in their midst concerning the coming disaster. Zedekiah seemed determined to avert if possible the divine will, and, in the face of exhortation from Jeremiah to submit, he broke faith with Nebuchadnezzar, attempted an alliance with Egypt, and angered the Almighty. It is under these conditions, during the last four years of Judah's existence, that this section of Ezekiel falls.

We must remember that Ezekiel's message is to "the whole house of Israel" rather than to either Israel or Judah distinctively, for captives of the northern kingdom were present in the Babylonian Empire, which had subdued Assyria, their captors. "Like Daniel and John, who both, like himself, prophesied outside of Palestine, he followed the method of symbol and vision; or rather God followed that method through him."

EZEKIEL'S CALL TO PROPHESY (CHAPTERS 1 TO 3:14)

"The circumstances connected with Ezekiel's call were of a most remarkable and supernatural character, impressing us, in advance, with the momentous importance and interest of his communications."

Vision of the Glory of the Lord (ch. 1:4-28)

"It is significant that his apparition came out of the north quarter of the sky. It is meant to signify the divine and celestial counterpart to the terrible invasion of the Chaldeans out of the 'north country,' under which Judah was to be overthrown."—Stevens. Too little note do we take of the relation between the invisible agencies of the heavenlies and earthly events (Daniel 4:35; 10:12,13,20,21). "Jerusalem's fall was no mere accident of earthly political success; it was divinely planned and energized. The invisible operations are here disclosed, at least symbolically, to the prophet's vision. Thus his standpoint is located, from the outset, in the heavens."

Note the vision which he beheld—whirlwind, cloud, fire, brightness, color (v. 4), living creatures (5-14), wheels (15-21), firmament (22,23), voice (24,25), throne, and a throne-sitter (26,27). An explanation of the vision is given in verse 28. "This was the appearance of the likeness of the glory of the Lord."

The living creatures are doubtless identical with the cherubim of Genesis 3:24 and the images, or figures, in the Holy of Holies in the tabernacle and embroidered on the veil and the curtains of the sanctuary (Exodus 25-27). They were probably familiar to Israel, since no description of them is given in Genesis or Exodus. Can this be accounted for by the fact that possibly down to the time of the Flood these beings continued to guard the approach to the tree of life? Shem was contemporaneous with Abraham 150 years and could have passed the description of them on to him, and through Abraham to his posterity. The first revelation of their appearance is given here in Ezekiel. The general form is human, "The likeness of a man," with the four faces of man, lion, ox, and eagle. Their movements were as swift as lightning. They had four wings, and underneath the wings the hands of a man.

They have a very definite connection with the divine presence and with the purposes of God in redemption, as revealed by their presence in the garden, in the tabernacle, over the mercy seat, here in Ezekiel in connection with Israel, and again in Revelation 4, where they seem to join the angelic host and the elders in ascribing praise to the Lamb. The four faces surely represent the highest orders of the creature world—man, the highest ideal of wisdom and knowledge; the lion, majesty and might; the ox, the highest type of patience and service; the eagle, dominion, loftiness of flight, courage. "If now, according to the ordinary principles of symbolic interpretation, we ask for the realization of all this, we may find it in our redeemed humanity when delivered from the curse and restored and glorified through Jesus Christ. The cherubim would seem to be the embodiment of that glory to which our humanity is destined in the resurrection state—that combination of powers and excellencies which shall be ours when our salvation is consummated in the life to come."—Christian Workers' Commentary.

"The Cherubim are always found in immediate connection with the surroundings of the divine presence, as declaring that those they represent have a right within the paradise of God—the blessed promise held out to our redeemed humanity."

The Commission of Ezekiel (ch. 2:1-8)

The majesty and awe of the vision caused Ezekiel to be prostrated (cf. Exodus 3:3,4; 1 Kings 19; Isaiah 6; Daniel 10; Revelation 1), but the voice of assurance bade him stand upon his feet. Note how clearly like New Testament experience in receiving the Holy Spirit is, "the Spirit entered into me" (v. 2). Ezekiel's commission was not an easy one, for it was to a "rebellious nation," "impudent children," and the "stiff-hearted" (2:3,4). His message was to be delivered fearlessly, regardless of the attitude of the Jews toward it, even though they should be as "briars and thorns," "scorpions" (2:6,7). Oh, that our ministry might be so fraught with power and the presence of the Lord that people would know that a prophet had been among them!

The Roll Given to Ezekiel (chs. 2:9 to 3:14)

This transaction is not to be taken literally, but as transpiring in the Spirit in the vision. However, the results of the experience were most manifest in the ministry of the prophet. Ezekiel is given the "roll of a book"—a scroll wherein was written lamentations, mourning and woe (the message of the Lord to Israel and the effect it would have upon them). He is bidden to eat it, and as he does the roll is as honey for sweetness in his mouth, but in his inner being it is bitter. This signifies that even the terrific judgments of God are precious to those in harmony with Him. Perhaps we ourselves have realized the righteous judgments of the Lord upon us individually, and we have joyfully magnified His justice and equity, though the chastening was bitter to our soul. This act of eating the roll signified the qualifying of Ezekiel to be the recipient of God's oracles and the channel through whom they were to be conveyed to the people. Note the effect of the incoming of the Spirit in fortifying and strengthening Ezekiel against the opposition and haughtiness of Israel (cf. Jeremiah 1:17-19). The incident closes with the supernatural catching away of Ezekiel, probably as was Philip in Acts 8:39,40.

SYMBOLICAL PREDICTIONS OF THE FALL OF JERUSALEM
(CHAPTERS 3:15 TO 7:27)

Introductory

After settling among the exiles at Chebar, Ezekiel is warned again of the seriousness of his commission as a watchman (3:17-21). A further interview between the prophet and the Lord takes place upon the plain, and he is bidden to shut himself up in his own house (v. 24), and instructed that he would only be able to speak as the Lord commissioned him, and at times only as the people permitted him, for they would bind him (vv. 25-27). How much we need wisdom to speak only when told by the Lord, and the ability to keep silent sometimes.

Chapters 4-7 record a series of prophetical actions or pantomimes which the prophet Ezekiel enacted before the assembled captives at the river Chebar. They vividly portrayed the terrible judgments about to come upon the city and people in the land. The nation is to be completely scattered and the city of Jerusalem laid waste. These portrayals took place within the period of a year.

The Portrayal on the Tile (ch. 4:1-3)

Ezekiel is instructed to make a drawing of the outlines of Jerusalem upon a tile and to depict the engines of warfare used in those days to besiege a city. The iron pan between him and the city probably refers to the separation between God and His people because of their iniquities, which are vividly brought to their notice in the second symbolical action.

Lying on His Sides (ch. 4:4-8)

The prophet then lies upon one side for 390 days symbolically bearing the sins of Israel, then upon the other side for 40 days bearing the iniquity of Judah. This pantomime gives the reason why God has forsken His people and given them over to their enemies.

Preparing His Food by Measure (ch. 4:9-17)

This act of weighing out his food and preparing it with a fire of dried cow's dung, is a symbol of the famine conditions to prevail during the coming siege.

Shaving His Hair and Beard (ch. 5:1-4)

This symbol is explained in the rest of the chapter. The razor is the "sword" of the enemy which God is about to use. The operation of shaving is a sign of the humiliation of the nation, as it was humiliating to the prophet to do this (2 Samuel 10:4,5). The hairs are the people. One third is to be killed, one third to perish by famine and pestilence, and the remainder to be scattered among the Gentiles.

The small number bound up in the prophet's skirts represents the remnant who are preserved (6:8). Chapters 6 and 7 are a continuation of the subject of chapter 5. They tell of the desolations to come upon the nation and the preservation of the remnant.

Smiting with the Hand and Stamping with the Foot (ch. 6:11)

This is possibly a symbolical action of Ezekiel, expressing intense emotion called for by the awful calamities to befall his people.

Making a Chain (ch. 7:23)

The chain which the prophet makes represents the bondage into which king and people are to be taken in Babylon.

Visions (Chapters 8 to 11)

These chapters record a series of visions which the prophet received as he sat in his house before the assembled elders, 14 months after the preceding series. The prophet is carried away by the Spirit to the city of Jerusalem, where are unfolded before his view the abominable idolatries secretly practiced by the people, elders, and princes of the kingdom. These revelations were given to show the exiles, who were expecting a speedy return to the land, the reason why the judgment of God must fall.

Secret Sins of Jerusalem (ch. 8)

In this chapter is recorded a progressive revelation of the secret sins of Jerusalem, practiced right in the temple courts. First, at the door of the inner gate on the north the prophet sees an idol image called "the image of jealousy," so named because it provoked the anger of a jealous God, whose place it usurped (v. 3). Next he sees the whole pantheon of heathen gods, which Israel had adopted, portrayed on the walls of a secret chamber, whose blind entrance is revealed to him by the Spirit (vv. 6-12). Following this he sees the idolatry of the women, "weeping for Tammuz"—probably Adonis or Osiris (vv. 13,14). These rites were always accompanied with the grossest immoralities, making them so nauseating to the Lord. Finally a group of men are seen, with backs turned toward the Lord, worshiping the sun contrary to the command of the Almighty (Deuteronomy 4:19,15,16).

The Man with the Ink Horn (ch. 9)

This vision follows as sequel to the foregoing. Judgment is now being prepared. Chapters 9 and 10 give us the celestial counterpart to the earthly means of judgment. Before justice should be visited upon the apostate nation, the faithful few who cried "for all the abominations that be done" must be sealed for protection. Then unsparing slaughter follows in vision, as a prediction of what was soon to take place in actuality in Jerusalem. Ezekiel's heart fails as he sees all this, but the Lord says that it must be, as the nation is utterly corrupted.

The Fire and the Cherubim (ch. 10)

The purpose of the revelation is to show that the coming judgment should proceed directly from the presence of Jehovah, under the figure of "coals of fire." ("Our God is a consuming fire.") Again a detailed description of the cherubim is given, identifying them with the vision seen by the prophet in the first chapter (v. 15). Note the prompt, unquestioning response of the "living creatures" to the will of the Spirit, which possessed them (vv. 16,17). Note also the gradual progressive departure of the glory of the Lord from His temple (9:3; 10:4; 10:18,19) until God's presence is wholly withdrawn from the city and removed to the Mount of Olives on the east (11:23). From the same quarter will the glory of the Lord return to Israel when the feet of Jesus shall stand on Olivet again (Zechariah 14:4).

The Guilty Princes at the East Gate (ch. 11)

Twenty-five men of the princes of the people are shown here to be the ringleaders "that devise mischief and give wicked counsel" in the city. Two men, Jaazaniah and Pelatiah, are mentioned by name, probably as the chief instigators (v. 1). As Ezekiel prophesies against these men and their abominations, forthwith he sees summary judgment visited upon Pelatiah who dies in the presence of his associates, probably as a warning to them (v. 13). The latter verses of the chapter show the purpose of God to restore the nation through the seed of those of the remnant who are faithful to Him. The final fulfillment of this promise awaits the last days, when they shall be gathered "from all countries" (v. 17) and given "the land of Israel." As pointed out in the previous chapter, the glory of the Lord is seen here (v. 23) completely withdrawn from any further fellowship with the house or people which bore His name.

Find four verses in chapters 8-11 which show the progressive withdrawal of "the glory of the Lord" from the midst of His people.

EXPOSURE OF THE SINS OF JERUSALEM, ESPECIALLY
OF HER LEADERS (CHAPTERS 12 TO 19)

*Ezekiel Made a Sign of the Removal of the King
and Kingdom of Judah* (ch. 12)

Ezekiel is called upon by the Lord to enact another scene before
the eyes of the exiles. He is instructed to prepare his household
goods for removal by day; and in the twilight, with face covered,
he is to carry forth his stuff through a hole in the wall, which he
has dug in their sight (vv. 1-7). The explanation of this is given (vv.
8-16) as typifying the removal of the people from the city, especially
of the attempted escape of "the prince" (cf. Jeremiah 39:4).

Again the prophet becomes a "sign" to the exiles in the eating of
his bread with anxiety and carefulness (probably by measure) as a
sign that thus the inhabitants of the city would be straitened in the
coming siege of the city (vv. 17-20). The final message of the chapter
is that the impending judgment, which the nation was foolishly
saying would never come, was to fall immediately (vv. 21-28).

*Message Against the Lying Prophets and
Prophetesses* (ch. 13)

The city, the princes, and the kings have been singled out for
judgment. Now the prophets speaking "out of their own hearts" are
dealt with. Their lying message of "peace and safety," upon which
the nation was building its hopes, is likened to a wall built with
untempered mortar. The first storm would wash it all out and the
wall would crumble. The Lord speaks through the prophet Ezekiel
that the "shower" of His wrath would soon fall upon the false prophets and their dupes. Verses 17-20 seemingly refer to some hypnotic
or mesmeric seances which were presided over by some women of
Jerusalem who were engaging in these false divinations for paltry
sums (v. 19). "They 'sew pillows to all armholes'—which might be
rendered to elbows and wrists—and the reference is thought to be
to the cushions which the prophetess made to lean upon, typifying
the tranquility they foretold to those who consulted them."—Gray.

The Hypocritical People (ch. 14)

The scathing rebuke of this chapter is called forth by the visit of
some of the elders to Ezekiel ostensibly to consult with him and
enquire of him certain things, but whose hypocritical motives are

revealed to the prophet. They are shown as being representatives of "the whole house of Israel," who were idolatrous at heart. Such hypocrites deserve no answer but the visitation of their own deeds on their heads (vv. 4,5). God promises supernaturally to darken the minds of the false prophets (v. 9; cf. 1 Kings 22:23; 2 Thessalonians 2:11,12). The intercession of a Daniel, a Noah, or a Job would be unavailing in the day of His visitation of famine, noisome beasts, sword, or pestilence, because the nation is utterly apostate. The mention of the name of Daniel points to the prominence with which he was already coming before the nation of Babylon (vv. 12-21). The comfort to the believing remnant spared from the slaughter is again given (vv. 22,23).

The Burning Vine (ch. 15)

The worthless state of the people of Jerusalem is pictured as the vine, dead and withered, useless for any purpose, even for firewood. The burning of the vine at both ends typifies the devouring of the evil generation by the fire of God's wrath.

Figure of the Foundling Child (ch. 16)

The reason for God's judgment upon the city and the nation is pictured under the figure of a foundling child of mean birth, left to perish, taken up in pity, washed, nourished, beautified, richly endowed, finally wedded—but proving unfaithful to her husband, receiving every lover. Her husband of necessity turns from her and becomes her judge, but finally upon her repentance receives her back into favor. Jerusalem is thus pictured as a city once Canaanitish but now chosen of God, richly blessed and made famous among the nations because of His rich endowments and power manifested, but also as a city proving ungrateful, turning to the abominable idolatries of the nations around her, even surpassing Israel, Sodom, and the Amorites. Judgment must fall, but on the ground of His covenant promise God will restore and fully reconcile her as she acknowledges her shame.

Riddle of the Cedar and the Eagles (ch. 17)

Jehoiachin, "the highest branch of the cedar," is taken to Babylon, the "land of traffic" and "city of merchants," by Nebuchadnezzar, "a great eagle." Zedekiah is pictured as "the seed of the land" planted by the waters of Babylon and becoming "a spreading vine of low stature," prosperous as long as "this vine did bend her roots toward him." But the king of Egypt, "another great eagle," attracted Zedekiah to make an alliance with him against Babylon and to break his covenant. This was the main complaint of the Lord against the kingdom of Judah under Zedekiah and the prophet foretells his speedy removal from the throne to the captivity of Babylon. Ultimate restoration is promised under a king who shall be exalted from the lowest place to the universal throne, bringing worldwide acknowledgment of Jehovah. This King is, of course, Messiah (vv. 22-24).

Parable of the Sour Grapes (ch. 18)

Rebellious Israel was evidently using the following parable as a complaint against the Lord, that His ways were not equitable and just. They were saying, "The fathers have eaten sour grapes, and the children's teeth are set on edge," meaning that the Lord was punishing an innocent generation for the sins of their fathers. He proves the equity of His ways by sparing the righteous son of a wicked father, and punishing the wicked son of a righteous father; also by sparing the wicked man upon repentance, and punishing a righteous man who turns rebelliously to wicked ways. "The soul that sinneth it shall die." The Lord calls upon the nation to turn from their evil ways and "make them a new heart and a new spirit," for He takes no pleasure in the death of the sinner (v. 32; cf. 2 Peter 3:9).

Parable of the Lioness' Whelps and the Fruitless Vine (ch. 19)

The princes mentioned here are evidently Jehoahaz or Shallum, the son of Josiah, who reigned three months and was taken captive by Pharaoh-necho to Egypt, and Jehoiachin or Zedekiah who was taken captive to Babylon (vv. 1-9). Jerusalem is pictured as a fruitful and flourishing vine, seemingly well and permanently planted, but plucked up by the nations in their anger. Both parables predict the speedy removal of the sceptre from Judah—the cessation of the kingly succession.

FURTHER WARNINGS GIVEN A YEAR LATER (CHAPTERS 20 TO 23)

Catalog of Israel's Idolatry (ch. 20:1-44)

When certain elders come to inquire of Ezekiel, the prophet is given a message rehearsing the idolatry and unfaithfulness of Israel all the way down from Egypt to the prophet's time. He refers to their days in Egypt (vv. 2-9), the wilderness (vv. 10-17), the borders of Canaan (vv. 18-26), the new generation in Canaan (vv. 27-29), the prophet's time (vv. 30-32). Repeatedly in these verses the elders are called to remember that God spared the nation for the sake of avoiding the reproach of the heathen nations ever saying that He was not able to sustain His chosen nation. (Cf. Moses' intercession, Exodus 32:10-13.) Therefore the Lord refused to be inquired of by them. Verse 32 is especially significant as it reveals the real heart attitude of the nation in their determination to "be as the heathen, as the families of the countries, to serve wood and stone." This purpose of theirs has ever been frustrated by the Lord. Israel has never been assimilated by other nations at any time during their history. Ever have they been kept a separate people by the unseen working of the Almighty. God declares His plan to purify the rebels from the midst of the nation, and from the purified remnant to begin the restoration (vv. 33-44).

Various Messages of the Severity of the
Coming Calamity (chs. 20:45 to 23:49)

1. Jerusalem, under the figure of the south forest, is to be utterly consumed, both the dry and withered trees and the green and flourishing (20:45-49).

2. Again the prophet, by enacting before the people the signs of sighing (v. 6), deep emotion in crying and howling (v. 12), and smiting his hands together (v. 14), depicts the dreadfulness of the distress of the people when the "furbished sword" shall be unsheathed against them (21:1-17).

3. This sword is designated as "the king of Babylon," who is unerringly directed by the Lord to come against Jerusalem even through heathen divination. King Zedekiah especially is warned of his doom, the removal of his crown, and the complete overthrow of the Davidic sceptre until the Messiah (He whose right it is) shall come (21:25-27). Ammon is to be slaughtered by the same sword (21:28-32).

4. Israel's abominations are summarized (ch. 22). The specific transgressions of princes, priests, prophets, and the people at large are catalogued here. For these things the Lord is about to scatter them among the nations, for they had become as worthless as is the dross after the refining process has been finished (vv. 18-22).

5. A final charge is made against Israel and Judah under the names of Aholah and Aholibah (ch. 23). Both kingdoms are alike indicted for their idolatries, and classed alike as "lewd and bloody," but Judah is pictured as exceeding Israel (Aholah) in her iniquity. Both had gone lusting after the idols of the heathen nations around about and had copied them in the immoral practices accompanying their idol worship. They had no place for Jehovah and had utterly forgotten Him. He purposes to recompense their deeds upon their own heads and let them drink to the full the cup of His indignation. The Assyrians (the lovers of Aholah) and the Babylonians (the lovers of Aholibah) were to be the agents of their destruction respectively.

MESSAGES GIVEN ON THE DAY OF THE BEGINNING
OF THE SIEGE (CHAPTER 24)

Ezekiel evidently had given forth no message for two years and five months. "Even when the Lord makes so definite a statement of His purpose as He had done in the last prophecies, yet He is wont to fulfill His words with such deliberateness as to lead superficial man to conceive that He is failing to act. But this deliberateness is all the more impressive. It is like the inevitable, irresistible approach of the slow-moving glacier. The messages of the present chapter are unlike any of the foregoing. They called to repentance; they looked forward to judgment; they left the door of providence open. Now doom has struck. . . . Ezekiel, after being directed to record the beginning of the siege that very day, is given the parable of the caldron being filled with the pieces of flesh. Every bit of flesh is to be thrown in; it is already seething and the scum is rising."— Stevens. Compare 11:3.

Ezekiel is also told that his wife, the desire of his eyes, will die that day and that he is to make no mourning for her. In this he is to be a sign to the people, when they inquire the reason for his strange action, that so would their sons and daughters fall by the sword and the city and sanctuary, the desire of their eyes, be destroyed. They would be so taken up with their own mourning one toward another that they would not lament for the city.

Ezekiel further is to be a sign to them in that he would be dumb until the messenger should arrive bringing the news of the fall of the city. This was for three years (cf. 33:21,22).

Lesson 39

Ezekiel 25-48

PROPHECIES GIVEN AGAINST VARIOUS GENTILE NATIONS DURING THE PERIOD OF THE SIEGE (CHAPTERS 25 TO 32)

A. *Against Ammon, Moab, Edom, and Philistia* (ch. 25).

They should have taken warning instead of haughtily lifting themselves up in pride and gloating over the misfortunes of Israel.

B. *Against Tyre* (chs. 26 to 28:19) *and Zidon* (ch. 28:20-26).

In the eleventh year, first day, of Ezekiel's captivity, Tyre is rebuked with the foregoing nations for her delight in Jerusalem's overthrow—for hoping to gain for herself in it. On this ground punishment is predicted.

1. The coming siege and overthrow of Tyre by Nebuchadnezzar is depicted (26:7-11). At verse 12 the theme changes, revealing other instruments of Tyre's overthrow. The city was besieged for 13 years (585 B.C. to 572 B.C.). The city was captured and laid waste, and the Tyrians withdrew to an island in the Mediterranean, near the old site. Here 240 years later verse 12 was fulfilled when Alexander the Great captured the stronghold. Though baffled at first by the situation of the island stronghold, he finally made a causeway out to the island from the mainland by dumping the ruins of the old city into the water, literally scraping the land bare. The utter consternation of the surrounding nations at the fall of Tyre and their bitter lamentation are pictured in verses 15-21. Nations are viewed here as being thrust down to the under realms of the earth (Sheol) in punishment (vv. 20,21).

2. Chapter 27 gives a wonderful description of Tyre as the "mart of nations" under the figure of a magnificent ship, strong and beautifully furnished in the interior. By their trade with Tyre, the surrounding nations are seen as contributing something to her pros-

237

perity (vv. 1-26). The wreck of this great ship and the lamentation of these nations at her loss is shown (vv. 26-36).

3. The prince of Tyre, probably Ittiobalus II, is indicted for his impiety and blasphemous self-security as he resides in his seagirt stronghold. His utter destruction is predicted. There is nothing in the section (28:1-10) but what might be applied to any great monarch. Note the irony of verses 3,4. But in verses 11-19, while the address is to "the king of Tyre," it is plain that a supernatural being of great wisdom, beauty, royal state, dignity, and exalted position is described. This king of Tyrus is doubtless used to depict the Antichrist, the great king of Tyre of the last days, as well as to depict the arch-adversary of God and man, Satan himself, who is incarnate in this last world-ruler. In the main, the verses describe the exalted position in the presence of God of Satan—his dwelling ("every precious stone was thy covering"), his royal state, his fall, his character in his fallen state, and his final doom.

4. The judgment of Zidon (Sidon) is described (28:20-26). Sidon was the mother of Tyre, but was outrivaled in prosperity and wickedness by Tyre. She was also a "pricking brier" unto the house of Israel and must be dealt with for Israel's sake.

C. Against Egypt various prophecies are spoken at different dates (chs. 29 to 32).

1. Prophecy in tenth year, tenth month (29:1-16). Egypt is here condemned for her utter self-confidence and reliance on her own resources, especially the richness of the valley of the Nile. Judgment is pronounced upon Egypt as a dragon or crocodile hauled out of its native element and left on the bank of the river to die and be devoured. This immediate judgment was to endure for 40 years, after which a restoration is promised, but from that time Egypt would be a "base kingdom," no more taking the place of prominence and preeminence which she once had (vv. 14-16).

2. Prophecy dated the twenty-seventh year, first month. This is a renewed prediction of Egypt's overthrow by Nebuchadnezzar, who had already taken Tyre. The long siege of Tyre (13 years) had so incensed him that he is spoken of as being rewarded (v. 20) by the Lord with the spoil of Egypt. The siege of Tyre had yielded no spoil at all. Again we have here another striking instance of the direct interference of the Almighty in events which, to the natural man, appear to have only human causes and instrumentalities in them

(29:17-21). The prophecy continues through 30:18, predicting the fall of all of Egypt's allies and the destruction of her magnificent cities, notably No (the ancient city of Thebes). (See *Wonders of Prophecy,* by Urquhart, for many interesting facts concerning the fulfillment of these prophecies and those in Isaiah concerning Egypt.)

3. Prophecy given the eleventh year, first month. Further revelation of the impending doom of Egypt (30:20-26). Egypt had already met defeat at the hands of Nebuchadnezzar at the battle of Carchemish, not far from Chaldea (605 B.C.), but the Lord promises further to strengthen the "arms of the king of Babylon," while the "arms of Pharaoh shall fall down."

4. Prophecy dated the eleventh year, third month (ch. 31). The coming destruction of Pharaoh by Nebuchadnezzar is confirmed by reference to the capture of Nineveh, the year before the battle of Carchemish, and the overthrow of the glory of the Assyrian Empire. Pharaoh and his hosts are pictured as going down into Sheol together (vv. 15-18).

5. Lamentation for Egypt made in the twelfth year, twelfth month (32:1-16). The theme is the same as the foregoing, except that the nations are seen as lamenting over the downfall of Egypt.

6. Prophecy dated fourteen days later than the foregoing (32:17-32). The overthrow of Egypt is pictured as the ignominious death of a tyrant. The nations are here shown as gathered together "into the pit," the "nether parts of the earth," i.e., in Sheol, the underworld.

PROPHECIES LEADING UP TO THE MILLENNIAL RESTORATION (CHAPTERS 33 TO 39)

Responsibilities of a Watchman (ch. 33:1-9)

This message to the prophet is just as applicable to all who have been placed by God in spiritual ministries.

Another Message Vindicating the Divine Justice (ch. 33:10-20)

This word is similar to that of chapter 18. In fulfillment of 24:26,27, after three years of silence the mouth of the prophet is opened when the messenger arrives among the exiles with the word that the city had fallen (vv. 21,22).

Message Subsequent to the Fall of the City (ch. 33:23-33)

There were those left in the land and among the exiles who thought that, because the Lord constituted the nation from Abraham as a beginning, He ought to take those remaining in the land and make them the nucleus of an immediate regathering. The word of the prophet was to show them that their character was directly opposite to Abraham's. Their hypocrisy was revealed again and the warning left them that when the word of the Lord to utterly lay waste the land was fulfilled, they then would realize that a prophet had been among them (v. 33). Jeremiah 40 to 42 is a fine commentary on these verses.

Rebuke of the False Shepherds (ch. 34)

The unfaithful rulers, princes, and nobles of the nation are here arraigned for their sin in leading the people astray (vv. 1-11). The Lord Himself promises to be the Shepherd of Israel, leading them back from captivity, establishing them in the green and fruitful places in the land, healing the sick ones, etc. Messiah (v. 23), or possibly David himself, is prophetically appointed to be the Shepherd of Israel. This all refers to the millennial estate of the nation. Jeremiah 23 is a fine parallel passage.

Judgment Against Mount Seir, or Edom (ch. 35)

The descendants of Esau are here judged for their perpetual hatred and vindictive spirit shown toward their own brethren in the flesh. Utter wasting of the land, and the sword upon the inhabitants, is to be the portion of Mount Seir.

The Physical Renewing of the Land and the
Spiritual Transformation of Israel (ch. 36)

The mountains (literal) of Israel are here addressed as being personified. They had been a reproach because of the idolatry of their high places, and desolate because of the judgment of the Lord (vv. 1-7). Now they are called upon to bring forth rich produce, to be the dwelling place of the multiplied inhabitants, and never more to be without tillers of their soil (vv. 8-15). The chapter continues in explanation of the reason for the scattering of the nation (vv. 16-19); it tells how the dispersion was a reproach to Him in the eyes of the nations (v. 20). Out of pity for them, and to glorify His name again among the nations, God promises to restore them (vv. 21-24), to regenerate their hearts, cleanse away all their sins, fill them with

His own Spirit, multiply their temporal blessings, restore the land to its original fruitfulness, and thus glorify Himself in the eyes of the nations (vv. 25-38).

Resurrection of Israel as a National Body to Constitute an Everlasting Kingdom Under Messiah (ch. 37)

Under the vision of dry bones filling a valley, the resurrection of the nation is shown and interpreted in verses 1-14. "The scattered, disjoined, and dry state of the bones pictures the denationalized state in which Israel has been in these centuries, until all national hope has come to be abandoned commonly by them. The graves are the Gentile nations among whom the Jews were scattered without any national articulation. But God promises to put a national spirit into them, make them awake unto national life, and place them in their land" (v. 14).—Stevens. This national revival has been going on for a number of years, as represented by the Zionist Movement. It has resulted in the reconstituting of the State of Israel. This regathering, as prophesied in Zephaniah 2:1-3, is in unbelief.

Under the figure of two sticks (scepters)—one to represent Judah and the other Israel (or Ephraim), i.e., the southern and northern kingdoms, separated from each other since the time of Solomon— the return and reunion of these kingdoms is promised. The reunited nation is to be presided over by the Davidic line in the person of Messiah, with David himself possibly as a vicegerent. The fulfillment of the Abrahamic and Davidic Covenants is again promised, and the return of "the glory of the Lord," who will dwell in His sanctuary in the midst of the people (vv. 15-28).

The Northern Hordes of Antichrist Summoned Prophetically Against the Land and Regathered People (ch. 38)

The vision of the restoration of Israel is followed by one of a great invasion of the land by a northern power and confederacy (vv. 2-6,15). Israel is seen prophetically settled back in the land, prosperous (v. 12), dwelling in fancied security without defense (v. 11).

The jealousy of this confederacy (vv. 3,5,6) of nations is aroused against Israel, and they conspire to despoil the land (v. 12) and wipe out God's chosen people. This invasion is from the north, literally "uttermost north" (v. 15). Magog (v. 2) was one of the descendants of Japheth (Genesis 10:2), also Meshech and Tubal. The descendants of these Japhetic nations were the ancient Scythians, who occupied the region around the Caspian and Black Seas, and were the progenitors of the present Russian peoples. A better rendering of verse 2 is, "Son of man, set thy face against Gog [a name probably corresponding to the Bible name Ahasuerus, or emperor], the prince of Rosh, Meshech, and Tubal." Students of ethnology (study of the division of men into races) see in these names references to Russia (Rosh), Moscow (Meshech), and Tobolsk (Tubal), the latter two being Russian cities.

Moscow is the present capital of Russia, the seat of government having been transferred from Petrograd by the Bolsheviks; and Tobolsk is the ancient Siberian capital. Moscow is on the Moskva river and Tobolsk on the Tobol. Here we see the names given to a people (Muscovites), to a river, and a town. Under the well-known laws of toponymy (place names of a region or language) there can be no doubt that the tribes with these names came and settled in the valleys that still bear their names.

Russia has been a chief persecutor and malignant enemy of the Jews for many years, and still is today despite her apparent aid, in a policy of expediency, of the new state of Israel.

Russia is seen in this chapter to be a "guard" (v. 7), or commander of a group of allies (vv. 5,6) who swoops down upon Palestine in the last days. They may be fairly well identified and include Gomer, which students of ethnology have reason to believe is Germany— Teutonic peoples of Central Europe.

Verse 13 indicates that there is also a group of nations which oppose this northern coalition. Many expositors, on the basis again of ethnological science, identify this coalition as headed by Britain ("lion") and the nations of the British Commonwealth ("young lions"), including the United States, a "young lion" which sprang from the British "lion."

At any rate, the present cleavage between East and West (Russia and the East on one hand; Western Europe, Britain, and the United States on the other) is significant.

The invasion of Palestine by this group of nations is not the same as the Battle of Armageddon (Revelation 19:11-21; 16:12-16). It is an end-time event which could occur at any time.

The Destruction of Gog (ch. 39)

The supernatural overthrow of these hordes is pictured here (v. 5), and it is so complete that the fowls of the air are summoned (vv. 17-20) to consume the flesh, doubtless to preserve the land from pestilence. Seven months will be consumed in burying these hosts (v. 12), and employment will be given to a special force of laborers to do this work.

The purpose of all this is to prove to the nations God's faithfulness to Israel, the truth of His Word (Genesis 12:3), and to cause Israel to know that Jehovah is truly their God and has watched over them (vv. 21,22,28). This event marks the close of Israel's long period of chastisement and the beginning of the loving favor of the Lord to be manifested forever in behalf of the spiritually renewed nation (v. 29).

VISION OF THE MILLENNIAL ORDER, RELIGIOUS AND POLITICAL, TO BE ESTABLISHED IN RESTORED JERUSALEM AND IN THE HOLY LAND AS ORIGINALLY PROMISED TO ABRAHAM (CHAPTERS 40 TO 48)

These revelations were received by Ezekiel 13 years after the fall of the city. The importance of these visions is emphasized by the solemn charge to the prophet as to their reception and transmission (40:1-4). The question arises, "Are these visions to be interpreted literally or symbolically?" If the important question of the resumption of sacrifices is viewed correctly there need be no trouble in rightly interpreting. There is nothing in the context to warrant our taking these visions symbolically. The clearest and most logical way to interpret any Scripture, unless definite statement is given by the context itself that the Word is symbolical, is to interpret it literally. In these chapters we will be saved from an endless confusion of symbolical interpretations if we look at them in their clear, literal sense.

Chapter 40:2 gives a definite beginning: "The frame (or structure) of a city." In the following outline the arrangement used by W. C. Stevens is quite closely adhered to. This city is seen on a "very high mountain" "on the south." Subsequent verses show us clearly that Jerusalem is the city before us.

The Temple (chs. 40 to 42)
1. The outer temple court: the wall, the gates—eastern, southern, and northern—their porches, lodges, etc. (40:5-27).
2. The inner temple court: the three gates, and the tables and chambers of the north gate, dimensions of the court, and position of the altar (vv. 28-47).

3. Porch of the house (vv. 48,49).

4. The temple: the Holy and Most Holy Place (41:1-4).

5. The house: its wall, side chambers, basement, doors, dimensions of the whole house, and of the separate place (vv. 5-14).

6. Comparative measurements of sacred buildings, ornaments, the altars, and the doors (vv. 15-26).

7. More specific details of the chambers for the priests at the north and south gates of the outer wall (42:1-14).

8. The great enclosure separating the sacred precincts and the common territory (vv. 15-20).

The Returning Glory of the Lord (ch. 43:1-12)

The temple and the whole surrounding mountaintop are thereby sanctified. In verse 4 you will note the direction from which the glory returns, "the east," which was the place of its outgoing. Doubtless this vision foreshadows the return of the Lord Jesus Christ, Israel's Messiah, when His feet shall stand upon Mount Olivet on the east.

Measurements and Ordinances of the Altar
(ch. 43:13-27)

"In this connection it may be said that the renewal of all the sacrifices of old in the millennial temple while at first thought unexpected, if not repugnant to our idea that all sacrifices are forever past, may be viewed as retrospective. In both cases their value consists in seeing through them the person of Jesus Christ in all the aspects of His sacrifice for us. Jesus implies, for example, that after He comes back He will keep the Lord's supper, for He promised to drink the eucharistic wine anew with us in the kingdom. So, there doubtless will be a most precious meaning in the renewed sacrifices gathered from His presence with Israel."—Stevens.

The ordinances will be carried out with the utmost spiritual import and blessing to Israel, the earthly people. The sin of Israel in the past had been that they lost sight of this intent and carried them on in outward form and as a beautiful ritual alone, until finally they gave them up altogether and worshiped idols.

Restrictions Relating to Entrance to and
Ministry in the Sacred Places (ch. 44)
The Oblation (ch. 45:1-8)

The oblation, or offering of territory, is to be 25,000 reeds (approximately 60 miles) square. Temple and precincts, 500 reeds square, to be in the heart of a strip 25,000 reeds east and west, by 10,000 reeds north and south, reserved for the priests (45:1-4). The same amount of territory, contiguous on the north, is to be reserved for the Levites (v. 5). City land, contiguous on the south of the priestly portion, is only 5,000 wide (v. 6).

Chapter 48:16-19 shows that the city was to be 4,500 reeds square, occupying the exact middle square of the entire strip of city land. Around this were 250 reeds on each side for "suburbs." The Prince's possession was all that lay to the east and to the west of the entire reservation thus far described.

Duties of the Princes (ch. 45:9-17)

The corruptive influence of her rulers was one of the troubles of old Israel. In the renewed Israel this shall be absent and they shall be examples of "probity and benevolence, as well as of faithfulness to God in religious matters."

Sanctification of the Sanctuary and the Institution of the Great Annual Feasts (ch. 45:18-25)
Further Regulations Concerning the Prince and the People (ch. 46)

"Here again the grand and exemplary character of the princes of the people in the new age is exhibited. It is also seen on how much more liberal a scale all religious observances will be. The prince will be near to God and near to the people after the gospel spirit (vv. 9,10)."—Stevens. The requirement that the people pass out of the gate opposite that by which they enter the court, is probably for the maintenance of order, because of the immense crowds passing through to worship Jehovah (v. 9).

Vision of the Holy Waters (ch. 47:1-12)

This Scripture is commonly viewed in a spiritual light, and often, though incorrectly, is made to refer only to the Holy Spirit as a river of water. The spiritual lesson is good, but the application here is doubtless to a literal river. "Even the old temple had its literal waters, that were typical of the Spirit; namely, the pool of Siloam. This pool was supplied by a conduit, a third of a mile long, entering into the heart of the mount on which the temple stood." Refusing "the waters of Shiloah that go softly" (Isaiah 8:6) was the figurative way of charging Israel with forsaking trust in the secret presence of God. The blind man was sent to wash in this pool, as a type of healing by the power of the Holy Spirit. It certainly is not incredible that from under the sanctuary shall flow, from the perennial spring, waters "the streams whereof shall make glad the city of God" (Psalm 46:4). Zechariah 14:4 clearly implies an upheaval of Mount Olivet, which shall result in the cleavage of the mountain in two, making a great valley. This valley, running from east to west, will doubtless form the channel for this river of Ezekiel. The waters of the Dead Sea are healed by the inflow of this pure river and it becomes full of schools of fish. The Dead Sea has been the source of the salt supply of Jerusalem, so portions of the southern extremity of the Dead Sea are left saline for this continued purpose.

Boundaries of the Millennial Holy Land (ch. 47:13-23)

Here at last Israel comes into the full possession of the territory promised to Abraham (Genesis 15:18; Deuteronomy 11:24). Strange to say, many commentators overlook or ignore the fact that his original grant extends far east of the Jordan, even to the Euphrates, and probably to the Indian Ocean as implied (v. 18). The western boundary is the Nile or "the river of Egypt," a small stream which rises in the Wilderness of Sinai. This extent of territory has never been occupied by Israel, even in the reigns of Solomon and David, who reigned over the fullest extent of land of any king. This great land will admit of the granting of liberty to non-Israelites to be incorporated in the Jewish body (vv. 22,23).

Apportionment of the Land (ch. 48)

1. Allotment to seven tribes (vv. 1-7). These tribes receive their inheritance in successive bands extending from the Mediterranean to the extreme east, north of the "oblation" described in chapter 45.

2. The oblation (vv. 8-22). This is a belt of territory 25,000 reeds in breadth, running clear through from east and west, allotted as a separate offering. Of this territory are the portions for the city with its suburbs, for priests, for the sanctuary, for the Levites, and for common use. The residue of the belt, both to the east and to the west, is for the prince. This whole belt is to be "holy unto the Lord."

3. The portions of the five remaining tribes (vv. 23-29). These all lie in belts south of the oblation, nearly filling up the south country

that used to be outside the Holy Land. Twelve tribes are numbered besides the Levites (instead of 12 with the tribe of Levi, as in Genesis 49). This is done by dividing portions between the two sons of Joseph. The two tribes, Judah and Benjamin, who remained true to David, are given places nearest the holy oblation, north and south.

4. The millennial city, Jehovah Shammah (48:30-35). The 12 gates with their tribal names are here given. Levi is the name of one, while Ephraim and Manasseh are included in the name of Joseph. The distinction of this millennial city is that "the Lord is there"— even Christ, the King of the Jews.

Lesson 40

Haggai

Haggai was the first of the prophets by whom God spake (Hebrews 1:1) after the return from exile. Haggai, Zechariah, and Malachi are the three post-exilic prophets. His prophecy is dated "in the second year of Darius" (Hystaspis), 16 years after the decree of Cyrus, from the sixth to the ninth month, covering a period of about four months.

This Darius was Darius Hystaspis, whose treatment of his Jewish subjects is recorded in Ezra 4:24 to 6:22.

Historical Background

In 605 B.C. Nebuchadnezzar took Jerusalem and carried off Daniel and his friends to help him in the government of his new, rapidly growing empire.

On March 16, 597 B.C. (according to Nebuchadnezzar's own records discovered by archaeologists), he again took Jerusalem and carried off Jehoiachin, Ezekiel, and 10,000 of the leading citizens of Judah. By taking away most of their leadership he hoped to forestall further rebellion.

Finally in 586 B.C., his patience exhausted, Nebuchadnezzar destroyed the city and the old temple of Solomon. The majority of the remaining Jews were then carried off into captivity where they joined those with Ezekiel who were settled by the Chebar canal east of Babylon.

In 561 B.C. Evil-merodach (Amel-Marduk), Nebuchadnezzar's son, came to the throne. Neriglissar, his brother-in-law, slew him in 560 B.C., and ruled to 556 B.C. Then Neriglissar's son Laborosoachard (Labashi-Marduk) took the throne but was slain the same year by Nabonidus, the father of Belshazzar, whom he appointed co-king in 553 B.C. In 539 Cyrus took Babylon, but did not enter until six months later. After proclaiming himself king he made Darius the Mede (Gubaru) subking, and in 538 issued a decree for the return of the Jews and the rebuilding of the temple (Ezra 1:1). About 42,360 of the exiles returned to Jerusalem at this time under the leadership of Zerubbabel (Ezra 2:2-70; Nehemiah 7:1-73) and began carrying out Cyrus' orders. Zeal and enthusiasm characterized this group as they cleared away the debris and began preparations to set up the foundations of the temple building. The altar was first erected for the burnt offering, and this sacred rite was reinstituted (Ezra 3:6), but the foundation of the temple was slow in taking shape. Two years later, however, the foundation was laid amid great rejoicing (3:8-11). Their ardor was cooled by the opposition of the Samaritans (ch. 4) and possibly by the hard labor entailed in such an undertaking. Each person became interested in his own work and in the building of a private house. Nearly 16 years passed before Haggai came to call them to build God's house (cf. Ezra 5:1). "It is almost unbelievable that God's people should have waited so long to do the very thing they came back to see accomplished."

Cyrus was followed by his son Cambyses. The suicide of this king precipitated disorder and rebellion in the Persian Empire. Psuedo-Smerdis, a usurper, claimed the throne, but reigned only a few months. Gradually the mighty hand of Darius the Great (Hystaspis) gained control, and order grew out of chaos. "His consolidation and organization of the empire, so diverse in its elements, was truly a monumental work."

"During the days prior to the coming of Darius the Jewish people worked frantically to make a living and build their own houses. Poor crops, blasting, droughts, opposition of neighbors, failing trade, turmoil, and misery, brought little comfort to the people who had come back to Jerusalem with such rosy dreams of a worthy building for God. They were slaving and worrying but finding no genuine happiness. They were not even getting the things for which they were striving with such feverish anxiety. In the meantime God's house was still in ruins. Zerubbabel was the temporal ruler and Joshua was the high priest in charge of the worship of the people. These two chosen leaders seem not to have had any influence with the people in enlisting their aid to build the Lord's sanctuary. God's prophet must be called out to bring His word to governor, priest, and people. Haggai and Zechariah stood side by side in this important task."—Yates.

The Man Haggai

Very little is known of the personal history of Haggai, this "patriotic Jewish layman who responded so enthusiastically to Yahweh's call." From 2:3 it may be gathered that he was an old man who had lived long in Babylon before coming to Jerusalem with the returning exiles. "He loved the Temple devotedly and understood something of the loss the people were suffering without it. He had deep conviction that he was right, a blunt way of driving home the truth, and an assurance that he was going to have his way. In a plain and unadorned way he presented his message. There was a note of urgency that elicited rapt attention and instant obedience. Though neither an orator nor a poet, he obtained results. Consciences were pricked; imaginations were stirred; the work was done.

"He was a man of one idea. God had set him on fire with a burning zeal. Peoples were compelled to follow his orders. In some unseen way he was able to put godly courage into the hearts of his kinsmen and to inspire the vital enterprise."—Yates.

The Book

The Book of Haggai is a collection of four brief messages written between the "sixth month" (Elul, corresponding nearly to our August-September) and the "ninth month" (Chisleu, corresponding to our November-December). Each oracle is exactly dated. One central purpose is clear, the rebuilding of the temple, and Haggai stirred the people to the work.

As a result of the Jew's neglect to rebuild the temple, they were punished with drought and barrenness. The inquiry of the people concerning the reason for these calamities gave Haggai the occasion for his message, in which he declared that their selfish indifference in regard to the needs of the temple was the cause of their misfortunes.

THE FIRST ORACLE (CHAPTER 1:2-11)

This message is one of rebuke and a call to action. The failure to prosecute the work of the temple was because of fear and selfishness. They had failed to honor Jehovah, so were being punished.

First the Lord revealed to the prophet the attitude of the people toward the rebuilding and the expression of it among themselves— "The time is not come, the time that the Lord's house should be built" (v. 2).

Possibly they were waiting for some special revelation from God before they would assume their clear duty and resume the work of building.

The cause of their neglect was their selfishness (vv. 3,4). They needed no special command to build and to embellish their own homes. "God's dwelling place still lay desolate, appealing in vain to their piety and patriotism, which had been overborne by selfishness and supineness."—McCurdy.

Next Haggai summoned the people to take spiritual stock—"Consider your ways." Something must have been wrong with their ways, for God's blessing was not upon them. They were to infer the nature of their conduct from its results (cf. Deuteronomy 28:1,2,8; Haggai 1:5-11).

The direct command is given to action (v. 8) with the clearest indication that God's hand has been upon them in chastisement— "I did blow upon it," "I called for a drought."

Historical Interlude (Chapter 1:12-15)

This historical interlude "describes the remarkable effect of this ringing challenge. Governor, priest, and people began immediately to do the will of God." It was a prompt response to a rousing sermon.

The Second Oracle (Chapter 2:1-9)

Three weeks had now elapsed since resumption of the work, and the enthusiasm of less ardent builders began to flag. The seventh month was the time of the Feast of Tabernacles, the close of the ingathering of harvest. "A certain degree of despondency would be excited by the recollection that the harvest of the present year had been so scanty."

Apparently some were still living who remembered the magnificence of Solomon's Temple and they were discouraged by the thought that the present temple would not equal it in beauty and glory (2:3).

Now came the strong assurance to Zerubbabel, the governor, and to Joshua, the high priest, and to the people, of the Lord's continued presence. His covenant promise has never failed (vv. 4,5). God reveals His purpose to extend His glory to embrace not only Israel but all the nations. Jerusalem and the temple is to be the focal point of a still greater glory than Solomon's day. Here He will give peace.

Undoubtedly this passage has messianic implications (cf. Malachi 3:1).

THE THIRD ORACLE (CHAPTER 2:10-19)

"The third oracle (2:10-19) contains another appeal to conscience
and in addition a call to patience. Haggai heard their complaints
that the promised blessings were slow in coming although they had
been working for three full months. He made it clear to them that
the land had been defiled and profaned by their neglect. Pollution
has a way of spreading far and deep. Evil manifests a power of
infection more serious than holiness. Their sin could not be so easily
and quickly expiated. Those years of selfishness, neglect, and sin
had rendered them unclean in God's sight. If they would persevere
in the work and be faithful to their God they could be certain of
victory. Fruitful seasons, good crops, and rich blessings were to be
theirs. The new day of fruitful gifts was dawning for them. (Zechariah
was now preaching by his side.)"—Yates.

THE FOURTH ORACLE (CHAPTER 2:20-23)

The prophet now brings a message of hope to Zerubbabel as the
leader of His people in those times of world upheaval (2:20-22). He
is to be protected in the midst of the national disturbances, which
may have caused his heart to fear for the perpetuity of his nation
and for their prosperous future. There is a possible double reference
(vv. 21,22) to the political upheavals of the prophet's immediate
time and the final "shaking" of nations preceding the second coming
of Christ (cf. Zechariah 2:6,7; Hebrews 12:26-28).

As the representative then of the house of David and as an ancestor
of the Messiah (cf. Matthew 1:12) Zerubbabel is assured of protection
for himself and his people.

Lesson 41

Zechariah

Historical Background

The historical background of Zechariah's prophecy is the same as that of Haggai. These prophets were contemporary and their mission was similar.

"A serious depression, with crop failures and apparent ruin, faced the Jewish people who had responded to the call of Haggai to build the house of God. Under the pressure of discouragement and want that faced them they found it easy to fall out. The blunt, prosaic hammering of Haggai had its effect, but a new voice was needed to lift them into the kind of enthusiasm that would keep them working to the finish line. Zechariah came to the rescue to supply the needed help."—Yates.

There were good grounds for the people's discouragement. They had been a free people with their own king. Now they were under vassalage to a foreign power (Persia) with no king of their own. They had returned to a desolated capital city.

"Their present condition presented a dark picture, but Zechariah made this serve as a dark background of a more glorious scene, as he, by a series of visions and prophecies, depicted a restored Jerusalem protected and indwelt by the Messiah, and capital of a nation exalted above all others. Besides the promise of future glory, the prophet gave promises of present success and achievement, for he assured the remnant that their temple would be rebuilt in spite of opposition. But Zechariah could offer no permanent encouragement short of the promise of Messiah's coming. Israel's present experience is but a foreshadowing of their future experience. As it was through the chastisement of the Babylonish captivity that the nation was purged of the sin of idolatry, so it will be by the fires of

253

the Great Tribulation that Israel will be purified from its sin of sins—the rejection of its Messiah and King (13:8,9; 12:10; 13:1)."— Pearlman.

The Man Zechariah

From 2:4 we gather that Zechariah was a young man, born in exile and brought back to Jerusalem under divine guidance to help spur the builders to action. He was intimately associated with his older friend, Haggai (cf. Ezra 5:1).

"He does not rebuke or condemn or berate the people. With striking colors and vivid imagination he paints glowing pictures of the presence of God to strengthen and help. Words of inspiration flow from his lips. His hope for a new kingdom rests upon the faith he has in his own people to respond with willing hearts to the wishes of God. Obedience will bring rich blessings."—Yates.

The Book

"The main design of Zechariah's prophetic activity was to administer consolation and encouragement to the people of God still in a condition of weakness and suffering. This plainly appears from the general tenor of the night-visions, from the promised change of fasts into festivals, and from the glowing pictures of future blessedness and honor which occur in the latter portion of this book. Yet it was necessary to prevent these consolations from being usurped by any to whom they did not belong, and to show that repentance and holy living were indispensable conditions of the attainment of any of these blessings. This thought is again and again expressed in the course of the prophetic revelations (3:7; 6:15; 7:7-10; 8:16,17; 10:1,2; 11:10; 14:20), but it is made especially prominent in these opening verses, which seem to be a kind of introduction both to the prophet's labors in general, and to the present collection of his utterances. In them Zechariah sounds the keynote of all spiritual religion, a return to God, and urges its importance by the mention of their fathers' sins and their fathers' punishments."—Chambers.

Three Divisions

The Book of Zechariah falls into three sections: Symbolical—Visions of Restoration (chs. 1-6); Practical—Oracles of Appeal (chs. 7,8); Prophetical—Disclosures of Destiny (chs. 9-14).

The first section (chs. 1-6) is composed of a series of visions designed to encourage the builders in their task. Both promises and warnings are found. The second section (chs. 7,8) is a discourse on the true fast, called forth by a special request from Bethel. The prophet warns Sherezer and Regem-melech against a formalism devoid of ethics and exhorts them to deeds of practical righteousness. "The third section (chs. 9-14) is a colorful unveiling of the future of Israel. God's shepherd is to be rejected and Israel must suffer severe tribulations, but glorious days will come when Israel shall be restored to spiritual supremacy among the nations of the earth."— Yates.

VISIONS OF RESTORATION (CHAPTERS 1 TO 6)

Opening Appeal (ch. 1:1-6)

Verses 1-6 of chapter 1 form an introduction to the book. This returned remnant, now granted divine favor so signally, is even yet in need of a wave of genuine repentance to sweep over them. They are admonished to take warning from the fate of their fathers, who disobeyed the voice of the prophets and suffered in consequence. They must recognize that the will of God abides, that threatened judgments came true and are coming true (cf. Haggai 1:2-11). "Let them realize that the only way to have the favor of God upon them is to repent and obey the call of God."

Three months after his first prophecy and two months after Haggai's last message, Zechariah saw a series of visions in the stillness of the night.

The Horseman and the Horses (ch. 1:7-17)

The rider or horseman in this first vision, together with the horses— red, sorrel, and white—represent God's agents in the earth. Power is an abstract quality, and not a subject of sight. It must put on shape or produce phenomena in order to be seen or apprehended. "Mere effects would not so well, so clearly, and in so summary a manner, display its character and movements." Zechariah beholds these symbolic pictures of divine power in action, apprehendable to the senses (vv. 7-10).

The rider on the red horse (red being an appropriate symbol of bloodshed and war) reports to the angel of the Lord, whom Zechariah interviews in the vision, that the world is now at rest (v. 11). The clash of empire against empire is silent for the present, and the time has now come for Israel's restoration.

In response to the angel's inquiry or intercession, Jehovah responds that He is displeased with the vindictiveness of Israel's enemies in exceeding the divine commission in punishing Israel. He is about to return now and rebuild the cities of Judah. Verse 17 seems to encompass a broader vision of Israel's final restoration.

The Four Horns and the Four Carpenters, or Smiths
(ch. 1:18-21)

The horn is the common scriptural symbol of strength and in prophecy usually represents a kingdom or political power. Zechariah sees the four hostile powers that have scattered Israel, Judah, and Jerusalem beaten down by four opposing powers that Jehovah is using to save Israel.

The Man with the Measuring-line (ch. 2:1-13)

As the second vision represented the destruction of Israel's foes, the third moves to the positive revelation of divine enlargement and prosperity for Jerusalem. Measuring always indicates a new order of some kind. Jerusalem is to be rebuilt without walls (that is, as suburbs outside the perimeter of the walls) because of increased population, and will be protected by the presence of God as a wall of fire. Verses 11-13 indicate a broader scope of blessing which will include other nations' participation in the millennial future. God will be there (cf. Ezekiel 48:35).

Joshua Accused by the Adversary (ch. 3)

The fourth vision "lays a sure foundation for the glowing assurances and promises contained in those that precede by revealing the fact of the divine forgiveness. Sin had been the cause of all the troubles of Israel, and its continuance would bring them all back. Hence the need and value of the great truth expressed in the dramatic form and rich symbolism of this vision."

Joshua, the priest, who represents the people, is seen in vision before the angel of the Lord clothed in soiled garments and opposed by Satan. He is divested of his filthy garments and reclothed with clean raiment. This pictures and also literally states Joshua's forgiveness, a type of the cleansing of the Jewish remnant (vv. 1-5).

He is now clothed in rich priestly attire and personally exhorted to be an example to the people to keep the statutes of God, to guard carefully the priestly office from perversion, and vigilantly to protect the "courts" of the Lord from intrusion of idolatry (vv. 6,7).

Joshua and his fellow priests are a type or a sign of the servant of Jehovah (Isaiah 42), the Branch of David (Jeremiah 23:5), who will effect the final purification of Israel.

Vision of the Golden Candlestick and the Olive Trees (ch. 4)

Zechariah's vision in brief was of a golden candlestick or candelabrum, with seven branches, and with a bowl or oil vessel on top, from which the oil flows into the seven lamps through seven tubes. On each side of the candelabrum is a living olive tree from which oil is directly supplied to the oil vessel.

The great spiritual principle taught by this vision is that the divine purpose is accomplished not by human might and power, but by the flow of the energy of the Holy Spirit Himself (4:6).

This message is one of encouragement to Zerubbabel, who, as leader of the returned Israel, is reestablishing the Jewish commonwealth against great opposition (cf. 4:7—"O great mountain"). Zerubbabel is truly God's anointed prince, and he is assured that he will be enabled to complete the work of temple building.

The two olive trees are symbols of these associated leaders, Zerubbabel and Joshua, who are divinely "anointed ones" (literally, "sons of oil") through whom God is pouring rich blessings upon His chosen people then and for the future. Remember that Zerubbabel was a prince of the house of David and a progenitor of the Messiah.

God through His chosen servants has undertaken to keep the light of Israel's redemptive testimony burning brightly by the power of His own Spirit. The seven eyes (3:9; 4:10) are the "eyes of Jehovah" which sweep through the earth. From Revelation 1:4; 5:6 we gather that they symbolize the sevenfold fullness of the divine Spirit, all-pervasive, all-discerning, and ever active as the divine Administrator to accomplish Jehovah's purpose in the earth.

The Flying Roll (ch. 5:1-4)

This vision teaches that Israel cannot enjoy the rich blessings promised them apart from practical righteousness. They must be free from violators of the divine laws. "Sinners and their sins must be purged from the land. Spiritual reformation must precede temporal prosperity."

The Woman and the Ephah (ch. 5:5-11)

Sin, or wickedness, personified as a woman, is seen sitting in an ephah (the Jewish dry measure of approximately one bushel) being transported to Babylon by two other winged women, who move like the wind.

The sense of this vision seems to be that Israel's sin—especially of idolatry and rebellion—which caused her to be removed as a nation to Babylon, will be concentrated in that very land, possibly in the last days. Babylon was the center of the first organized blasphemous rebellion against Jehovah (Genesis 11:1-9), and many believe that the pendulum, after centuries, will swing back to that point, and that a great pagan commercial center (world capital) will be established there.

Dr. Joseph Seiss sees in the details of this vision a symbol of commerce being centered in the last days in Babylon, in connection with a universal religious sytem—idolatrous, blasphemous—where sin and rebellion against God in all its hideousness will be concentrated. (See Revelation 17,18.)

Vision of the Four Chariots (ch. 6:1-8)

Zechariah now sees a vision of four chariots coming forth from between two mountains of brass. These chariots are drawn by horses—red, black, white, and speckled bay. They go in all directions and are symbolic of the "four winds of heaven" (ASV), under the direct control of God, as He manifests His divine providences or judgment among the nations of the earth. Here we have, in contrast with 1:8-11, not exploring scouts but chariots of war which actually execute the divine will.

The mountains of brass, as Dr. Chambers suggests, are "an adequate symbol of the strength and permanence of the divinely guarded theocracy." The colors of the horses may signify war, famine, pestilence, etc., as in Revelation 6. The same "Spirit of prophecy" inspired Zechariah and John.

The Symbolic Coronation (ch. 6:9-15)

This symbolic action of crowning Joshua, the high priest, with a double crown, typified the crowning of Messiah, the Branch, as king-priest and the building of His spiritual temple. It was a prediction of the combination of these two offices in one individual— church and state united—something that has never been successfully done in human history, because of sin in priest or ruler.

Peace will be established in the glorious reign of Messiah, in whom both offices of king and priest will be combined.

ORACLES OF APPEAL (CHAPTERS 7, 8)

An interval of nearly two years elapsed between this and the preceding messages, during which time the work upon the temple had been steadily prosecuted.

Hypocritical Fasting (ch. 7)

"As the building rose before the eyes of the people and gave promise of a speedy restoration of the ancient worship in its integrity, they became doubtful about the propriety of continuing to observe the solemn fasts by which they commemorated calamitous epochs in their former history, especially the anniversary of the burning of the city and temple by Nebuchadnezzar on the tenth day of the fifth month. Accordingly a message of inquiry was sent to the priests and the prophets, to which the Lord vouchsafed a direct and abundant answer by the hand of Zechariah."—Chambers.

The occasion of the oracle is first given (7:1-3). Verse 2 is clearer in the ASV: "Now they of Bethel had sent Sharezer and Regemmelech, and their men, to entreat the favor of Jehovah."

It could well be that these men were honestly seeking light on the matter of continued fasting, but the answer of the prophet clearly reveals that they did not represent the real motivation of the majority of the returned exiles. The prophet rebukes them for the mere formalism of their services (vv. 4-7) and reminds them of the stubborn disobedience of their fathers and the sad doom which followed (vv. 8-14).

"When the cause of fasting and mourning—sin—is removed, then Israel's fasts will be turned into feasts."

Israel's Glorious Regathering (ch. 8)

In chapter 7 the prophet had rebuked the people for their formalism and had set forth the dreadful consequences of disobedience. Now he paints a remarkable prophetic picture of the results of obedience to the divine will.

While Jehovah had returned in measure to Zion in the events of the recent return of the exiles, the language of verses 1-3 is so specific it undoubtedly depicts Jerusalem in a future day of restored purity, when the divine presence shall be visibly manifest (cf. Isaiah 4:4-6; Ezekiel 43:1-5).

A lovely era of tranquility for the aged and joyous play for the children is seen by the prophet in Jerusalem (vv. 4-6), as a result

of a regathering of a spiritually transformed people from every quarter
to a permanent residence in the land (vv. 7,8). General fertility and
fruitfulness, with attendant agricultural prosperity, will characterize
this restoration (vv. 9-13). The future execution of these promises
is to be as sure as the past execution of the divine threats of judgment
(vv. 14,15). The moral conditions of prosperity are emphasized (vv.
16,17). Fasts in commemoration of tragic events in their history,
will be transformed into joyous feasts of recognition of the divine
favor (vv. 18,19). Jerusalem will become the religious center of the
earth, with Gentile nations participating in the blessings of Israel's
restoration and of the divine presence (vv. 20-23).

DISCLOSURES OF DESTINY (CHAPTERS 9 TO 14)

Chapters 1-8 refer chiefly, though not entirely, to the prophet's
own time. While these prophecies had a historical relationship to
that period, they also took cognizance at times of the distant future.
However, the discourses of this latter section deal almost entirely
with the future.

Chapters 9-14 are diverse from 1-8 in so many ways that even
devout scholars believe that some inspired writer other than Zechariah produced them.

"In chapters 1-8 the author speaks in the first person, the utterances are dated, the style is didactic instead of apocalyptic, almost
every paragraph refers clearly to the events of the [post-exilic] years,
there are visions in which angels play a part. In chapters 9-14 the
author's name is never mentioned, the first person is not used, the
city is threatened with siege, no data for determining his age are
given, the method is apocalyptic, there are no angels or visions
mentioned and no reference to the building of the Temple."—Yates.

Be that as it may, these points are no final argument against the
authorship of Zechariah. He may have written them in his later
years, under the guidance of the Holy Spirit, to describe events
relative to the coming Messiah and the final setting up of His kingdom.

Dr. James M. Gray in his *Synthetic Bible Studies* makes a logical
division of this section into historical periods in Israel's history: Israel
under Grecian rule (chs. 9,10); Israel under Roman rule (ch. 11);
Israel under Messiah's rule (chs. 12-14).

Israel Under Grecian Rule (chs. 9,10)
Alexander the Great (ch. 9:1-8)

In our study of the Book of Daniel (see ch. 8) reference was made to Alexander's favor to the Jews. Verses 1-7 record his conquests along the plains of Phoenicia and Sharon on the west coast of Palestine. Verse 8 describes the deliverance of Jerusalem out of his hands. We give a further digest of Josephus' account of Jerusalem's escape:

He tells us that, after the conquest of Tyre and Gaza (mentioned in 9:1-7), Alexander set out for Jerusalem to punish Jaddus, the high priest, who had refused to submit to him. The Lord in a dream commanded Jaddus to open the gates to the conqueror and, dressed in his high priestly garments, and attended by his priests, to receive Alexander in triumph. Jaddus obeyed, and Alexander, seeing this imposing procession, saluted the high priest and adored the God whose name was on the golden plate attached to the priest's headgear. Alexander then explained that, while in Macedonia, he had had a vision of this procession, and this vision had been brought to his mind by what he had just seen. He afterwards treated the Jews with great kindness.

Messiah the Greater (ch. 9:9-12)

On the background of Jerusalem's deliverance from Alexander, whom the ablest generals of that day were able to halt only briefly, the prophet imposes a prophetic picture of a greater King, Messiah, "a royal personage, who is to appear without armies or weapons," coming without pomp and display, to establish a general peace and a kingdom universal in extent (vv. 9-12).

Victory over the Syrian Greeks (ch. 9:13-17)

This passage seems to refer to the defeat of Antiochus Epiphanes of the Greek dynasty in Syria of the Seleucidae. We have already described him, his sacrilegious acts and his defeat by the Maccabees, in the study of Daniel.

Expanded Prophecy (ch. 10)

This chapter expands the foregoing prophecy, and is an integral part of it. Verse 1 seems clearly to belong with 9:17 as well as with 10:3. First, there is a promise of rain and fruitful seasons (v. 1); followed by a reference to idolatry under misguided leaders as the cause of Israel's afflictions (vv. 2,3); deliverance by divine strength imparted to good rulers (vv. 3-5); ancient mercies restored (v. 6); the participation of the united nations—Ephraim and Judah—in

these promises of growth and enlargement (vv. 7-9); further promises of deliverance and enlargement, "couched in historic allusions
to their former experiences, and fulfilled only in the Messiah's kingdom" (vv. 10-12).

Israel Under Roman Rule (ch. 11)

The context of chapter 11 indicates the prophet's viewpoint is the
first advent of Christ as the true "Shepherd of Israel"—whom they
rejected. These events took place in the period of Roman supremacy.
Since this was the time of Israel's crowning act of unbelief (the
rejection of their Messiah, under the guise of the worship of God)
we may expect a note of judgment upon their false shepherds. "In
words arranged with great rhetorical power, full of poetic imagery
and lively dramatic movement," the ruin of the entire land under
these false shepherds is described (vv. 1-6). It is altogether possible
that here is a prophetic forecast of the Pharisees, Sadducees, and
the scribes (cf. John 10).

The Shepherd of Israel Rejected (vv. 7-17)

With verse 7 the prophet becomes a dramatic impersonator and
representative of the messianic Shepherd. "He undertakes to dis-
charge the functions of a shepherd to a flock which is in a very sad
condition,—so much so as to be already devoted to destruction. His
commission is to guide and feed and defend a people so wicked and
hardened that they are on the point of being given over to the just
retribution of their sinful ways."—Chambers. Who the "three shepherds" of verse 8 are, is difficult to determine.

Probably in pantomimic action, as did Ezekiel so frequently, the
prophet in the presence of the people takes two staves such as the
shepherds use. One of these he names "Beauty," or Loveliness,
denoting the loveliness of God, or idealistically of His people. This
staff he breaks as a sign of the broken covenant between Jehovah
and His people (vv. 10,11).

The prophet continues to impersonate the Shepherd and is eval-
uated by the people at the price of 30 pieces of silver, the price of
a slave (vv. 12,13. Cf. Matthew 26:14-16; 27:3-10).

Zechariah now breaks the second staff, designated "Bands," which
signified the disruption of the unity of the 12 tribes and probably,
too, the breaking up of the nation into parties bitterly hostile to
each other in Christ's day. These were the Pharisees, Sadducees,
Herodians, etc. This disunity was a marked peculiarity (and still is

today) of Jewish history and has greatly accelerated their ruin in times when national unity was imperative (v. 14).

The action of verse 15 is of the same symbolic character as that recorded in verses 7ff. The nature of the implements assumed is not specified, but they were doubtless of a character fitted to indicate injury rather than benefit to the flock. "Foolish" carries with it a scriptural implication of "wicked."

Many see in the idle (worthless) shepherd of verses 16 and 17 a reference to the Antichrist, who deceives the flock of Israel only to devour them, but who meets swift and just retribution.

Israel Under Messiah's Rule (chs. 12 to 14)

Many of the prophecies of this section of Zechariah are yet to be fulfilled. They refer to the time when Israel is once more in the land in the national sense and in possession of the city of Jerusalem. Even though Israel has returned in a condition of unbelief as to Christ, the stage is being set for the fulfillment of these great prophecies. How vivid are the shadows being cast before in our day by the newly constituted Israel!

It is at this point when the nations are besieging Jerusalem (cf. 14:1-3) that this "burden (oracle) of the word of the Lord" begins (12:1,2). It will be peculiarly true in those days, when the nations attempt to annihilate Israel and to settle the issue of anti-Semitism once for all, that Israel will be a "burdensome stone," too heavy for the "people of the earth" to lift (v. 3).

Jehovah will come directly to their defense in a supernatural way (12:4-9; cf. also 14:3). Israel will be deeply repentant as their Messiah comes forth for their deliverance in answer to their heartfelt plea for help (12:10 to 13:1; cf. Isaiah 63:17 to 64:12; Revelation 1:7). In that day they will apprehend the meaning of their Messiah's sacrifice, at His first advent, to provide a fountain for the cleansing of their sin (13:1).

The nation will be purged of its unbelieving element by the fires of the Great Tribulation. A faithful remnant will come through those fires, purified as gold and silver is refined (13:7-9; cf. Revelation 7:1-8; Ezekiel 36:33-38).

Chapter 14 continues with a description of the tribulation of Israel brought about by an invasion of enemy nations from every quarter— a converging upon Palestine of peoples hostile to the Jew, when anti-Semitism reaches its climactic surge of power (14:1,2). But in this desperate, apparently hopeless situation, Jehovah moves against these nations, "as when he fought in the day of battle" (v. 3). This means active supernatural intervention as was displayed in the days of Gideon, Deborah and Barak, Jehoshaphat, and Hezekiah against the Assyrians.

The feet of our Lord, in that momentous day will touch the Mount of Olives, whence He departed for the heavenlies 19 centuries ago (v. 4).

Verses 4-11 predict certain topographical changes in the immediate area of Jerusalem. An earthquake produces a valley, through which will probably flow the river of Ezekiel 47 into the Dead Sea, an arm of which also reaches the Mediterranean (v. 8). Verse 10 speaks of further topographical change. The outstanding truth of those verses is the fact that "the Lord shall be King over all the earth: in that day shall there be one Lord, and his name one" (v. 9). Glorious day for a sin-cursed world!

The enemies of Israel will be punished (vv. 12-15) and then will begin the wonderful thousand-year era of righteousness and peace. Other nations will participate in the annual tribute to and worship of Jehovah in the Feast of Tabernacles (v. 16). Proof is positive that this era is not the final, absolutely perfect one, for nations have to be summarily dealt with to remind them of their duty to honor the King (vv. 17-19).

"Holiness unto the Lord" will characterize that day. No longer will there be degrees of holiness, but every instrument used in the service of the Lord, lowly or highly esteemed, will be sacred.

Lord hasten this joyous day!

Lesson 42

Malachi

The Times

The exact date of the prophecy of Malachi is not known, but all are agreed from the internal evidence that it was after the exile, which is not mentioned in the book. The temple was rebuilt, and its service, together with the sacrifices, feasts, and fasts, restored. It is generally accepted that he belonged to the times of Ezra and Nehemiah.

Over 100 years earlier (536 B.C.) a remnant of Jews had returned, under the leadership of Zerubbabel, from the Babylonian captivity to reestablish their national life in their homeland. The walls of Jerusalem were later rebuilt under Nehemiah's leadership. The temple had been rebuilt (520-516 B.C.) by Zerubbabel, the governor, and Joshua, the priest, under the encouraging preaching of Haggai and Zechariah, the prophets.

In the year 458 B.C. Ezra had come to Jerusalem, bringing with him many of the rolls of Scripture. He had initiated certain reforms. Malachi dealt with the same evils that troubled Ezra and Nehemiah: neglect of God's house, idolatrous marriages, defiled priesthood.

Malachi, the last of the prophetic voices, testifies to the sad fact of Israel's failure, as did his predecessors.

Economic, Social, Religious Conditions

Economic depression prevailed. Crops were poor and pests ruined the plants. "The priests were so corrupt and immoral that a spirit of skepticism pervaded the entire population. The people complained against God, bemoaned their sad plight, refused to pay their tithes and offerings, were guilty of social injustice, and had mixed themselves with the heathen people of the land. Divorce was common, Jehovah's covenant had been forgotten, and a low type of

behavior was the common order of the day. Worship had degen-
erated into empty and indecent formalism. The nobles of the land,
who wanted the profit from religion without being willing to pay
the cost, caused the serious trouble. The example and conduct of
the nobles and the priests affected the whole community. Everybody
was disposed to question the authority and the method of God. It
was a serious situation that called for a fearless servant of God.
Malachi was God's man for the crisis."—Yates.

The Man Malachi

The name *Malachi* means "messenger of Jehovah," or, if a shortened form of Malachiah, means "servant of Jehovah." "He was a
fearless reformer who spoke directly to the sinners of his day without
hesitation or embarrassment. We may rest assured that he was a
strong, vigorous, clear-cut personality who was strongly opposed to
any person who treated the temple and the things of the Spirit with
indifference and carelessness. He was on fire with spiritual zeal to
bring about the sort of reform that would guarantee justice and right
for all the people, and bring them to worship Yahweh as their own
loving God. Perhaps Nehemiah influenced him to put forth such
strong efforts on behalf of righteousness and godliness. It is probably
best to place him in the period during Nehemiah's return to the
Persian court, where he served as a strong ally in the vigorous
reforms instituted by Ezra and Nehemiah."—Yates.

The prophet denounced the very evils that existed in Nehemiah's
time (cf. Nehemiah 13:10-12 and Malachi 3:8-10; Nehemiah 13:29
and Malachi 2:4-8; Nehemiah 13:23-27 and Malachi 2:10-16).

The Book

"Malachi's book differs greatly from the other prophetical trea-
tises. He does not present certain independent sermons or addresses
but launches into an argument with his contemporaries. We can
see and hear the audience respond to his open-air preaching with
comments, questions, objections, and excuses. The master debater
takes each objection and answers it before going forward with another. Priest and people are charged with specific crimes while the
weak replies continue to come back at him. Throughout the entire
dialogue he is describing the divine love, revealing the faithlessness
and ingratitude of the people, calling for genuine repentance, answering the skeptics, challenging the current godlessness, and making glorious promises for those who are faithful."—Yates.

The book begins with a direct statement by the Lord through the prophet to Israel: "I have loved you." The answer of the people of that time is, in effect, a slap in the face for God—"*Wherein* hast thou loved us?"

Note the recurrence of the word *wherein* which expresses the defiant attitude of the people and becomes really the key to the book (1:2,6,7; 2:17; 3:7,8; cf. 3:13).

Dr. G. Campbell Morgan observes: "That word 'wherein' . . . is a startling revelation of the attitude of the people. To every charge brought against them they replied by using the word. In other words, Malachi was speaking to people who protested against the charges he was making. The whole prophecy reveals a calloused people and a sensitive God."

The message of Malachi is to the whole nation of Israel. When the people returned from captivity they consisted not only of the tribe of Judah, but of members of all the tribes.

The book may appropriately be divided into two parts: Messages to the Rebellious and Messages to the Faithful.

MESSAGES TO THE REBELLIOUS (CHAPTERS 1 TO 3:15)

Message to the Whole Nation (ch. 1:1-5)

In the opening statement of verse 2, "I have loved you, saith the Lord," the force of the Hebrew original is lost in our English translation. It is incomplete. The tense here employed suggests something far more than "I *have* loved you," which is past tense. The Hebrew tense marks continuity. "I have loved and do love you," is the force of the words.

The people were insolently questioning God's love for them. They were exhibiting their base ingratitude and failing to recognize that the afflictions through which the nation had passed were but the chastenings of the Lord to purify them. They apparently reasoned that if God loved them He would pay no attention to their sin, but just continue to bless them despite their flagrant violations of His law, given peculiarly to them.

As proof of His love to the nation, the Lord points to the election in grace of their forefather Jacob and the rejection of Esau. The word *hated* as used here does not signify hatred in the sense that we now understand it. It is used in the sense of "lesser love," which in comparison to the great love for Jacob seemed as if it were not love. God blessed and prospered Esau. Leah, Jacob's wife, is called "hated" in Genesis 29:31, yet Jacob did not literally hate Leah; he loved and cared for her as his wife, but he preferred Rachel before her. Compare Luke 14:26 and Matthew 10:37, where the word *hate* means to love with a lesser affection.

God gave both nations over to the Chaldeans for the punishment of their sins, but He brought the Jews back and left Edom unrestored (1:4,5).

Message to the Priests (chs. 1:6 to 2:9)
Irreverence (ch. 1:6)

A son, by the instinct of nature, by the unwritten law of the heart, will honor his father. If he fails to do so he is considered to be an unnatural son. To God the Father, reverence was due; to Him as Master, submission was due; but the priests rendered neither. They were exhibiting a spirit of self-satisfied insensibility, ignoring their responsibility to God and to their sin, when they challenged God: "Wherein have we despised thy name?"

Blemished Sacrifices (ch. 1:7-11)

The prophet answers their hypocritical question and exposes their irreverence for God by showing that they had offered polluted bread or meal-offerings upon His altar, along with blemished and imperfect animal sacrifices (1:7). While undoubtedly well supplied with these necessary sacrificial animals by decree of the Persian king (Ezra 6:8-10), they presented only the worst (v. 8). They offered God what out of mere propriety they would never have dared to offer to a fellow creature.

The prophet proceeds to make an application of the illustration (v. 8). If the governor will not receive worthless gifts, much less God. The challenge of the prophet (v. 9) is not a call to repentance, for he assumes that God would not accept them. It is rather irony— "Go now, seek the favor of God, as ye would not that of your governor." These sins had, indeed, been committed by them, not by their fathers, or by aliens. The responsibility was clearly theirs and how could they expect God to regard them?

Verse 10 seems clearly to indicate that the Lord is "so provoked by their illegal offerings, and the spirit which actuated them, that He would gladly see His whole worship discontinued," the doors closed.

In contrast with these sacrifices which Jehovah rejects, Malachi declares that the hour is coming when true worshipers, not only in

Jerusalem but in every place, will offer unto Him a pure offering, and His name will be honored even among the Gentiles (v. 11).

Indifferent Worship (ch. 1:12-14)

The priests were regarding their service at the altar not as an honorable privilege, but as an irksome, oppressive drudgery, so they dishonored it by bringing blemished offerings.

Death of the Levitical Covenant (ch. 2:1-9)

The prophet pointedly addresses these unfaithful priests (2:1) reminding them of their holy honor and privilege in being Levites (2:5). They had been called to a close walk with the Lord; like their ancient fathers (Exodus 32:25-29) they should have a zeal for righteousness and be able to teach the law (2:6,7). In these rugged qualities the priesthood of Malachi's day was sadly lacking (v. 8).

His disfavor, yea, His curse will be upon them (vv. 2,3) and they will be made contemptible in the eyes of the people (v. 9).

Messages to the People (chs. 2:10 to 3:15)
Unlawful Divorce, Heathen Wives (ch. 2:10-16)

Many of the people had divorced their lawful Israelitish wives in order to marry foreign women (cf. Nehemiah 13:23-28). The prophet stigmatizes their unlawful divorce as an abomination, and as such to be classified with idolatry, witchcraft, and adultery (cf. Ezra 9:2), for Israel was to be holy to the Lord (Jeremiah 2:3).

Skepticism (ch. 2:17)

"This verse forms the transition to 3:1. The skeptics of the day were insinuating that God delighted in evildoers since the latter seemed to prosper. Then, if that was the case, why should they serve God? (3:14,15). Where is the God of judgment? they ask. The answer is forthcoming (3:1-6). The Lord whom they seek (whom they challenge to appear) will come suddenly (when they least expect it) to His temple and will visit judgment on priests and people. Not because Jehovah had changed was judgment delayed, but because He had not changed in regard to His covenant promises, and because of His unchanging mercy (3:6)."—Pearlman.

Withheld Tithes (ch. 3:7-12)

After announcing the coming judgment for long-continued transgressions of the people, Malachi adds a gracious promise as in Zechariah 1:3—"Turn ye unto me, saith the Lord . . . and I will turn unto you." But in self-righteous delusion, supposing they need no repentance, they inquire, "Wherein?"—in what particular? (3:7).

The prophet shows them that they are doing what no man should even think of attempting—they have defrauded God in the tithe and the heave-offering (cf. Nehemiah 13:10-14; Leviticus 27:30; Deuteronomy 14:22).

They have withheld tithes, despite the fact that God had already visited them with severe punishment, which aggravated their guilt. They had been cursed with failure of harvest and famine (vv. 9,11).

The prophet now directs them to the mode of recovering the divine favor. It is simple. Bring the whole tithe, not a part only, keeping back more or less, and the blessing of God will follow in copious abundance, because the devouring instruments, sent by God, will be restrained (vv. 10-12).

Challenging God (ch. 3:13-15)

Impudent and presumptuous, indeed, are those who challenge God or charge Him foolishly on any issue! But this is what these returned Israelites were doing. They were saying that it was profitless to serve God and keep His ordinances since He was not righteous. The wicked were prospering, the nations around them were abounding in all things, and they themselves were in adversity. They evidently felt that the mere religious performance of rites and sacrifices was sufficient. It is evident from the looseness and carelessness with which they did even this that their hearts were far from God.

MESSAGES TO THE FAITHFUL (CHAPTERS 3:16 TO 4:6)

Promises to the Righteous (chs. 3:16 to 4:3)

There were the faithful few who feared God with reverent fear, honored His name, and recognized His righteousness. The proud-speaking of the ungodly called out the piety of the God-fearing. The darkest days of Israel's apostasy produced a faithful remnant, true to God and His way. So was it in Malachi's day when the fires of holy worship were burning low. These fellowshiped together and kept the holy flame burning. Of them God was fully aware and mindful. He was keeping records (3:16).

They are His "jewels," His peculiar treasure (3:17).

They will be preserved in the day of judgment, both national and individual, when the wicked, the skeptics are destroyed (4:1). The

Sun of Righteousness in the full-orbed day of His millennial glory will arise to burn up the wicked as stubble and to establish the righteous in joy, simple and childlike, as of calves let loose from the stall to pasture, who frisk and leap for sheer joy (4:2,3).

Closing Old Testament Exhortation (ch. 4:4)

"Remember . . . the law of Moses!" Until the Sun of Righteousness rises! The last message of the Old Testament was to remember the Law given to their illustrious leader, Moses. In the absence of prophetic voices, the Law is all the more important to remember as their rule of life and conduct. There will be no more prophetic ministry until "*the* Prophet" comes. Four hundred years are to intervene.

Last Prophecy of the Old Testament (ch. 4:5,6)

Before the coming of the great day of judgment at the end of the age, Elijah will return as the forerunner of Messiah. He will prepare the people for Messiah's coming. This prophecy was partially fulfilled in John the Baptist, who came "in the spirit and power of Elijah" (Luke 1:17; Matthew 11:14).

When the disciples, at the time of the transfiguration when Elijah appeared on the mount, called Jesus' attention to this prophecy, He stated plainly that "Elijah truly shall first come, and restore all things" (Matthew 17:11), but He indicated also a prefulfillment of this in John the Baptist, His forerunner. Many expositors of Scripture believe that Elijah is one of the witnesses of Revelation 11; and that, as John was the forerunner of Messiah's first coming, Elijah will be of His second appearing.

STUDY QUESTIONS—UNIT SEVEN

LESSON 23

Introduction to the Prophetic Scriptures

1. What basic procedure must one follow to understand the prophetic Scriptures?
2. What was the threefold purpose of God's call to Israel?
3. What was the twofold ministry of the prophets?
4. Give a reason for their messages concerning Gentile nations.
5. For what purpose were prophecies recorded in writing?

Joel

6. Explain the occasion of Joel's prophecy.
7. Give the meaning of the term "day of the Lord."
8. What is Joel's threefold outlook of that day?
9. Explain the import of the immediate, the imminent, and the future "day of the Lord" in Joel.
10. What is the relationship of Joel 3:9-16 to Matthew 25:31-46?

LESSON 24

Jonah

1. Where do we locate Jonah historically?
2. Give some facts to prove that a man could be swallowed by a whale.
3. Tell something of the times of Jonah.
4. Tell something of the literary value of the book.
5. Give reasons for Jonah's disobedience.
6. What divine attributes are revealed in the Book of Jonah?
7. Give reasons for the possibility that Jonah actually died in the great fish.
8. What in the religious life of the Ninevites would make Jonah's ministry more effective?
9. Give some arguments in favor of the fact of the repentance of the Ninevites.
10. Give some typical lessons from Jonah.
11. Name seven practical lessons.

LESSON 25

Amos

1. Tell all you can of the man Amos.
2. Tell something of the political conditions of his day.
3. How does God use the nations in accomplishing His national purposes?
4. What was the reason for the judgment of Israel, and what made their sin more awful?
5. Tell the story of Amos' experience with Amaziah the priest.
6. Give the significance of the basket of summer fruit and the vision of the sanctuary.
7. Give some of the details of Israel's restoration.

LESSON 26

Hosea

1. Describe the social, economic, religious, and moral conditions of the time of Hosea.
2. Relate Hosea's unique personal experience and give its significance.
3. Give the key words to the threefold division of Hosea.
4. Explain the significance of the names of Hosea's children.
5. Give a brief exposition of chapter 3.
6. What is the main message of chapter 4:13? Give a few details.
7. Upon what basis is Israel to be restored?

STUDY QUESTIONS—UNIT EIGHT

LESSON 27

Isaiah 1-35

1. During the reigns of what kings did Isaiah prophesy, and what was the character of each king?
2. Can you see any ways in which the Book of Isaiah is a miniature of the whole Bible?
3. What sins of the people are rebuked in chapter 1:2-4, and to what are the people likened in verses 5-7?
4. Does God see any hope of result from His appeal? What follows of necessity and with what final outcome? (1:21-27)

5. How are the shadows of the Tribulation banished and what glories of the messianic kingdom does the prophet see? (4:2-6).
6. How is the nation of Israel symbolized in chapter 5?
7. Why do you think God gave Isaiah such a vision of His majesty?
8. What was the import of Isaiah's message, and why do you believe the Lord intervened in behalf of such a wicked king as Ahaz (7:4-9)?

LESSON 28

Isaiah 36-66

1. Tell the story of chapters 36 and 37.
2. Tell the story of Hezekiah's healing and his sin of pride.
3. How is Part II connected with Part I? To whom is Part II addressed?
4. How may the last 27 chapters be divided structurally, and what is the main theme of each division?
5. Point out several passages showing clearly the main theme of chapters 40 to 48—the return from Babylon.
6. Give the theme of chapter 40.
7. Give the theme of chapter 41.
8. Of chapter 42.
9. Of chapter 43.
10. Of chapter 44.
11. Of chapter 45.
12. Of chapter 46.
13. Of chapter 47.
14. Of chapter 48.
15. What change of vision occurs in chapters 49 to 57?
16. What is the theme of chapter 49?
17. Of chapter 50?
18. Explain the main themes of chapters 52:13 to 53:12. How does 53:4-6 explain the Atonement?
19. What is the theme of chapter 54?
20. What are the three main themes of chapters 55:1 to 56:8?
21. What is the change of vision in passing to chapters 58 to 66?
22. Who is speaking in 62:1,10; 63:3,7; also in 63:15 to 64:12 and 65:1?
23. Explain the four national views of chapter 66.

STUDY QUESTIONS—UNIT NINE

LESSON 29

Micah

1. Write a brief sketch of political events in Micah's time.
2. Tell all you can about the man Micah.
3. Outline the social conditions of Micah's day.
4. Give scriptural illustrations of important points.
5. Outline the religious conditions of Micah's time.
6. Give scriptural illustrations of important points.
7. What is the general message of the book?
8. Point out five important predictions of the book.

LESSON 30

Nahum

1. What is the relation of the Book of Nahum to the Book of Jonah?
2. Tell something of world history in Nahum's day.
3. Describe briefly the city of Nineveh.
4. Give a brief character sketch of the man Nahum.
5. What is the theme of the book and its purpose for Judah?
6. Learn one of the three outlines suggested.
7. How is the character of God revealed in chapter 1?
8. Tell something of the overthrow of Nineveh.
9. How is God's justice and vengeance vindicated in chapter 3?
10. Name five practical lessons of value to us.

LESSON 31

Zephaniah

1. What group of prophets did Zephaniah follow, and with whom was he contemporary?
2. Describe the social and religious conditions of Zephaniah's time.
3. Give a brief character sketch of the prophet himself.
4. Give the fourfold outline of the book.
5. Comment upon each point, especially the "day of a pure language."

LESSON 32

Jeremiah 1-25

1. Give a brief account of the historical background of the Book of Jeremiah.

2. Cite briefly the social and religious conditions under which Jeremiah prophesied.
3. Tell something about the man Jeremiah.
4. Tell about the circumstances of Jeremiah's call and commission.
5. Give the substance of Jeremiah's first message (2:1 to 3:5).
6. Give briefly the importance of Jeremiah's second discourse (3:6 to 6:30).
7. What sin is particularly condemned in 7:1 to 8:3?
8. Give the substance of the second charge (8:4-22).
9. Give the substance of the third charge (chapters 9,10).
10. Tell the import of the discourse on the broken covenant (chapters 11,12).
11. What was the message of the linen girdle (chapter 13)?
12. Tell briefly about the prophet's two petitions and Jehovah's two refusals (chapters 14,15).
13. What is Judah's removal likened to (16:16-18)?
14. For what did Jeremiah pray (17:14-18)?
15. What blessing is promised if the people sanctify the sabbath, and what warning if they continue to desecrate it (17:19-27)?
16. Tell the story of the potter and the broken vessel (chapters 18-20).
17. Tell the story of Jeremiah's experience with Pashur (19:14 to 20:6).
18. Give the account of Jeremiah's discouragement (20:7-18).
19. Tell the story of the curse on Jeconiah's household, and why Jesus has a right to sit on the throne of David (22:24-30).
20. What does the prophet say about the unrighteous kings and the Righteous King (23:1-8)

LESSON 33

Jeremiah 26-39

1. Tell the story of Jeremiah's experiences in chapter 26.
2. What is the meaning of the wooden yokes (chapter 27)?
3. Describe briefly the contest between Jeremiah and Hananiah (chapter 28).
4. What was the import of Jeremiah's message to the exiles in Babylon (chapter 29) and what were the consequences?
5. Give the main themes of chapter 30.

6. Give some of the main themes of chapter 31.
7. Tell the story of chapter 32 and point out its prophetic significance.
8. Give some of the salient items of the prophetic forecast of chapter 33.
9. Show the duplicity of the people of Jerusalem as recounted in chapter 34.
10. What is the practical lesson of chapter 35?
11. Tell the story of chapter 36.
12. Tell about the four stages of Jeremiah's imprisonment (chapters 37,38).
13. Tell of the events in chapter 39.
14. Give briefly the story of chapters 40,41,42.
15. Where were Jeremiah and Baruch forced to go, and what prophetic act did Jeremiah perform (chapter 43)?
16. What horrible example of persistent sin is recounted in chapter 44?
17. Name the foreign nations prophesied against in chapters 46-51.
18. Give a few of the salient points in each prophecy.
19. What does chapter 52 contain?

STUDY QUESTIONS—UNIT TEN

LESSON 34

Lamentations

1. Who is the author of Lamentations?
2. When was the book written?
3. Sum up briefly the story contained in the first poem (chapter 1).
4. Whom do the words "friends" and "lovers" indicate?
5. What form do the last three verses of the first poem take?
6. What is the prominent element in the second poem (chapter 2)?
7. What does the third poem contain (chapter 3)?
8. To what does the fourth poem especially relate?
9. Bring out some of the main points of Part One of the final poem (5:2-7).

LESSON 35

Habakkuk

1. Tell something of the background of the book.
2. Give a brief character sketch of the prophet.
3. Tell something of its literary excellence and importance.
4. What can you say as to its form?
5. Explain Habakkuk's first perplexity and God's answer.
6. To what further perplexity did God's answer lead?
7. What wise attitude did Habakkuk take?
8. How did Jehovah dispel Habakkuk's doubts?
9. Catalog four of the national sins of the Chaldeans.
10. Describe Habakkuk's experience in chapter 3, and the results in his own concept of God.

Obadiah

1. Give a brief account of the origin and history of the Edomites.
2. Give a brief character sketch of Obadiah.
3. What is the theme of the book?

LESSON 36

Daniel 1-5

1. Tell something about the judgments upon Judah.
2. Discuss the man Daniel in relation to his great moral and religious decision.
3. Cite briefly the reformation activities of Josiah the king.
4. Give proof of Daniel's training as shown by his courtesy.
5. What are the two divisions of the book, and what does each deal with?
6. Tell the story of Nebuchadnezzar's dream of the image.
7. What four empires are represented by the different metals?
8. Explain the "toes" of the statue, and tell how and by whom they shall be broken.
9. Give briefly the gist of Dr. West's comments on 2:42-44.
10. Prove that the Messianic kingdom was not fulfilled in the first advent of Christ.
11. Why does Scripture pass over in silence all the intervening centuries since the first advent of Christ?
12. Why do you believe Nebuchadnezzar set up the image of chapter 3?

13. Show the progression in Nebuchadnezzar's religious experience.
14. What was Nebuchadnezzar's dream in chapter 4, and what was the interpretation?
15. How was this dream fulfilled?
16. How was Daniel's record of Belshazzar as the last king of Babylon proven to be true?
17. Tell the story of the mysterious handwriting on the wall (5:5-9).
18. What kind of woman was the queen mentioned in 5:10-12?
19. Give the interpretation of the mysterious writing (5:25-29).

STUDY QUESTIONS—UNIT ELEVEN

LESSON 37

Daniel 6-12

1. What position did Daniel hold in Darius' Kingdom (6:1,2)?
2. Tell the story of the plot against Daniel, and its final outcome.
3. What is the significance of the striving of the winds upon the great sea, in the vision of chapter 7?
4. What were the characteristics of the first beast, and by whom was this fulfilled (7:4)?
5. Tell the same about the second beast (7:5).
6. Also the third beast (7:6).
7. The fourth beast (7:7).
8. What are the "ten horns" and the "little horn"? Have these already appeared, or are they yet to appear?
9. Tell about the ram in 8:3,4; and about the goat and its conspicuous horn (8:5-8).
10. Tell about Antiochus Epiphanes and his sacrilegious actions.
11. What are the proofs that "the little horn" was not exhaustively fulfilled by Antiochus?
12. Discuss the following countries in relation to prophecy and history:
    (a) Turkey
    (b) Syria
    (c) Egypt
    (d) Greece

13. Bring out the main features of Daniel's prayer (9:1-19).
14. Whom does the prophecy of the 70 weeks concern (9:24-27)?
15. What does the word "weeks" mean? How do we determine that Daniel is thinking of "years" rather than "weeks of days"?
16. What is the sixfold purpose of the 70 sevens of years?
17. How is the entire time period of 70 "sevens" divided (9:25,27)?
18. What marked the beginning of this total period?
19. What marked the ending of the seven "sevens" plus 62 "sevens"?
20. How is the length of a year determined?
21. How were the words "Messiah shall be cut off" fulfilled?
22. What followed the cutting off of Messiah?
23. Tell what events will take place during the time of Daniel's seventieth "week."
24. What were the conditions that caused Daniel's extraordinary season of prayer and fasting (10:2-4)?
25. What two things does this vision reveal?
26. Who is the "man clothed in linen" thought to be (10:4-6)?
27. What are the great truths behind this vision?
28. Tell about the deeds of the Maccabees (11:21-35).
29. What does 11:35 indicate concerning the testing of Israel?
30. Tell something about the last and supreme persecutor of Israel (11:36-39).
31. From where shall Antichrist come (11:40)?
32. What does God's final purpose for "the kingdom of God" upon earth involve (12:1-13)?
33. Who will be in the resurrection of "them that are Christ's at His coming"?
34. Who are the "Maskilim" of 12:3?
35. Give two possible meanings of the verse, "Many shall run to and fro, and knowledge shall be increased" (12:4).
36. Give the main points of the final revelation (12:10-12).

STUDY QUESTIONS—UNIT TWELVE

LESSON 38
Ezekiel 1-24

1. Discuss the man Ezekiel as to the meaning of his name, his call to the prophetic office, etc.
2. Tell some facts about the times in which he prophesied.
3. How were most of Ezekiel's messages communicated to him?
4. Give the three main divisions of the book.
5. According to Stevens, what is the key to the book?
6. Discuss Ezekiel's vision of the glory of the Lord (1:4-28).
7. To whom was Ezekiel's message to be directed, and how (2:1-8)?
8. What does Ezekiel's eating of the roll signify (2:9 to 3:14)?
9. Discuss the five symbolic pantomimes Ezekiel was to do before the people, and tell the meaning of each (chapters 4-7).
10. Name and explain the visions contained in chapters 8-11.
11. Find four verses in chapters 8-11 which show the progressive withdrawal of "the glory of the Lord" from the midst of His people.
12. What do Ezekiel's actions in 12:1-7 signify?
13. Who is singled out for judgment in chapter 13? Why are they to be punished?
14. What called forth the rebuke of chapter 14?
15. Discuss the picturing of Jerusalem as a foundling child (chapter 16).
16. What is the main complaint of the Lord against Judah under Zedekiah? Who shall bring about their ultimate restoration?
17. What parable was Israel using as a complaint against the Lord? How was this answered?
18. What does 20:1-44 consist of?
19. Tell about the various messages of the severity of the coming calamity (20:45 to 23:49).
20. What were the messages given on the day of the beginning of the siege (chapter 24)?
21. Why was Ezekiel not to mourn for his wife?

LESSON 39

Ezekiel 25-48

1. Why was Tyre rebuked (26:1 to 28:19)?
2. How was the prophecy against Tyre partially and then completely fulfilled?
3. Who does the king of Tyrus depict?
4. Why was Egypt to be overthrown? By whom?
5. What do chapters 33-39 contain?
6. Discuss the rebuke of the false shepherds (chapter 34).
7. Explain chapter 37.
8. What is the theme of chapter 38?
9. Who are the nations generally considered to fulfill this vision?
10. Give the general theme of chapters 40-48.
11. What is the significance of the glory of the Lord returning from "the east"?
12. Discuss the renewal of the old sacrifices.
13. Draw a diagram of the "oblation."
14. Explain the vision of the holy waters (chapter 47).
15. What are the boundaries of the millennial Holy Land (47:13-23)?
16. What is the distinction of the millennial Holy City?

LESSON 40

Haggai

1. Name the post-exilic prophets.
2. Tell about the historical background of the book.
3. Give some details about the man Haggai.
4. What is the central purpose of the book?
5. What is the message of the first oracle (1:2-11)?
6. What was the attitude of the people toward the rebuilding of the temple?
7. What does the historical interlude describe (1:12-15)?
8. What factors were causing despair and despondency among the people (2:1-9)?
9. What assurance was given?
10. What does the third oracle contain (2:10-19)?
11. Give the message brought to Zerubbabel (2:20-23).

LESSON 41
Zechariah

1. Discuss the historical background of the book.
2. Tell about the man Zechariah.
3. What is the main message of the book?
4. Give the three divisions of the book, and tell what each section is composed of.
5. Tell about Zechariah's vision in 1:7-17.
6. What does the third vision indicate (2:1-13)?
7. Tell the story of the vision where Joshua is accused by the adversary (chapter 3).
8. Explain about the vision of the golden candlestick and the olive trees (chapter 4).
9. What was the meaning of the vision of the woman and of the ephah (5:5-11)?
10. Describe and explain the vision found in 6:1-8.
11. What did the symbolic coronation typify (6:9-15)?
12. What was the prophet's answer to the inquirers in chapter 7?
13. Give some of the blessings seen by Zechariah for Israel (chapter 8).
14. To what period of time do chapters 9-14 refer?
15. Give Dr. Gray's division of chapters 9-14 into historical periods.
16. Tell about Israel under Grecian rule (chapters 9,10).
17. Where is the prophet's viewpoint in chapter 11?
18. Tell about the prophet's representation of the Messianic Shepherd.
19. When are the prophecies of chapters 12-14 to be fulfilled?
20. Give a brief sketch of the contents of chapter 14.

LESSON 42
Malachi

1. Discuss the times of the Book of Malachi, and its subject.
2. Tell some facts about the economic, social, and religious conditions.
3. Give some characteristics of the man Malachi.
4. Discuss the use of the word "wherein."
5. How may the book be divided?
6. What does the word "hate" mean, as used here (1:1 to 3:15)?

7. Tell about the blemished sacrifices.
8. What were some of the sins of the people as set forth in 2:10 to 3:15?
9. What is the gist of the message to the righteous (3:16 to 4:3)?
10. Discuss the closing Old Testament exhortation, and the last prophecy of the Old Testament (4:4-6).

Notes

Notes

Notes

Notes